VINTAGE
SEVEN DECADES OF INDEPENDENT INDIA

Vinod Rai served as the eleventh comptroller and auditor general (CAG) of India. He is credited with some scathing audit reports on the allocation of spectrum (2G) and coal blocks, and inefficiencies in the preparation of the XIX Commonwealth Games. He is presently a distinguished visiting research fellow at the Institute of South Asian Studies in the National University of Singapore and a trustee on the IFRS Foundation Board. He has been entrusted by the Supreme Court of India with the mandate to put in place a credible and transparent management structure in the Board of Control for Cricket in India. His autobiographical account, *Not Just an Accountant*, is a widely acclaimed book.

Amitendu Palit is senior research fellow and research lead (trade and economic policy) at the Institute of South Asian Studies (ISAS) in the National University of Singapore (NUS). An economist working on trade policies, regional developments, China–India relations and political economy, he is a columnist for *Financial Express* and a regular contributor for various global media outlets. His books include *The Trans Pacific Partnership*, *China and India*, *China–India Economics* and *Special Economic Zones in India*. He appears as an expert on the BBC, Bloomberg, Channel News Asia, CNBC, Doordarshan (India) and All India Radio.

SEVEN DECADES

of

INDEPENDENT INDIA

ideas and reflections

edited by

VINOD RAI
and
AMITENDU PALIT

VINTAGE
An imprint of Penguin Random House

VINTAGE

USA | Canada | UK | Ireland | Australia
New Zealand | India | South Africa | China

Vintage is part of the Penguin Random House group of companies
whose addresses can be found at global.penguinrandomhouse.com

Published by Penguin Random House India Pvt. Ltd
4th Floor, Capital Tower 1, MG Road,
Gurugram 122 002, Haryana, India

Penguin
Random House
India

First published in Viking by Penguin Random House India 2018
Published in Vintage 2021

10 9 8 7 6 5 4 3 2 1

ISBN 9780143456384

Typeset in Minion Pro by Manipal Digital Systems, Manipal
Printed at Replika Press Pvt. Ltd, India

www.penguin.co.in

Contents

Preface

Putting together a volume on seven decades of independent India might appear a far-fetched notion given the depth and range of issues that the task would entail. As editors, therefore, we began with the assumption that however hard we tried we would not be able to do justice to the scale. Several subjects of significant importance for India would be left untouched by the book as would diverse opinions on the subjects that are included. As we pen these words, we realize the gaps that we were not successful in filling up. We hope there would be more opportunities for us to look back at India and the wonder that she is.

At the same time, we found the journey exciting and pleasant. As we went through the contributions, we realized the richness of thoughts that we have been able to gather. Rarely can one hope to achieve the unique blend of scholastic opinions with practitioner insights that the pages to follow would reveal. We feel elated at having been able to gather expertise across a vast spectrum of subjects for reflecting on how India was, is, and might be, after seventy years of its independence.

The book has deliberately been developed with a broad perspective on the subjects covered. But we had to do justice to a core theme within the broad canvas. As the reader will realize, public policies and institutions have been the implicit, if not the explicit, context of the entire book. All contributors have examined policies and their applications, notwithstanding whether they have been written on economic, social, political, external relations or governance issues. While we expect the book to generate interest among all readers given the issues it covers, we are certain about its contribution to the discourse on policies and institutions in India. Our effort has been to ensure that policy enthusiasts on India should get to consume insights and ideas from a group of experts whose views are not only much sought after, but also unique given their vast experience and knowledge on what they have written.

The idea of this book began from our conversation with Ambassador Gopinath Pillai, chairman at the Institute of South Asian Studies (ISAS) in the National University of Singapore. The book can be rightfully called an ISAS product. As research faculty of the ISAS, we would like to thank all our colleagues at ISAS for their invaluable help that we received at various points in time during the work on the book. Specifically, we would like to thank Ambassador Gopinath Pillai, Professor Subrata Mitra (director, ISAS) and Hernaikh Singh (senior associate director) for their unfailing support and encouragement at all stages. Quite a few of the contributors in the book are either with ISAS, or have been associated with it at various stages. The book is an example of the excellent scholarship and commendable expertise on India and South Asia that ISAS has cultivated over the years and the contribution that it would continue to make in this regard.

We can hardly thank the distinguished contributors of this volume enough for their time and effort. They have been most supportive, diligent and patient in all their responses and communications to our repeated queries. We cherish the experience of working with a wonderful team of authors. We have learnt a great deal from what they have written for this book and we are sure that the readers would benefit as much as we have from their writings.

As editors, we owe large debts of gratitude to some without whom this book would not have been seen the light of the day. Our colleague Faiza Saleem, research assistant at ISAS, has worked on the manuscript with precise care. Her rigour and attention has gone a very long way in giving the book its final shape. Indrani Dasgupta, copy editor at Penguin Random House India, has been prompt and detailed in scrutinizing the book as thoroughly as possible. Last, but not the least, in our list of those to whom we are deeply grateful is Lohit Jagwani, commissioning editor, Penguin Random House India. Right from the beginning, Lohit has tended the book with great affection and has spared no efforts to ensure its timely evolution and progress. Finally, like in all our other endeavours in life, this work too, would not have come to fruition without the support and encouragement of our respective better halves—Geeta and Parama. All the lapses and lacunae in the work remain entirely ours.

Vinod Rai and Amitendu Palit

Introduction

Policy, Governance and Institutions: Mapping India after Seven Decades of Freedom

Vinod Rai and Amitendu Palit

Public policy discussions on India present formidable intellectual challenges given the great variety of issues and perceptions involved in their objective analysis. The challenges become more daunting given the expansive backdrop of a few thousand years, over which India has produced individuals and ideas—Aryabhata in space exploration, Chanakya in governance, emperor Akbar in religious coexistence, Ramanujan in mathematics, Gandhi in ahimsa, Tagore in humanity—to name only a few. They have become examples for the world to emulate and admire. The world has kept looking at India for new sources of admiration even after Independence, notwithstanding the substantive changes in its sociopolitical and economic context.

Comprehending India's journey over the seven decades that it has travelled since 15 August 1947 is not possible unless contextualized in the light of the pain and the trauma characterizing the milieu in which independent India took its first steps. Partition sowed seeds of hatred to a great depth among the country's major religious communities. The animosity, which was difficult for the young country and its new leaders to contain, remains a significant challenge even today with communal harmony a major governance goal for political leaderships and administrations across the country. The importance of building a secular, independent India and making its institutions work in a fashion uninfluenced by religious tensions and biases have been a key objective of Indian public policies. Most of the public policy is shaped by the tenets of the Indian Constitution.

India chose to go down a path like most other countries at the time, which were emerging from and embarking on independent futures. Providing effective governance and building efficient institutions were major public policy challenges that India encountered upon becoming a sovereign republic. The intensities of these challenges were, in many respects, more for India than its peers given its remarkable decision to grant complete political freedom to all in the country. The grant of democratic liberty, along with a series of Constitutional rights guaranteeing freedom of speech, opinion and religious practices for individuals, wasn't accompanied by a similar freedom for economic activity. For four decades after Independence, India relied on the state as the main driver of economic growth. The seeds of state-led economic development sown in the Industrial Policy Resolution of 1956 were carried forward over the next decades into greater dominance of the public sector and contracting role of private enterprise. By then, India had nationalized its banks, insurance companies and coal mines, and regulated private capacities in heavy industries through licences. The government was steering towards reaching the overarching goals of tackling poverty, reducing unemployment and ensuring self-sufficiency in food production. The way it decided to do it was through greater state control, which then laid the foundation for a 'licence and inspector raj' through the regulatory apparatus it spawned. In a sense, it created more governance and institutional challenges for India, primarily by generating bottlenecks in economic expansion and efficient delivery of public services, which the country could have well avoided. Most of the economic reforms that India effected since the early nineties were aimed at undoing the deeds of the past four decades. The energy and time spent in creating unproductive regulations and disbanding them were costs that the country could have well avoided.

Politically, the wheel appears to have turned the full circle in India. The tallest leaders at the time of Independence—Mahatma Gandhi and independent India's first prime minister, Pandit Jawaharlal Nehru—represented the Congress party that dominated Indian politics. Nehru was succeeded by Lal Bahadur Shastri and Indira Gandhi, prime ministers who ensured political sustenance of the Congress well into the decade of the seventies. Imposition of an internal emergency by Indira Gandhi during the mid-seventies (25 June 1975 to 21 March 1977) was responsible for changing the character of India's politics as a disillusioned electorate voted out Congress in the elections that followed to usher in a non-Congress government for the first time in the history of independent India. Though the Congress rebounded to regain primacy in the eighties, the general elections to the Parliament held in 1989 marked the onset of multiparty coalition governments in India. Regional parties began occupying prominence in the governments at the Centre as the Congress realized the inevitability of aligning with smaller parties for mustering numbers in the Parliament.

The 1989 election also marked the emergence of the Bharatiya Janata Party (BJP) on the national political scene. The growth of the BJP underscored the resonance of a right-wing nationalistic political agenda with a significant section of the electorate. This was in marked contrast to the centrist political posturing of the Congress and the left-of-centre positioning of the Left, comprising mainly the Communist Party of India (CPI) and the Communist Party of India (Marxist) (CPI-M). The BJP went on to displace the Congress as the leading political party of India and formed coalition governments at the Centre with regional parties in the late nineties under Prime Minister Atal Bihari Vajpayee. Coalition governments refused to fade away as the Congress under Prime Minister Manmohan Singh stitched multiparty alliances to run governments at the Centre for most of the last decade and into the current one. The 2014 elections again marked a watershed as the BJP under Narendra Modi came to dominate the arithmetic in the Parliament with an absolute electoral majority of its own. While the BJP still has some regional parties supporting it as part of a broad alliance at the Centre, the last Parliament elections, and the electoral success of the BJP in most state elections held thereafter, marks its emergence as the most prominent political party in the country. While still not as overwhelming as the Congress was in the first four decades after Independence, the BJP's electoral success at both national and sub-national elections has enabled it to significantly reduce political opposition in various legislatures of the country, making both regional parties and the Congress struggle for political survival.

While it might be adventurous to correlate the economic and political transitions, the fact that state control of the economy was the highest when the Congress was the undisputed political authority in the country can hardly be overlooked. Generational changes in leadership did impact Congress's views on economic management with Prime Minister Rajiv Gandhi being among the earliest to visualize economic liberalization. But it was actually a Congress government supported by some regional parties that implemented the most decisive economic reforms in the nineties under the leadership of Prime Minister P.V. Narasimha Rao. Some of the politically sensitive reforms were facilitated by the prospects of the country defaulting on external payment obligations due to paucity of foreign exchange arising from precarious balance of payment conditions. But the Rao government and its successor coalition counterparts kept working on reforms even after economic conditions improved. Challenges in this regard have often been significant for various governments given that they needed to muster sufficient numbers in the Parliament for legislating major economic policies. Lack of adequate numbers often stifled the pace of reforms, like in the early years of the current decade when 'policy paralysis'[1] afflicted the Manmohan Singh government. Indeed, this was the time when the political economy of the country began showing stress with intra-coalition relations becoming tenuous leading to dissensions and tensions within the government. Turf issues began emerging with regional parties that were exercising influence disproportionate to their strength in the coalition. Quite often regional interests dominated national interests perpetuating policy paralysis. This was in marked contrast to the leverage enjoyed by the current Modi government. The latter's political authority enabled it to implement the rather audacious 'demonetization' of more than 80 per cent of the Indian currency in circulation on 8 November 2016. Political goodwill for the Prime Minister and for his party following the resounding electoral victory little more than two years ago, helped the government to push ahead with the measure despite the hardships it created for people and the setbacks it meant for the economy, at least in the short term.[2] While the benefits of demonetization in terms of its impact in making the economy less cash-intensive, more digitized, flushing out ill-gotten wealth and counterfeit currency will require to be examined over the long term, the importance of solid political authority in administering 'bitter' economic pills was evident from its implementation.

The extent by which the changing character of the polity and visions of political leaderships has impacted the quality of governance and the functioning of institutions—India's major challenges that she inherited and continues to live with—is not easy to answer. But some vital institutions are worth taking a close look in this regard. Notable among these are Indian *banks*. Prime Minister Indira Gandhi nationalized fourteen banks in 1969 on the pretext of breaking their control and ownership by a few business families, to mobilize savings from the masses and to cater to priority sectors of the economy like agriculture and small enterprises. The move resulted in more than 80 per cent of Indian banks coming under government control. This also set in motion lending among banks, in particular public sector banks. While private banks came up after the economic reforms of the nineties, state-owned banks remained the major entities in the sector, handling both government and private corporate businesses. Financial difficulties of public sector banks were usually rationalized by political parties and governments as inevitable side effects of their role in aiding the development of priority sectors, where lending decisions were not guided by the principle of maximizing returns.

Indian banks were also praised for being relatively immune to catastrophic developments in the global banking industry, notably the global banking crisis of 2008, as they were not plugged into the toxic assets circulating in regional financial markets. However, Indian banks began experiencing their own crisis of existence soon after as they became inundated with non-performing loans due to excessive lending to businesses lacking domain experience in building infrastructure assets. They also borrowed heavily from markets for maintaining their lending and became financially overleveraged. This factor got further compounded by inordinate delays in projects being given statutory clearance, leading to time and cost overruns and thus defaults on advances from banks. Build-up of stressed assets of around Rs 6 trillion has eroded the capital of Indian banks.

The situation reflects the failure of not only vital state institutions like public sector banks to manage their capital and lending, but also the political reluctance of decades to reform banks. This could also be since banks have been performing politically 'important' functions such as lending to electorally important constituencies like farmers, small businesses and scheduled castes and tribes, as well as large businesses that are major funders of political parties. Indeed, fear of persecution has made executives of public sector banks slow in resolving or restructuring stressed assets, leading to a huge amount of capital remaining locked up in defaulting accounts.

The challenge for public policy in India emanates essentially from the requirements of good governance. Banks exemplify the challenge better than most other institutions. Despite most of India continuing to remain unbanked, banks have brought forth critical challenges for governments. These include their recapitalization and tackling financial stresses for ensuring that basic banking facilities are extended to the vast numbers that would gradually become part of the banking system as the economy formalizes. Significant initiatives such as the Insolvency and Bankruptcy Code, time limitations for National Company Law Tribunals and an ambitious recapitalization plan for public sector banks have been steps in the right direction. However, these steps need to be administered in a manner that enables banks to perform efficiently while reaching out to more and more people. This, then, reemphasizes the persistence of challenges that India took on right since it obtained independence and as alluded to earlier in the chapter: *providing effective governance through efficient institutions.*

The issue of governance and institutions in India can hardly be addressed without looking closely at individuals entrusted with the responsibility to govern. Civil administration in modern India has increasingly become more and more complex as most of the country's shortcomings, particularly in the areas of public service delivery, are being attributed to lack of good governance by scholars, practitioners, civil society activists and international organizations. The heightened focus on governance has enhanced challenges for administrators with citizens now empowered with the Right to Information that calls for a far more responsive *bureaucracy* than the legacy carried from the days of the Raj. It is unfortunate that recommendations of multiple administrative reforms commissions for overhauling the bureaucracy have been either left untouched, or if implemented, then flouted more than adhered.

One of the best examples is the recommendation to have fixed tenures for some key appointments. While incumbents have been shifted out before the end of their fixed terms upon change of governments, the contrary instance of incumbents being retained well beyond their fixed terms is also available. Furthermore, little attention has been paid to the differences in expertise and skills required for governing India at the national and sub-national levels. While for states, administrators need to be proficient in ensuring timely delivery of key services (e.g. education, health, water, sanitation and local rural and municipal services), the demands at the national government level are more of conceptualizing and designing programmes with an eye on their reach and target. Delivering to people what they need in the right mix of quantity and quality, irrespective of agencies formulating the schemes, can fail if states are poor in implementation. State bureaucracies must be trained accordingly with a greater focus on the 'field' as opposed to the 'ivory tower'. Needless to say, the emphasis for national level bureaucrats has to be different with greater focus on conceptualizing schemes, studying efficiently devised projects in other parts of the world and customizing them to Indian requirements. But innovative and 'out of the box' thinking are unlikely to figure easily among a bureaucracy accustomed to thinking and acting in set moulds.

The need of experienced technocrats, particularly in key infrastructure sectors (e.g. electricity, roads, ports, telecommunications, urban services) in this regard can hardly be overstated. Such lateral and technocratic expertise can be attached to major infrastructure ministries. The problem though is 'lateral' infusion of external skills is not welcomed by the existing bureaucracy given that it is considered encroachment on turfs. Indeed, on many occasions, technocrats have found working in government agencies frustrating and counter-productive given the resistance they have encountered. The half-hearted attempts to implement suggestions of administrative reform commissions combined with the reluctance of bureaucracies to accept external expertise reflect formidable challenges in improving the quality of governance in the country.

India has come a long way from the days when it depended on other countries for supply of essential foodgrain.[3] 'Green' and 'White' revolutions have ensured self-sufficiencies in foodgrains and milk production. While chronic food shortages have become distant memories, the Indian state has fallen well short in providing its citizens *clean and hygienic living conditions*. Notwithstanding the advances of the country in nuclear science, space exploration and high-end technological solutions, India's failures are conspicuous in human waste management and environmental pollution. Around 40 per cent of the Indian population still practice open defecation[4] and until recently, building toilets and improving sanitation facilities were not among the topmost priorities of the state. The 'Swachh Bharat' mission—one of the most important flagship public policy programmes initiated by Prime Minister Modi for creating a 'Clean India' by 2019—targets eliminating open defecation, building modern toilets, eradicating manual scavenging and bringing behavioural changes among people. The mission focuses on extensive people participation and combining good habits and clean practices of individuals and households with expansion of sanitation capacities. Quite a few Indian states, notably Sikkim, Himachal Pradesh, Kerala, Uttarakhand and Haryana, have declared themselves Open Defecation Free (ODF) in rural areas. While achievements and rate of progress under the programme will be keenly followed across the world, the salience of 'good governance' in making it successful can hardly be reiterated. In the context of the earlier discussion on bureaucracy, the importance of commitment and dedication of local administrators to the otherwise mundane, but incredibly important civic objectives of shifting people from open defecation and ensuring appropriate garbage disposal, can hardly be overstated.

It is also important in this context to consider the role of political parties, their contributions to the causes of *waste management and environmental preservation* in the country. Elections in India are not fought on the issue of pollution. India's global commitment to bringing down carbon footprints through the Paris Protocol Agreement on Climate Change is accompanied by a striking absence of discussion on pollution and environment in the domestic political discourse. Indeed, nonchalance of political parties to control of pollution in the country is remarkable and is best borne out by the appalling situation in the national capital of Delhi. Since November 2015, and in the aftermath of the Diwali celebrations, Delhi has been experiencing intense air pollution. The situation has persisted leading to serious repercussions on public health. Courts appeared to be the only actors keen on finding an end to the problem providing directions on limiting vehicle movements on the roads of Delhi. Two years later in October 2017, alarm bells began ringing again as dense smog engulfed Delhi, presumably from burning of crop stubble by farmers in neighbouring Punjab. Over the next few weeks, everyone watched in stunned disbelief as regardless of pollution assuming crisis proportions, the affected state governments failed to thrash out a solution and the Central government too refrained from proposing corrective measures. While the prospects of a long-term solution to curbing pollution in Delhi seem remote, it reinforces the limitations in quality of governance that continue to affect provision of public goods in the country. Indeed, environmental pollution, including the lack of preservation of waterbodies, has been a great concern. Pollution levels in the country's major snow-fed rivers like the Ganges and the Yamuna do not show any signs of abating despite millions having been spent on action plans for cleaning them. Elsewhere in the country, waterbodies such as lakes and backwaters are getting choked with water hyacinth destroying marine life. What is worrying is the scant concern of local governments, administrations and commercial developers to the fact that Indian residents enjoy a right to clean and healthy habitats and ensuring such conditions is a collective responsibility.

Regardless of disappointment over governance and functioning of critical institutions in India, there are occasions which provide hope. One of these, undoubtedly, is the effort by the Centre and states to come together for putting in place a uniform indirect tax system in the country. What had begun as the Value Added Tax (VAT) has eventually taken shape as the Goods and Services Tax (GST) after nearly two decades of labour. The existing GST is hardly perfect and several sectors are facing teething problems. Nonetheless, the fact that states and the Centre could rise above political differences and short-sighted economic calculations to agree to far-reaching constitutional amendments for institutionalizing a common indirect tax framework gives hope for more cooperation between Centre and states and a greater display of *cooperative federalism* in improving governance. As far as improvement of quality of delivery of public services is concerned, much in this regard will depend on how central and state agencies and bureaucracies act together in administering a federal framework. The experience of the GST would be a great example in this regard. Not only would it involve extensive coordination between national and sub-national institutions, but also embrace of technological solutions by the latter. Both of these are substantive challenges for people and agencies not accustomed to change.

About the book

Hope, more than anything else, reverberates across the various themes discussed in this book. Written by some of the most distinguished public policy practitioners from India and noted scholars with years of expertise on India, the chapters that follow bring together a gamut of issues integral to seven decades of independent India. These include India's external security and its engagement with the world, particularly Asia-Pacific; evolution and management of India's elections and the democratic process; India's globalizing economy and the planning experience; prospects and issues in agriculture and industry; critical challenges in land market and employment; regulations and issues in health, education, skill development, tax framework and corporate governance; and the changes and churnings characterizing Indian media, sports, civil services and caste and society.

While critical and candid, these essays are objective commentaries on India's course followed thus far and the course corrections that might be required as it goes ahead. Given the connection between public policy, governance and institutions highlighted in this chapter earlier, the papers weave around them the synergy between India's visions of itself in the current century as evolving from the journey it has traversed and the experiences it has had in policy and governance. And while reflecting, the papers do not fail to touch upon the obvious notwithstanding their honesty: resilience is what has seen India through till now and hope is what will take it forward.

I

India's External Security Challenges

Shivshankar Menon

Today, India is in the fortunate position of not facing any existential threat to her security. In that respect it is better placed today than in the past. She also has an increased capacity to deal with external challenges to her security now.

This cannot, however, obscure the fact that the international environment in which India makes her foreign policy and national security decisions has worsened recently. At the same time, her internal security challenges, many of which have strong external linkages, have also increased. Despite her improved capacity to deal with these challenges, it appears that India is entering a new era, which will require new responses from the country.

The Regional Context

A major determinant of India's external security is the international context within which it operates and seeks to develop and transform itself.

Today's world is less supportive and offers more difficult choices than the binary ones of the Cold War. Nor does it offer the economic opportunities of the years before the world economic crisis of 2008. Both world politics and the world economy are fragmenting and becoming increasingly regional. Protectionism has grown around the world. The rise of China, and her quest for primacy, first in Asia and then globally, along with a hierarchical view of an international order centred on herself, epitomized by the Belt and Road Initiative (BRI), pose a new set of questions and challenges to the established order and to Western supremacy. China now uses economic means, such as the BRI programme, to pursue geopolitical outcomes. In effect, economics and politics are no longer separate in today's world. Indeed, politics may now be driving economics.

Pressing issues for India are the disequilibrium or accelerated imbalances of power in the Asia–Pacific, sub-regional vacuums created by the rise of China and other powers, and the Trump administration's effective disengagement from the world. While these imbalances and vacuums will be corrected, recalibrated or filled over time, it is a slow process of adjustment that creates friction and tension. China seems to have decided that the time has come for her to reorder the broader region. The United States administration under Trump is yet to clarify its approach to China and the region. The initial signs are of a more transactional and less geopolitical US approach, driven by what it can get out of China and the Asia–Pacific rather than by the effect of its policies on other states, friends or allies, or on regional order. It remains in doubt whether these will amount to a long-term approach that other states can base their policies upon. These processes will, therefore, take time to work themselves through to a new equilibrium.

In the meantime, disequilibrium is liable to: ignite flash-points like the Korean Peninsula; invite overreach by one power or another in territorial and maritime disputes like the South China Sea, the East China Sea, the India–China boundary; or create space for insurgents, extremists and terrorists to exploit fragile societies and states like Afghanistan, Pakistan, Myanmar and southern Philippines. Whether they admit it or not, states in the Asia–Pacific today face unparalleled uncertainty. They are responding by tightening internal controls and building up their own defences, in what amounts to the world's greatest arms race, seeking partners who share their security concerns, and hedging their relationships with great powers like China and the US.

The commons in the Asia–Pacific are now increasingly contested, whether on the high seas, or in cyber and outer space. Since the commons are increasingly critical to the prosperity and security of the region, and for India, this poses a real problem for all the countries of the region. The traditional regional security architecture, of a hub-and-spokes arrangement centred on the US, or even a new G-2 of the US and China, is unable and unlikely to be able to address these issues. The Asia–Pacific is a crowded geopolitical space with several established, re-emerging and rising powers jostling in close proximity, all of whom have to be part of a solution, if that solution is to be lasting.

Secondly, domestic developments in many large countries have heightened the uncertainty and complexity created by the regional imbalance of power.

Since the 2008 financial crisis there has been a rise of authoritarian centralizers to power in several large countries, including China, Japan, India, Russia, Turkey, the UK and the US. They base their legitimacy on a heightened appeal to nationalism or nativism. In a slowing global economy, and in spite of the diminishing capacity of their governments to deliver domestic growth, they promise more and more and rely on nativist appeals (like 'America first' or 'The Great Rejuvenation of China'). In southern Asia, this phenomenon takes local forms. India is no exception to the global trend; in Pakistan, the power, influence and role of the army has been considerably enhanced at the expense of civilian governments nominally in power.

One result of this phenomenon is to accentuate the fragmentation and regionalization of world politics. As the powers' capacity to compromise and negotiate is lessened, relations between competitive powers become more fraught than in the past. Some of this dynamic is visible in India–Pakistan and India–China relations over the last year or so. Neither relationship is as smooth or predictable as it was a few years ago, and today pose new challenges to Indian security policy, separately and together.

The 2003 ceasefire along the LoC between India and Pakistan has broken down and political communication between the two states is minimal. As a consequence, the South Asian Association for Regional Cooperation (SAARC) summit has been postponed and cooperation in SAARC has been driven down to subregional levels, which excludes Pakistan. Even if there were to be a warming of India–Pakistan relations, the underlying causes of tension—cross-border terrorism from Pakistan and its quest for 'strategic parity' with India, and strategic depth in Afghanistan—are rooted in Pakistan's internal condition. Therefore, they are likely to repeatedly assert themselves, and any warming is likely to be temporary. The prospect of difficult India–Pakistan relations is a geopolitical fact that affects and will affect the geopolitical choices of India and other Asian countries.

The last few years have also seen a considerable strengthening of China's ties with Pakistan, her only ally apart from North Korea. As China steps out into the region, and as China–US strategic contention strengthens, it has hinged the BRI on the China–Pakistan Economic Corridor (CPEC). Not all projects under the BRI seem viable economically, which suggests that they have been included for geopolitical or other reasons. CPEC, for instance, lacks economic justification, and its strategic portions like Gwadar Port that have been implemented first, give the Chinese navy, which is now building a base at Djibouti, access and presence in the northern Arabian Sea and the approaches to the Hormuz Strait. This changes India's security calculus. The CPEC is to traverse some of the most lawless and insecure parts of the world. For India there is the added complication that it goes through the Indian territory under Pakistani occupation, and by making a long-term investment on that basis, seeks to solidify and legitimize that occupation. This is clearly unacceptable to the Indian government.

India–China relations have always had elements of both cooperation and competition, and are undergoing a shift, though the prospect is more positive than for India–Pakistan relations. The older modus vivendi from the eighties is no longer sufficient.[1] Several signs of stress in the relationship have surfaced in the last two years such as China's attitude to India's National Security Guard (NSG) membership (in contrast to her attitude in 2008 to the special exemption by the NSG for India), the listing of Masood Azhar as a terrorist in the UN, India's attitude to the BRI, and so on. As India and China have grown and their definitions of their own interests have expanded, they increasingly rub up against one another in the periphery that they share, whether on the southern Asian landmass, in archipelagic and mainland southeast Asia, in the Indian Ocean, or in the seas near China such as the South China Sea. However, a new strategic framework for this relationship will probably be worked out by the two countries. Since both countries have other domestic and international priorities, their core interests are not in fundamental conflict, and their differences can be managed.

Today, as a result of reform and rapid growth, both India and China need and see the world as essential for their domestic purposes—Chinese Dream and single-party rule, or New India and economic transformation. Therefore, expect more interventions, expeditionary and activist external politics playing to the nationalist gallery at home relatively soon, and backed by the military in China's case. India and China will try and shape their world, China alone, and India working with coalitions.

The future does not hold only doom and gloom. One effect of the economic growth spurt in India in the last three decades is that it today has tools and abilities it never had before. It may face new problems but there are also new ways of dealing with them. And the new problems in themselves possess potential opportunities.

This becomes evident when considering security issues facing India, such as cross-border terrorism, maritime security, or cyber security, all of which need primarily domestic capabilities and responses. They have a significant external element and also bring opportunities in their wake.

Security Issues

Consider national security, internal security and personal security—three domains where Indians expect their government to deliver security.

National security: India's real threats to national security today are internal, but with strong external linkages. Cross-border terrorism from Pakistan, and the corrosive effect that extremism and radicalism can have on a plural and diverse society like India's, are major security concerns. The situation in West Asia, which has deteriorated over the last decade, is further fuelling terrorist, extremist and radical religious forces in the subcontinent.

Given transborder ethnicities, there is fertile ground in the region for separatist movements and insurgencies. Many of these insurgent groups operate in less governed spaces and across national boundaries. Fortunately, cooperation among southern Asian states in dealing with these movements has improved considerably in the last decade, and India is getting better at mastering the techniques to deal with such problems through a combination of political and other means. Deaths from terrorism and internal conflict in India have declined steadily over the last decade.

The risks of interstate conventional conflict in the Indian subcontinent have been managed successfully for over four decades now, and its costs and risks are better appreciated than in the fifties and sixties. The fact that there are two declared nuclear weapon states in southern Asia has actually stabilized the situation as far as conventional conflict is concerned. It has driven conflict to other sub-conventional levels—to terrorism, covert action and forms of asymmetric warfare.

Another aspect of national security that is increasingly relevant for India is maritime security in the Indian Ocean. When India began reforming in 1991, external merchandise trade accounted for less than 18 per cent of the Gross Domestic Product (GDP). By 2014 that proportion had risen to 49.3 per cent, and well over 80 per cent of that was carried by sea.[2] This indicates the importance of the Indian Ocean to India's security and well-being. Fortunately, the security situation in the Indian Ocean is not as acute as it is in the seas near China with their territorial and maritime disputes, or in the western Pacific where a real struggle for naval mastery and dominance is unfolding. The Indian Ocean's issues arise mainly from troubles on land, particularly around its seven choke points, and the resulting piracy and instability that threaten the security and safety of critical sea lanes. Around 50 per cent of the world's trade passes though crucial Indian Ocean choke points and its sea lanes carry a large proportion of the world's energy flows. The open geography of the Indian Ocean means that no single power can or is likely to dominate it. But this does not prevent great powers from trying, and their contention is growing.

Internal security and ICT: The most significant security threats to India today are internal. They arise from a loss of social cohesion due to the very rapid growth and change that has been experienced in the last few decades, and external attempts to exploit those from Pakistan and West Asia. They also arise from the effects of new technologies, particularly Information and Communication Technology (ICT) which empower small groups and individuals, irrespective of whether they intend harm or benefit. ICT has breathed new life into older insurgencies, terrorist groups and rebellions (like the Naxalites in India or ethnic insurgencies in Myanmar). ICT also creates new opportunities for criminals. In 2012, for instance, threats and malicious rumours spread on the social media drove almost 80,000 people from northeast India to return to their homes from Bangalore and Mumbai. They were soon back at work and the government put in place systems to prevent such misuse of social media in the future, but that was an early example of the power of ICT to spread social panic.

Of course, ICT is a welfare enabler as well. ICT has helped to deliver benefits from the government directly to the most needy, through the unique biometric identity number, Aadhaar. ICT has also greatly enhanced the country's ability to manage disasters and respond to extreme weather events, and accelerated financial inclusion. The list of benefits is long and far outweighs the dangers. And these economic benefits and platforms also have security advantages, vastly increasing the state's reach and capacity. But the long list also makes it all the more important to treat cyber security with the seriousness that it deserves. Cyberspace is one domain that recognizes no national boundaries or man-made sovereignties. Cooperation across boundaries is essential if there is to be success in managing cyber security.

ICT also has a broader political effect. It helps to create and spread expectations and aspirations among the young, uprooted and mobile population of all our countries. History (and Alexis de Tocqueville) has shown that revolutions are produced by improved conditions and rising expectations, not by mass immiseration. This is exactly what globalization has given—a world where everything is amazing and nobody is happy; where life is better than ever before for most people but anger and dissatisfaction are high. This is especially true in case of India, which has just undergone its fastest economic growth spurt in history, thus accentuating inequalities just when ICT spread knowledge of what is possible and available elsewhere and thus raised expectations. Traditional elites and establishments are under attack everywhere. The resulting pressure on governments to deliver security and growth is, therefore, at unprecedented levels.

Personal security: It is also probably true in several countries that individuals no longer feel as secure in their persons as they used to. Statistics and polls, when available, bear this out. Crimes against the person and violence against women are increasing in all our societies. Some of this is the result of the uprooting that comes with massive urbanization and migration. As women join the workforce and social norms change, personal security and policing face new challenges. Traditional policing no longer suffices.

Fortunately today, India and the world have the means to tackle these problems, if there is political will to work together.

Next Steps

What should India and the region do about the security issues that have been mentioned above?

- There is certainly much more that the region could do against multinational threats such as terrorism, and against state sponsors of terrorists. Information sharing and joint actions against cross-border terrorism, its financing and support come to mind as immediately feasible.
- The time is also probably ripe to make much more use of the extended ASEAN Maritime Forum (AMF) to work together on maritime security. A start should also be made in capacity building and in cooperation on border and coastal security and policing that require collaboration across boundaries.
- Sharing of best practices of community policing and finding effective ways of cooperating against internal security threats and the new crimes that an interconnected globalized world makes possible to enhance cyber security and personal security.
- New legal instruments or multilateral initiatives are more difficult. Experience shows that they are unlikely to be effective in practice without the necessary political will among all the states involved. Instead, coalitions of those affected who share the same approach may be the best way forward on issues like radicalization and maritime security.

Conclusion

India is at a moment when the threats that she faces have evolved and changed. Most of these demand more, not less, engagement by India with her neighbours in southern and southeast Asia, and a new approach to managing her big power relationships. Fortunately, the international context, though complicated, also makes clear to several powers their common interest in working together to limit uncertainty and deal with security issues in the region. Besides, capabilities and awareness of these security issues have improved considerably throughout the region. It now remains for these countries to display the political will to tackle these security issues in order to continue the Asian march to prosperity that has already changed so many lives in the Asia–Pacific.

II

India in a Globalized World:[1]
Maximizing Benefits and Minimizing Costs

Duvvuri Subbarao

The year 1991 was a watershed in India's economic history when it made a decisive break from the past and shifted from a dirigiste regime of heavy protection, extensive controls and tight regulation to a more open, liberalized and market-oriented regime of economic management.

Motivation for the 1991 Reforms

The trigger for this radical shift, at any rate in popular perception, was the external payments crisis consequent on the first Gulf War, but that was just the proximate cause. The more substantive motivation for embracing wide-ranging structural reforms, going beyond merely stabilizing the external sector, was the realization that the economic philosophy that had guided India since Independence—self-sufficiency, protection and public sector dominance—had run its course. India needed to institute sweeping reforms in order to accelerate growth and reduce poverty.

According to the government's discussion paper on economic reforms[2] published in July 1993, the objective of the reforms was:

. . . to bring about rapid and sustained improvement in the quality of life of the people of India. Central to this goal is the rapid growth in incomes and productive employment . . . The only durable solution to the curse of poverty is sustained growth of incomes and employment . . . Such growth requires investment: in farms, in roads, in irrigation, in industry, in power and, above all, in people. And this investment must be productive. Successful and sustained development depends on continuing increases in the productivity of our capital, our land and our labour.

Within a generation, the countries of East Asia have transformed themselves. China, Indonesia, Korea, Thailand and Malaysia today have living standards much above ours . . . What they have achieved, we must strive for.

Reforms in the Nineties

The early big-bang reforms straddled a wide canvas. Industrial licencing was dismantled, save for a few exceptions; it was accompanied by a government policy for reducing the 'commanding heights' role of the public sector. Import restrictions were largely removed and tariff and non-tariff barriers were sharply scaled down. Following the steep two-step devaluation of the rupee, heavy management of the exchange rate gradually yielded to a market-determined exchange rate while the foreign investment regime was substantially eased.

Recognizing that it was the fiscal profligacy of the eighties that was at the heart of the external payments crisis, the government vowed to adhere to fiscal responsibility by reducing the fiscal deficit by two percentage points of GDP and laying out a road map for further consolidation. The fiscal reforms catalysed monetary reforms, including the dismantling of the administered interest rate and credit allocation system towards a market-based system. These were accompanied by financial sector reforms aimed at the development of deep, wide and vibrant financial markets. Significantly, the banking sector was opened up to new private sector players to enhance competition.

Post 1991, those early reforms were widened and deepened, to give a market orientation to most sectors and dimensions of economic activity, substantially relieving India from the tag of 'the most closed and heavily controlled economy in the world'. Over the years, the agenda shifted gradually, if also logically, from first generation reforms, having to do mostly with product markets, which are largely within the control of the Central government, to second generation reforms centred in factor markets, where progress depends on the active cooperation, if also explicit involvement, of states, as exemplified most recently by the implementation of the Goods and Services Tax (GST).

Reforms—Unique Indian Context

Implementing economic reforms is politically difficult, always and everywhere. India was no exception. Its reforms were criticized for being hesitant, cautious and slow. That may well have been the case. But they were also arguably unique inasmuch as they were negotiated through a vigorous, if also noisy, democracy, and through the complex labyrinth of India's federal structure where narrow regional interests clashed with collective economic virtue, and short-term political compulsions often militated against the national optimal. This may have slowed the process but it ensured that the reforms were robust and that the benefits were widely disbursed. That, at any rate, was the hope and expectation.

Democracy, in this sense, was, and remains, both India's strength and weakness as far as reforms are concerned. The democratic process ensured that a plurality of opinion informed the content and process of reforms even if it meant contentious, and even vexatious, debates and difficult compromises. Some people hold that India reformed by stealth. This is far from the truth. Except for market-sensitive reforms like devaluation of the currency, all other reforms were implemented in the best traditions of the sunshine law.

Globalization at the Heart of India's Reforms

One consequence, admittedly intended, of the economic reforms, even those centred in domestic sectors, was to integrate India with the global economy. For example, industrial delicensing or de-reservation of products for the small industry sector, even though domestic in content, was aimed at enabling the Indian industry to compete in the world. With the forces of globalization blowing hard and strong through the eighties, India surmised that staying out of globalization was no longer an option; on the other hand, the dazzling experience of the East Asian tigers (Hong Kong, Korea, Singapore and Taiwan) showed the rewards of global integration. The early successes of China, which opened up over a decade ahead of us, eroded India's export pessimism by demonstrating that even a large, continental-size economy can be nimble enough to compete in the world if it gets its act together.

Globalization—Emerging Market Experience

Globalization comes with costs and benefits as indeed evidenced by the experience of virtually all emerging market economies across space and time. The Latin American countries were the first to break out of the low income trap and dependency syndrome by liberalizing their external sectors. But throwing caution to the wind cost them heavily in the form of several episodes of the Tequila crisis.[3] The East Asian Miracle, riding on exporting value-added goods to the world to overcome the limitations of small home markets is a spectacular example of the positive side of globalization. On the other hand, the Asian financial crisis of the late nineties and the devastating toll it took on growth and welfare is a telling reminder of the pitfalls of misguided liberalization.

China's astonishing success over the last two decades in turning itself into the 'factory of the world', which helped it accelerate growth and lift hundreds of millions out of poverty, is truly unprecedented. It is also a striking demonstration of the benefits of globalization. On the other hand, the growing stress in China in recent years arising from its efforts to rebalance the economy from external to internal demand, from investment to consumption, the rapid debt build-up and depletion of foreign exchange reserves are evidence of the challenges of coping with the vagaries of globalization.

India's experience with globalization over the last twenty-five years is consistent with that of our peer emerging market economies. India experienced unprecedented growth acceleration in the first decade of the 2000s and clocked real output growth of nine plus per cent on average in the five-year period—2003–08.[4] The India growth story was so persuasive that the country was on the verge of being christened the next miracle economy. There were many reasons for this remarkable performance—enhanced productivity, growing entrepreneurial spirit, rising domestic savings rate and improving financial intermediation. But underlying all of these factors was India's deepening integration into the global economy manifesting the positives of globalization.

That sense of glory didn't last long as the negative side of globalization caught up soon thereafter with the outbreak of the global financial crisis following the collapse of Lehman Brothers in September 2008. The crisis hit virtually every country in the world and India was no exception. There was dismay and disbelief over the setback in India. The financial sector in the rich world was in deep turmoil because of reckless risk-taking in pursuit of quick profits but Indian banks had no exposure to the toxic assets. There was also a global recession but that should have hit big exporters like China, Japan and Germany; not India whose exports are only a small proportion of GDP. So went the popular narrative.

So why did India get hit by the crisis? The reason was that by 2008, India was more integrated into the global economy than we consciously recognized. India's two-way trade (merchandise exports plus imports), as a proportion to the gross domestic product (GDP) more than doubled over the previous decade: from about 20 per cent in 1998–99, the year of the Asian crisis, to over 40 per cent in

2008–09, the year of the global crisis. The deep trade integration was accompanied by an even deeper financial integration. Measured by the ratio of external transactions (total of all inflows and outflows in the current and capital accounts) to GDP, financial integration had more than doubled from 43 per cent in 1998–99 to 111 per cent in 2008–09. What this integration meant was that if global financial and economic conditions were in turmoil, India could not expect to remain an oasis of calm.[5]

International experience as noted above, including that of India's, shows that the adverse effects of globalization arose mostly out of financial liberalization rather than trade liberalization. On balance, trade liberalization has benefited developing economies whereas financial liberalization has been a mixed bag. In any case, past experience makes the challenge of globalization obvious— maximize the benefits and minimize the costs.

Benefits of Globalization

The benefits of globalization are obvious enough. The competitive forces generated by globalization improve productivity while also allowing the economy to operate to its comparative advantage. The resultant higher exports and faster output growth make the economy more attractive to foreign investors thereby giving the domestic economy access to a more diversified and competitive resource base. At the same time, domestic investors can diversify their risk by investing abroad. While higher investment engendered by globalization will expand the production base and employment opportunities, access to better technology and management practices will potentially put the economy on a virtuous cycle.

Does this theory work in practice? In other words, has India benefited from globalization as predicted by theory? Some broad indicators will be instructive.

Real GDP growth accelerated from 5.6 per cent per annum during the eighties to 6.9 per cent per annum in the post-reform period (1992–2016). Acceleration in per capita income was even more striking, rising as it did from 3.2 per cent per annum in the eighties to 5.1 per cent during 1992–2016. Underlying these broad parameters was a host of macroeconomic indicators—savings and investment rates, tax base and tax buoyancy, fiscal and current account deficits, credit growth and financial intermediation—all of which showed significant improvement consequent on reforms.[6]

How much of this improvement in the overall macroeconomic situation is due to India's integration with the global economy? Put another way, could similar results have been obtained if reforms were restricted to the domestic sector? It is difficult to give a precise answer in the absence of a counterfactual. But the reality is that domestic and external sector reforms are two sides of the same coin; it is difficult to reform on one side without reforming on the other side as well.

Costs of Globalization

Just as with benefits, the costs of globalization too are obvious enough but difficult to estimate in quantitative terms. With globalization, India's macroeconomic fortunes get linked to the vagaries of global forces. Entire industries can die because of import competition causing extensive job losses and destruction of regional economies. A case in point is the large steel imports that flooded Indian markets in the last two years forcing several factories to shut down, resulting in a huge negative multiplier effect. Similarly, exports can suddenly lose established markets because of abrupt and unforeseen supply-demand imbalances or innovation of new products and processes. Exports are also subject to periodic threats of protectionism as is the case presently.

While the volatility associated with trade integration can take a formidable toll, volatility arising from financial integration can be even more unforgiving. Capital flows, in particular, are notoriously fickle, subject to sharp surges, sudden stops and abrupt reversals, all of which can impair macroeconomic and financial stability, erode competiveness and hurt growth and welfare.

Volatile capital flows have been a common and recurrent feature of India's macroeconomic experience over the last ten years. In the years immediately preceding the crisis (2003–08) when the India growth story was on a roll and the world was experiencing the so-called Great Moderation, foreign capital inflows into India surged beyond its absorptive capacity. The result was a sharp appreciation of the rupee out of line with fundamentals and the threat of an asset price bubble and financial instability. The Reserve Bank of India (RBI) had to intervene in the market to prevent undue appreciation of the rupee.

That story changed abruptly with the outbreak of the global financial crisis in 2008 when, unnerved by the turmoil in the advanced economy financial markets, capital fled emerging markets to the safe haven of the US, giving India the reverse problems. The rupee depreciated steeply, inflation pressures intensified and fiscal pressures were exacerbated. This time round, the RBI had to intervene in the market to sell dollars in order to prevent volatility in the exchange rate.

The same story was repeated during the so-called Taper Tantrum triggered by a statement in May 2013 by Ben Bernanke, then chairman of the US Federal Reserve, that they were considering gradually tapering their asset purchase programme, popularly known as 'quantitative easing'. That the Federal Reserve would unwind its unconventional monetary policy once financial markets started stabilizing was known from the beginning. Nevertheless, global financial markets were shaken by the Bernanke statement setting off the Taper Tantrum.

Amidst the ensuing fear and panic, emerging markets, including India, experienced capital flight. The rupee tumbled, depreciating by as much as 17 per cent in just a little over three months, forcing the RBI once again to mount a fierce exchange rate defence.[7]

Managing exchange rate volatility caused by capital flow volatility is always a complex and costly challenge. Emerging market economies have tried a variety of options—capital controls, foreign exchange intervention and, on occasion, even monetary policy. But experience showed that no option is benign.

On capital controls, for example, there are always questions about what type of controls, when and indeed whether they will be effective. Similarly, when it comes to foreign exchange intervention, a central bank is concerned about maintaining its credibility since a failed defence of the exchange rate can be worse than no defence at all. If the exchange rate does not correct in spite of intervention, the central bank runs the risk of hitting a tipping point when it forfeits market confidence and the exchange rate goes into a free fall. This explains why central banks are always anxious to ensure that they have sufficient ammunition by way of foreign exchange reserves to counter any threat to exchange rate stability.

Global Cooperation to Manage Globalization

Volatile capital flows are a characteristic of globalization—in particular, a consequence of spillover from the advanced economy central bank policies into emerging market economies. Quite understandably, this is a contentious issue that has regularly figured in international meetings such as those of the IMF and the G20.

The consistent refrain of emerging markets at these meetings would be that the unconventional monetary policies of advanced economies are taking a heavy toll on their economies and that advanced economies must factor in this spillover impact in formulating their domestic policies. They argue that these cross-border capital flows are a consequence of globalization—maintaining open borders for trade and finance. Both sides, advanced and emerging economies, benefit from globalization and so they also must share the costs of globalization; it is unfair to leave the entire burden of adjustment to emerging markets.

Advanced economies, led by the United States, have largely been dismissive of these grievances. Their main response would be that their policies are driven entirely by the need to stimulate their domestic economies, and the argument that it is a cover for deliberately debasing their currencies for export advantage is vacuous. They would not deny the existence of the spillover impact but would argue that such spillover is an inevitable by-product of their policy effort to revive their domestic economies. Moreover, the argument goes, revival of advanced economies is an international public good inasmuch as emerging markets too benefit from such revival through increased demand for their exports. Their response would typically end with advice to emerging markets that they should set their own houses in order to cope with the forces of globalization rather than find a scapegoat in the domestic policies of advanced economies.

This has largely been a dialogue of the deaf. Global problems require global coordination; but in a world divided by nation states, there is no constituency of the global optimal. Consequently, emerging markets have had to fall back on their efforts to manage the negative impact of globalization, especially the macroeconomic instability caused by volatile capital flows. India has been in the forefront of putting across the case of all emerging market economies.[8]

Managing the Costs and Benefits of Globalization—India's Agenda

The above synopsis defines the task clearly: what should India do to maximize the benefit-cost ratio of globalization. Here is a five-point template in that regard.

- **Keep the fiscal and current account deficits in check:** Both in 1991 when we had a severe balance of payments crisis and in 2013 when we had a near crisis, the root cause was the 'twin deficit' problem—unrestrained fiscal profligacy spilling over into the external sector[9] pushing the current account deficit beyond sustainable limits. On the fiscal side, it is becoming increasingly clear that it is not enough if the Central government puts its fiscal house in order but the states too must do so, because what matters for macroeconomic purposes is the combined deficit of the general government.

- **Maintain macroeconomic stability:** The objective is to manage the basic macro parameters—interest rate, inflation rate and exchange rate—in such a way as to drive rapid and sustained growth consistent with low and steady inflation. This requires, in particular, managing the 'impossible trinity' which asserts that a country cannot simultaneously maintain all three policy goals of free capital flows, a fixed exchange rate and an independent monetary policy.[10] As an emerging economy steadily integrating with the world, India should manage the impossibly trinity flexibly and predictably to preserve macroeconomic stability.

- **Keep financial stability always on the radar screen:** A big lesson of the global financial crisis was that financial instability anywhere was a threat to financial stability everywhere. The crisis held out many other lessons as well. Steady growth and macroeconomic stability does not guarantee financial stability; indeed an extended period of stability can itself sow the seeds of instability. Moreover, the financial system can contain pressure for longer than we think possible and as a result, when the inevitable implosion takes place, it can be quite disastrous, even catastrophic. The challenge for regulators is to ensure that the systemic risk is within acceptable limits without choking growth and innovation.

- **Improve productivity:** The importance of improving productivity in order to be competitive in the world is obvious and India's agenda in this regard is huge—improve education and health outcomes, reduce gender gaps, improve skills and infrastructure and most of all create an environment and establish a regulatory framework that fosters innovation.

- **Improve ease of doing business:** One of the prime motivations for globalization is to attract foreign investment. The frustration and harassment that investors face in implementing projects in India is now the stuff of folklore. While India has now improved its rank to 100 out of 189 countries in the World Bank's ranking by way of 'ease of doing business', it still has a long way to go in making the country an attractive place for doing business. Empirical evidence shows that countries gain as much as one percentage point of growth when they move up fifty places in the ease of doing business ranking. Here again the agenda is huge and obvious; the challenge lies in implementation.

Globalization—a Double-Edged Sword

Globalization is a double-edged sword. It offers immense opportunities but also poses harsh challenges, making it tempting for emerging markets to believe that they would be better off withdrawing from globalization. That would be throwing away the baby with the bathwater—exactly the wrong response. Managing globalization boils down to keeping borders largely open for flows of goods and services, and keeping borders only cautiously open for financial flows. The challenge for India, as indeed for all emerging economies, is to manage this balance in such a way as to maximize the benefit-cost ratio.

III

India's Elections and Electoral Reforms at Seventy

S.Y. Quraishi

A thriving and vibrant electoral democracy has been India's distinct and durable identity, long before it asserted itself as an economic, nuclear or information technology (IT) major. This institution, which was founded by our freedom fighters and makers of the Constitution, has been nurtured by the Parliament, judiciary, political parties, media and above all by the people of India, with some distinct contribution from the Election Commission of India (ECI).

Despite doubts and fears from many quarters, the founders of modern India adopted universal adult suffrage from day one, thus reposing faith in the wisdom of the common Indian to elect his/her representative to the seats of power. The choice of electoral democracy was variously termed: 'a giant leap forward', 'a bold enterprise', 'an unparalleled adventure'. The common people in India were politically empowered to vote at a time when 84 per cent of Indians were illiterate and poor, living in an unequal society fractured by a caste-based hierarchical system.[1] The poor masses of India had voted in many elections before Switzerland allowed its women to vote in 1971 and Australia did so for its aborigines in 1967. The United Kingdom, the 'mother' of modern democracies, granted equal voting rights to women only in 1932, about 100 years after its first elections. On the other hand, the United States of America had its first presidential elections in 1789, but its women had to wait till 1920, till the nineteenth amendment of the Constitution, before being able to vote. France and Italy did so only in 1944 and 1945 respectively. Indeed, in this regard it is worth iterating Nobel laureate Amartya Sen—'A country does not become fit for democracy, it becomes fit through democracy.'[2]

Over the past sixty-seven years, the Election Commission has delivered sixteen elections to the Lok Sabha and over 400 elections to state legislative assemblies and has facilitated peaceful, orderly and democratic transfer of power. In India, the rise of leaders belonging to the marginalized sections of the society, farmers, women and minorities to head national and state governments, and to other important Constitutional positions has been a direct outcome of the practice of electoral democracy. Heterogeneity of political parties and multiple instances of government formation through coalition of different political parties reflect a bouquet of diverse aspirations. The upward trend of participation of women, backward castes, tribal communities and the economically marginal in India's politics and governance can be traced to elections. It is a matter of pride and satisfaction that secular India has had Muslim and Dalit presidents and vice-presidents, a Sikh prime minister and a Christian defence minister.

India is large, perhaps 'extra-large', in many respects, but the significance of its size would not dawn upon many without some elaboration. There were around 835 million electors on the electoral roll of India, as on 1 January 2014, which is more than the voting population of every continent. The elections to the Indian Parliament held in 2014 were described as the biggest management event in the world involving 835 million voters, 932,000 polling stations, 1.18 million electronic voting machines (EVMs) and 11 million polling personnel. While these are the statistics for the general elections to the Lok Sabha, corresponding statistics for many state elections would exceed those for national elections in several countries.

India's mind-boggling electoral statistics should not obliterate the painstaking administrative efforts for reaching voters. Some of these are remarkable, like having a stand-alone polling station for a lone voter from the Gir Forest area in the state of Gujarat, and twelve electoral staff trekking forty-five kilometres in knee-deep snow to reach a polling station for only thirty-seven voters in the Ladakh region in the Himalayas. All modes of transportation, including elephants, camels, boats, bicycles, helicopters, trains and aeroplanes have been used to move men and material during Indian elections.

India is a country of great diversities, be it geographical—deserts, mountains, plains, forests, islands, coastal areas—or in being multireligious, multicultural, multilingual and multi-ethnic. It has been a great challenge for the Indian state to meet the demands of this diversity. Equally difficult have been the challenges of fighting terrorism, external and internal security threats, adjusting to the impact of economic globalization and the rapidly rising expectations of an information-savvy, growing middle class. It is a daunting task to ensure the neutrality and credibility of elections for all stakeholders amidst conflicting claims, particularly when each political actor in a multiparty parliamentary system devotes full energy and prime time to demonstrating the inability of other parties to govern. And the methods used in this respect are not always above board. It, therefore, becomes the key responsibility of the election management body to deliver free, fair, transparent and peaceful elections, ensuring inclusiveness and participation. Indian elections are invariably marked by rivalry and revelry, serious and melodramatic campaigns, adherence and violation of codes but, finally, by happy acceptance of the verdict.

Electoral Reforms through the Years

The Election Commission's journey has witnessed change in both the quality and the quantity of its operations. The management of elections in India has continually evolved and still does, matching the colossal proportions and ever-increasing complexity of task. In the first general elections held in India in 1952, there were separate ballot boxes used for candidates. In 1962, the marking system of voting was introduced. Multi-member constituencies have given way to single-member constituencies. Computerized photo-electoral rolls have now substituted printed electoral rolls. The Elector's Photo Identity Card (EPIC) is by now a cherished possession of all citizens. By 2014, the coverage of both had already reached over 99 per cent of the electors.

In 1982, EVMs were used on an experimental basis. Since 1998, these have been used for all state elections and since 2004 in all general elections. During this period, EVMs have withstood judicial, administrative and technical scrutiny. Continuous improvements in EVMs have been taken up through an independent committee of technical experts and in consultation with political parties. Manufactured by the public sector in India, EVMs are simple, voter-friendly and cost-effective and give faster and error-free voting and quick counting. At every stage of handling of EVMs, candidates of all political parties are present. Use of the Braille strip on EVMs has made them popular with the visually challenged. EVMs are increasingly catching the attention of election management agencies across the world. In 2013, the EVMs incorporated a Voter Verifiable Paper Audit Trail (VVPAT) as an additional feature to enhance transparency and public confidence. The next general elections in 2019 will be held entirely with VVPAT.

Year after year, through engagement of technology and a sense of innovation, and, more importantly, matching with the dynamics of the sociopolitical and economic processes of the Indian society, the art and craft of election management has been chiselled further. In the highly charged arena of competitive elections, where distrust is the best guarantor of fair-play, the Election Commission spares no effort in election tracking, preventing intimidation, ensuring security of voters and facilitating votes. The latest effort in this regard is to have webcasting from polling stations at the time of polling for public view of the proceedings.

One major instrument that contributes to peaceful, free and fair elections in India is the Model Code of Conduct (MCC), which the Indian political class, particularly candidates in elections, is in awe of. The MCC ensures a level playing field and is a unique instrument that has evolved with the consensus of political parties in India and is a singular significant contribution to the cause of democracy. With the seal of approval put by the Supreme Court on the MCC, the Election Commission enforces it from the day it announces any election schedule, whether for a general election or bye-election. Provisions of the MCC facilitate the Election Commission in preventing misuse of state resources. While the MCC has no statutory backing and many of its provisions are not legally enforceable, public opinion is the moral sanction for its enforcement and, hence, it has evolved into a 'moral' code of conduct. Neutrality is the soul of any election management body and the fierce neutrality of the Election Commission constitutes the core of its strength, compounded by the MCC.

In its evolution, the ECI is presently at a new crossroads. While India's election management apparatus has quite effectively neutralized the challenges of muscle power and incumbency power, the Commission is aware of the battles that remain to be won. Foremost among these is corruption that can and does pollute the electoral process. It is a striking coincidence that when an agitated debate on corruption was raging across India, the Commission stepped up its efforts with some determined measures to curb the use of black money during elections. This also covers the new menace of 'paid news'—a corrupt nexus between political parties, candidates and media houses that seeks to hoodwink the expenditure rules and causes undue influence on electors. It warrants mentioning a few instruments for transparency in campaign finance, some of which already existed but required serious enforcement and some others that were introduced with the new resolve to fight money power. There is a prescribed ceiling on expenditure for the elections to the Parliament as well as the legislatures of the provinces/states. The candidates are required to maintain their day-to-day account of election expenses and lodge the same with the district election officer within thirty days of declaration of results. They are also required to file an affidavit declaring their assets and liabilities, along with affidavits about their educational and criminal antecedents at the time of filing their nomination. Such affidavits are displayed on the ECI's website. Expenditure observers are appointed to keep a check on the expenditure incurred by the candidates and the political parties.

For curbing corruption and use of black money in elections, the Commission has also issued directions that candidates must open a separate bank account for all their election expenses and should make payment for major expenses by cheques. It also directed its managers to maintain a 'shadow observation register' of election expenses for each candidate, which is compared with the candidate's statement of election expenses and the statement of expenditure provided by the political parties, for checking unmentioned excesses, if any. This is in line with the ECI's efforts to promote stringent auditing of the accounts of all political parties and publishing of their annual accounts. Starting from 2010, it set up district-level committees to operate 24/7 during the election period to account for the acts of paid news, while all the time walking on the razor's edge of not encroaching on press freedom.

Excessive money power has led to the clamour for state funding of elections, which is not desirable simply for the reason that it does not guarantee an end to the inflow of black money to the election arena. It might result in double jeopardy of both the honest taxpayer's money and black money getting mixed up in financing electoral campaigns. However, since democracy cannot run without funds being spent on election campaigns, state funding of political parties (not elections) based on the votes obtained by them can be seriously considered. If all parties were to get Rs 100 for every vote obtained, based on the last election turnout of 55 crore votes, they would get Rs 5500 crores without resorting to private fund collection using force or foul means. Awareness campaign for ethical voting without falling for bribes and inducements is a new dimension of the Election Commission's efforts, for which civil society has come forward with exemplary support.

Another issue that has engaged the serious attention of the Commission starting from 2010 is voter participation in elections. Elections have to be not only free and fair, but also socially just and more participative. Otherwise there may remain a democracy deficit despite a correctly conducted election. From the first general election onwards, India's voter participation, measured by the voter turnout has remained close to 55–60 per cent. While this might be a reasonably good figure compared to the declining voter interest in several other countries and societies, it is definitely far less than the country's aspirations. The theme that the ECI adopted in celebration of its diamond jubilee in 2010 was 'greater participation for a stronger democracy'. All elections ever since have registered record turnouts—states like Bihar and Uttar Pradesh have jumped from approximately 30 per cent to 55–60 per cent, whereas the northeastern states that were already high have crossed 80–90 per cent.[3]

The Indian Constitution from its very inception provided every twenty-one-year-old the right to vote in direct recognition of the role of the youth in the democratic process. The voting age was further reduced to eighteen years in 1989 through a Constitutional amendment. Unfortunately, the potential of the wide-ranging revolutionary step is far from being realized. This is evident from the low registration and turnout of young voters. Apart from the problems of youth enrolment and participation there is also the issue of a visible apathy among the Indian urban middle class that prevents many young voters from casting votes. Moreover, women voters also lag behind their male counterparts in certain parts of the country. Weaker sections, vulnerable groups, people in difficult situations of life, and voters from the defence forces are particularly in need of special facilitation.

The ECI's response to the above predicament, while a bit late, has been decisive enough. Replacing token gestures on voters' education in the past, a Systematic Voters' Education and Electoral Participation (SVEEP) wing was set up that rolls out comprehensive community outreach and multimedia campaigns for increasing electoral participation of all citizens. The attempt aimed at filling up all possible gaps in information, motivation and facilitation. In every election now, the ECI carries out a scientific survey of Knowledge, Attitude, Behaviour and Practices (KABP) of voters before launching targeted interventions in partnership with a host of governmental and civil society organizations. In a very short time, these efforts have become a central part of the election management operations. This initiative has returned impressive dividends in terms of higher registration and higher turnout in each of the recent state elections, including record turnouts in some states.

In a historic measure, the Commission declared 25 January, its foundation day, as the National Voters Day (NVD) from 2011 with the avowed purpose to increase enrolment of voters, especially of the newly eligible ones. In five NVDs, nearly 120 million new voters have been added. Each year, around 800,000 functions were organized at the polling booth level to give new voters their voter cards. All the participants took a pledge to vote without fail and without any bribe or inducement. It is heartening to note that several countries of the world are adopting this model of National Voters Day.

It does not require any explanation that aspiring democracies around the world look forward to sharing the knowledge, skills and expertise at the ECI's disposal. Responding to increasing global demands, especially from Afro-Asian nations, the Commission launched the India International Institute of Democracy and Election Management (IIIDEM) in 2011. IIIDEM serves as a training and resource centre in the critical sector of elections and democratic processes for both national and international participants. In the first year itself, the institute hosted over forty courses and had enthusiastic funding and technical partners joining in. Within five years, nearly seventy-five countries sent their election officials to get training here. The institute receives calls from developing democracies in Asia and Africa and also from countries that have witnessed the Arab Spring for capacity development and sharing of knowledge and skills. Teams from Egypt, Jordan, Iraq, etc., have received training and guidance from the ECI. The Commission is rising to this new role with conviction and humility.

Electoral Reforms: Emerging Concerns

With the type of constitutional mandate that the Commission has, it cannot afford to sit on its laurels. There are several long-pending reform proposals and some recent ones from the Commission that aim at cleaning up the electoral process, so that the foundation can be laid for good governance and a corruption-free polity. The ECI in association with the law ministry organized countrywide consultations on these reforms, paving the way for adoption of due legislation. Some of these proposals deal with criminalization of politics and regulation of campaign finance, publicity and opinion polls, etc. Groups from civil society have vociferously come out in support of early electoral reforms.

The electoral reforms being demanded can be grouped into three categories:

a) Ones that will reinforce the independence of the Election Commission.
b) Those that will help cleanse politics.
c) Those that will make the working of the political parties more transparent.

a) **Reinforcing independence of the ECI:** The proposal is that the appointment of the commissioners should not be done unilaterally by the government of the day, but by a collegium just like all other Constitutional and statutory bodies. The elevation of the chief election commissioner of India should be automatic—by seniority. The two other election commissioners should be removable only by the process of impeachment like the chief election commissioner.

b) **Cleansing of politics:** Though the law of the land provides for disqualification of convicted individuals from contesting, the

ECI has been demanding that the persons against whom heinous criminal cases are pending should be debarred from contesting—provided the court has framed the charges.

c) Enhancing transparency of political parties: The ECI must be given the power to deregister a political party for violation of the terms of registration and any gross indiscipline. Inner party democracy must be honestly followed. The funds of the political parties must be audited by an independent auditor and must be put on a website for the public to see. An act should be passed to ban hate speech that can arouse communal tensions, especially during elections. Funding of elections must be made transparent both in terms of fund collection and expenditure. Paid news must be made an electoral and a criminal offence. Government promotional advertisements must be banned six months before the elections. These are some of the suggestions that the Election Commission has been sending to the governments for over two decades. But the governments have been sitting over them.

Several national-level committees have given a number of suggestions on electoral reforms during the past four decades. These should be examined without further delay and implemented if the declining faith of the people in democracy is to be restored.

If the largest democracy on the planet wishes to become the greatest, the electoral reforms are the way to achieve it.

IV

India's Media 1947 to 2017

Robin Jeffrey

India's first general elections in 1951–52 enrolled 175 million eligible voters, lasted for six months, and led Jawaharlal Nehru across 40,000 kilometres of the country to speak to 35 million people. Election speeches on the radio were ruled out because Nehru reckoned there were too many parties to allow fair access, and, anyway, the country only had two radios for every 1000 people. Forty-six per cent of eligible citizens voted and Nehru's Congress Party won three-quarters of the 479 seats.[1]

In India's eighteenth general elections in 2014, 547 million voters—66 per cent of the electorate—cast ballots on EVMs. It took only five hours to declare the results, though polling had happened over six weeks. There were 650 television sets and 800 mobile phones for every 1000 people.[2] Narendra Modi, who became prime minister, covered 300,000 kilometres, addressed 400 rallies, and using two helicopters and a private jet, was back in his own bed in Ahmedabad nearly every night![3]

In seventy years of Independence, India's people have experienced varying and uneven benefits, but what is unquestionable is that their media world—their ability to communicate—has been transformed. That continuing transformation results from unpredictable collisions between controls, technology and capitalism. These contests have worked themselves out in three identifiable phases. The first extends from 1947 to the end of Indira Gandhi's 'Emergency'. The second dates from her return to power in 1980. Her government continued loosening of regulations. Capitalists acquired greater room for manoeuvre; 1982 was declared 'the year of productivity', and new technologies drove expansion of print publications and eventually a semi-legal explosion of television. Visual and print media began to reach mass audiences. The third stage arrived at the beginning of the twenty-first century when the arrival of digital communication in mobile phones blew apart all the comfortable predictability that went with 'old media'.

Word-of-Mouth World, 1947–77

India in 1947 inherited the apparatus of a colonial state that sought to control information. Print could be censored and printers and publishers imprisoned. Post, telegraph, telephones and radio were government monopolies. The Nehru vision of a planned economy propelled by the state added new layers of government direction. Thus, radio, television and telephones continued to be state-owned and intended for the didactic tasks of 'development' and 'improvement'. Consumer goods were a low priority. Newspapers had to apply for funds to buy foreign-made equipment and for permission to draw a quota of newsprint. The first amendment to the Constitution of 1950 prompted by the horrors of the Partition and the threat of communist insurrections made it easier to limit freedom of the press. A Central Board of Film Censors, set up in 1951, viewed all films before release and made the film industry 'a medium of national culture, education and entertainment'.[4]

The vaguely socialist Congress governments of the time regarded English language newspapers as a bastion of capitalism—the so-called 'jute press' (alluding to proprietors with investments in various industries) or the '*jhooth* press' (the lying press). Governments tried encouraging smaller newspapers by requiring a publication to raise its selling price to reflect the number of pages in that specific issue. This was to prevent bigger newspapers with generous advertisements from selling below cost, increasing circulations and expanding advertising revenues at the expense of smaller newspapers. Indira Gandhi's governments seemed to believe that many small newspapers would be less troublesome than a few big ones, a notion she later decided was wrong. The 'price-page' effort failed in the Supreme Court. Governments, however, still had devices such as newsprint quotas to use as levers against unsympathetic newspapers. And eventually the Emergency brought full-scale censorship.

Flourishing newspapers need advertising, and advertisers spend their money where they think will be buyers. This made the English-language press the dominant force in news media for the first thirty years of Independence. In the late fifties, only three daily newspapers sold more than 100,000 copies a day, two in English and one in Tamil. Only sixteen newspapers sold more than 50,000 copies a day, seven of them in English.[5] With production of consumer goods limited by the controlled economy, such advertising as there was went to English-language newspapers. There was little incentive to expand circulations. For proprietors who owned an Indian-language newspaper in 1947, the next thirty years were predictable and unimaginative. Between 1957 and 1977, the population grew by 240 million people to a total of 650 million. Daily newspaper circulations rose from 3.3 million to 10.6 million or from eight dailies per 1000 people to sixteen per thousand.[6]

Figure 1: Indian Daily Newspaper Circulations, 1957–2010 (Total, Hindi and English)

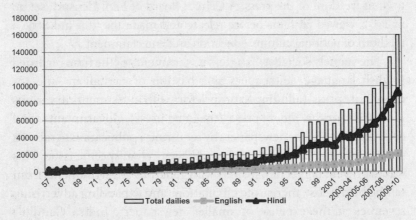

Source: Registrar of Newspapers for India, *Press in India*, for relevant years.

Government controls and scarce advertising limited the growth of the media. The third impediment was printing technology. Most newspapers were printed on ancient flatbed presses using metal type, set by hand. The process was slow, and because imports of good newsprint were restricted and Indian language fonts were ancient and limited, the results were unattractive. Metal type required skill and investment. Since publications in Indian languages offered few rewards, most languages suffered from limited investment and had only a few basic fonts. Until the sixties, for example, Gurmukhi, the script used to print Punjabi, was available only in a single twelve-point font with nothing larger for headlines and display.

Film was the only medium, other than newspapers, where private investment was permitted and it had two big advantages over print. First, and in spite of the government's high-minded intentions, it was pure entertainment and did not require literate audiences. Second, producers drew profits from the sale of tickets, whereas newspapers, notwithstanding a selling price, needed advertising for profits. Popular films raked in money even if governments took a hefty share through taxes. The film industry boomed. At the time of Independence, India was producing over 200 feature films a year in ten or more languages.[7] By 1980, that had risen to more than 700, and the industry was netting ticket sales worth Rs 335 crores of rupees. Films were censored for sex, violence and politics, but there were no limits to how many films a producer could make or how much could be invested.

Television in 1977 was in its black-and-white infancy, with broadcast centres only in Delhi (1959), Mumbai (1972), Srinagar (1973), Kolkata (1975), Chennai (1975) and Lucknow (1975).[8] An official in the Ministry of Information and Broadcasting warned sternly that the 'objective' of the television was 'not the amusement or entertainment of the urban elite, but the service and instruction of the rural masses'.[9] Since there were only 1.1 million TV sets in the entire country, more than half of them in Delhi and Mumbai, the rural masses were some way from being served and instructed.

By 1980, however, politicians began realizing the power of television. Stations were set up in Mumbai and Srinagar partly in response to the popularity of Pakistani television, viewed across the border during the 1971 war. When Indira Gandhi's chances of re-election were clearly doomed in February 1977, officials were ordered to air the hit film *Bobby* on Delhi television at the same time as a giant opposition rally. A damaged print was screened. But the rally was still a great success and the Congress Party lost the election. However, when Indira Gandhi came back to power in 1980, one of her election promises was to introduce colour television across the country.

Tightly controlled by the government, radios had spread slowly in the first thirty years of Independence, though accelerated a little by the arrival of the transistor in the mid-sixties. At Independence there were 250,000 licenced radios; 3.6 million by 1963; and 20 million by 1979.[10] From 1967, a few programmes were eligible to accept limited sponsorship, but the only news was government news, and AIR's reputation for boring programming was well established.[11]

At the end of the seventies, Indian Post and Telegraphs (IP&T) provided the most accessible means of communication for most Indians. IP&T carried 8 billion items a year (up from 2.3 billion in the fifties) and ran more than 120,000 post offices, with more than 100,000 of them in rural areas. IP&T was also the monopoly provider of two million telephones and managed the antiquated copper-wire telephone network for 680 million people.[12]

'Modern' World, 1979–2005

Three developments in the seventies brought dramatic changes in India's media. First, a relentless growth in population and expansion of the numbers of literates created huge potential markets for whatever consumer goods were available. The literate population increased from 60 million in 1951 to 240 million by 1981. More than 95 per cent of the literates spoke only Indian languages. Advertisers in the years after Independence chose to equate English language newspaper circulations as a proxy for the number of people with sufficient purchasing power to buy most consumer goods. Major advertising, therefore, flowed to English language publications. In 1970, an alliance of advertising firms and business advertisers commissioned the first National Readership Survey (NRS-I). It showed that about a quarter of urban Indians read print media regularly and pointed to a huge potential for Indian language publications to reach new categories of buyers.[13] A few proprietors began looking for ways to expand their circulations and increase advertising rates. The Kanpur-based Hindi daily *Dainik Jagran* opened a second publishing centre in Gorakhpur in eastern UP in 1974. The new Telugu daily *Eenadu* started a Hyderabad edition in 1975. In Kerala, where newspapers were more widely published and purchased than anywhere else, the two Malayalam dailies, *Malayala Manorama* and *Mathrubhumi*, had set up additional publication centres in 1962 and 1968. There were signs—and a few success stories—to indicate that there was purchasing power among readers of Indian languages outside the major cities.

The second incentive for the spread of newspapers came from the Emergency itself. Because of censorship and fear, people were immensely curious to know what had *really* happened in those months. What was Indira Gandhi's government suppressing? When the Emergency ended, media boomed. Circulation of Hindi dailies almost doubled in four years (from 1.9 million a day in 1976 to 3.6 million in 1980) and squeaked ahead of English for the first time in 1979.

Technology provided the third element in the growth equation. Indian manufacturers started to make offset presses under licence from foreign companies from the mid-seventies, and photocomposition of Indian scripts arrived in the eighties.[14] Together, they liberated Indian languages and their scripts from the prison of metal type where Gutenberg technology had confined them. Metal moulds for every letter were no longer necessary. An infinite array of characters could live in a computer's memory, called up when needed and printed on an offset press that transferred ink to paper by a chemical process, not a mechanical one. Offset also enabled fast, effective colour printing. Indian language dailies could for the first time have big picture-laden colour layouts with a variety of typefaces.

Table 1: Daily Circulations; All Languages, Hindi and English, 1958–2010 (in millions)

	1958	1971	1981	1991	2001	2010
All Languages	3.4	9.0	15.2	24.1	56.3	159.7
Hindi	0.5	1.5	3.7	9.3	23.0	71.9
English	0.9	2.2	3.4	3.1	8.5	21.1

Source: *Press in India* for relevant years.

When Indira Gandhi returned to power in 1980, there had already been an easing of some regulations on economic activity and import of equipment. And, as the *Bobby* incident during the 1977 election campaign illustrated, she and her advisers had had a change of heart about the utility of television. TV had been regarded as a toy for the well-off or a possible tool for educating peasants. The country had 160,000 television sets when the Emergency began.[15] Colour TV was introduced to telecast the Asian Games in Delhi in 1982. Doordarshan, the government television monopoly, had started accepting commercials in 1976. In the eighties, it became 'hooked to its new cash cow', from which it extracted more than Rs 500 crore in revenue by the end of the decade.[16]

Technology, control and consumption met in an awkward mating ritual in 1991. The first Gulf War in 1991 gutted India's foreign exchange reserves and forced a Congress-led government to abandon more of the old 'socialist' economic controls. Television, delivered by satellite, was a feature of the Gulf War, and CNN beamed into homes around the world. In India, enterprising technicians put dishes on roofs, captured satellite signals and ran copper wire to surrounding households—for a fee. It worked, and people loved it, but it was against the law for anyone other than Doordarshan to telecast to India, and only it had the right to use the communication satellites that India had put in space from 1981. But Indian authorities could not prevent video recordings, made in India, from being flown to Hong Kong or Russia where studios staffed by Indians would send them via non-Indian satellites back to viewers in India hooked up to enterprising (and illegal) cable distributors capturing signals on illegal dishes and funnelling them to subscribers' homes.[17] These telecasts carried advertisements for Indian products that were paid for in various inventive ways. Indian satellite TV developed an immediate following because it was not government-controlled, and it offered livelier programming than Doordarshan could aspire to. For an economy that was now encouraged to cater to consumers, and a middle class that was encouraged to consume, lively television was the place to advertise. Successive governments searched for ways to control these offshore broadcasters, but by the year 2000, they had recognized independent Indian television channels.

The tortuous arrival of competitive television did not harm newspapers.[18] Indeed, some proprietors thought television encouraged literacy and newspaper readership by making people curious to read about what they had seen. Between 1995 and 2005, daily newspaper circulations rose from 35 million a day to 87 million.[19] Households with television sets increased from 35 million in the early nineties to 100 million by 2004.[20] More importantly, the expenditure on advertising increased from about Rs 9 billion in the early nineties to Rs 110 billion by 2003. Print publications still harvested nearly half.[21] This was a dynamic and profitable world in which to be a media proprietor, but from about 2004, digital media in the popular form of the mobile phone began to blow it apart.

Digital World, 2005–?

In July 2013, IP&T (Indian Posts and Telegraph) shed the T in the acronym when it closed the telegram service. Western Union, the famed US company, had ended telegrams seven years earlier. The reason was obvious: now 'everyone has a mobile phone'. Cheap digital technology brought a new and unpredictable media world.

The first allocation of radio frequency spectrum (RF) to private companies to provide mobile phone services was carried out in 1995. It was a fiasco that ended years later with corrupt politicians going to jail. The bungled allocation process, and the stringent charges and conditions imposed on successful companies, meant that the inept, government-owned landline telephone system had no serious challenge until 2004.[22]

If 1979 was a landmark year for print when Hindi daily circulations surpassed English, 2005 was the landmark for the new world of digital electronic media. Mobile phone connections exceeded landlines for the first time (52 million to 41 million). The change was breathtakingly fast and widespread. By the end of 2015, there were 997 million telephone connections, 97 per cent of them mobiles. Landline connections fell to 24 million.[23]

During these ten years, up to ten companies were competing for customers pushing 2G and 3G phones into every corner of urban India and much of the countryside. It was a classic 'fortune at the bottom of the pyramid' story—vast numbers of clients, each generating a tiny revenue. By the end of 2016, however, average revenue per user (ARPU) had fallen to about Rs 100 a month.[24]

2G phones were immensely attractive in a country with large newly literate or illiterate people and a multiplicity of scripts. Consumers valued the ability to communicate without having to write, and especially liked the fact that a 'feature phone' could perform as a torch, camera, photo album, and audio and video player—and that it could be used privately and spontaneously. In some regions, mobile phones allowed local performers to create far wider audiences for their music in ways that the cassette recorder had done more modestly thirty years earlier.

When Mukesh Ambani's Reliance acquired major interests in a group of TV channels and print and entertainment enterprises in 2012, a rival media organization concluded that 'Ambani is the new media mogul'.[25] The company acquired appropriate spectrum in all regions in 2010 and began laying more than 200,000 kilometres of fibre optic cable across the country for launching mass-market 4G telecom that would allow users to watch events in real time on their handheld devices. The business plan was to own the toll way—a fast fibre optic network that would transmit vast amounts of data at lightning speed and charge a monthly fee to use 'the road' or 'the pipe'. Anyone sending deliveries (data) along it, and receiving such deliveries (as games, movies, calls, music, weather reports, etc.), would pay usage fee for the traffic initiated.

While the companies with rights to radio frequency for 2G and 3G phones expanded telecom industries and subscribers after 2004, Mukesh Ambani was laying the groundwork for a hugely ambitious scheme, which, if successful, would enable consumers to connect with real time, or 'live' video and interactive materials from throughout the world. The Reliance Industries Limited (RIL) already owns conventional television channels and has interests in an old-fashioned newspaper chain. If the telecom gamble with Reliance Jio succeeds, RIL will have a superior influence over what is transmitted on their network of fibre optic cable.

By April 2017, Reliance Jio had more than 70 million customers and had provoked the predicted 'consolidation' of telecommunication companies. Vodafone (British owned) said it would merge with Idea (A.K. Birla), and a similar merger was in the works between Aircel and Reliance Communications. It is likely that India will go from more than a dozen telecom providers to three major private providers, with government providers BSNL and MTNL struggling to stay afloat.

The attractions of a complete 4G service would be overwhelming if the speed of data transfer could be maintained and the cost of handsets kept low. In April 2017, a new 4G phone could be bought for less than Rs 5000 making it affordable for the poor. Would they be able to afford the cost of data, which is from where revenues would come for telecom providers?

Two words dominate such discussions: consolidation and convergence. In both print and telecommunications, the small tend to get smaller and are eventually taken over or disappear. The Times of India group (officially, Bennett Coleman and Company Ltd—BCCL) had become a veritable giant in the newspaper industry during the nineties. By 2017, it ran the largest English language TV news channel, had half a dozen specialist channels; the largest newspaper chain—*Times of India*—and owned daily newspapers in Hindi, Marathi, Kannada and Bengali, along with FM radio stations. Its great rival of former times, the *Statesman* of Kolkata, had all but disappeared, and the *Hindustan Times* of Delhi, *The Hindu* of Chennai and the *Indian Express* (of many places) were left far behind.

But print in India continues to make profits and retain subscribers, in contrast to much of the rest of the world.[26] Most big print companies ventured into other media to try to anticipate where consumers would put funds and their advertising in future. India has no regulations prohibiting 'cross-media ownership'—the control of various media by a single company.

The stunted radio industry benefited from removal of economic controls and digitization. But all national governments struggled to retain control of the radio. Private radio stations were licenced only in 2000, and even in 2017 the only news that the more than 240 stations were permitted to broadcast was feeds from the All India Radio.[27] Television, of course, had been doing news from the early nineties, even if the early efforts had to be beamed in from foreign-owned satellites. But television in 2017 was fully commercialized with more than 800 channels arriving in 185 million households via satellite, cable and land-based broadcast.

The film industry had adapted to different conditions for making revenue. With more than 10,000 screens, most with digital projection and housed in multiscreen locations, the practice of seeing films in cinema halls had not died with television and the Internet. And as converging technologies brought daily audiovisual experience into the lives of more people, India's large pool of film-making and computer-literate talent found possibilities for earning a living and creating new forms of media.

Summing up Three Worlds

The growing ability of people to use media in the first seventy years of Independence was revolutionary. When Nehru made his 'Tryst with Destiny' speech in August 1947, fewer than 60 million people could read and write. In 2017, there are more than 800 million literates. Most of the literate people in 1947 would have rarely seen a telephone, heard a radio, read a newspaper or gone to a movie. The stamps, postcards and rare telegrams of IP&T provided the only ways to communicate, besides occasional face-to-face meetings at marriages and religious festivals. In Narendra Modi's India of 2017, mobile phone connectivity was 88 per cent; more than 150 million newspapers were produced every day; and two-thirds of households had a television set, the vast majority hooked up to cables or satellites giving access to hundreds of television channels.

Indians want what consumers of media everywhere seem to want: to see themselves reflected, to communicate with friends and relations, to be entertained and informed, and to be enabled to use services, to buy and to sell. Along with the potential to connect with the rest of the world, the other great change since 1947 lay in the control of the media. In 1947, government controlled the miniscule system of radio and telephones; newspapers were rare, their presses vulnerable and censorship when invoked was relatively simple. Movies had offered possibilities to test the authority of foreign rulers, but producers had to couch nationalist themes in classical metaphors to slide messages past the censor. In 2017, some of the controls remain, but often they have become meaningless. The Central Board of Film Certification may ban a film, but it will become available via the Internet or informal transfers from one device to another.

Technological leaps affect political campaigns. The Bahujan Samaj Party (BSP) won an unexpected victory in the vast state of UP in 2007 because its cadre was hooked up and widely organized for the first time through mobile phones. Five years later, everybody had the same idea, the faithful cadre was dispirited and the party lost heavily.[28] Narendra Modi's BJP used hologram technology to beam him into hundreds of small towns during the 2014 national elections and create jaw-dropping small-town spectacles that people came from miles around to see.

Perhaps more important for long-term change, the prevalence of the handheld communication device and the potential autonomy it brings, disrupt tens of millions of households and communities with the question: 'Who should be allowed to have one and how should they be allowed to use it?' The intrusion of the media into people's lives leads to questions being asked and behaviour sometimes having to change. In 1993, a frustrated policeman in Andhra Pradesh explained why the rapid spread of Telugu newspapers made a policeman's life more difficult. 'Once,' he said, 'if one policeman went to a village, the people were afraid. Now, six police may go to a village and people are not afraid. Newspapers have made them know that police are not supposed to beat them.'[29] What will the digital world let people know?

V

India–ASEAN Relations at Seventy

Tan Tai Yong

Close Rapport through Shared Ideals

Relations between India and Southeast Asia have deep historical roots. On the day India became independent, most of Asia was still under colonial rule. Years later, when Lee Kuan Yew was delivering the Nehru Memorial Lecture in 2005, he recalled listening to Jawaharlal Nehru's stirring 'Tryst with Destiny' speech when he was a student at Cambridge. 'I belong to that generation of Asian nationalists who looked up to India's freedom struggle and its leaders, Mahatma Gandhi and Pandit Jawaharlal Nehru. [. . .] Nehru's speeches resonated with me.' Lee said. '[I] admired Nehru for his vision of a secular multiracial India, a country that does not discriminate between citizens because of their race, language, religion or culture.'[1] As the first Asian country to achieve independence from colonial rule, India was regarded by Southeast Asian nationalists, most of whom aspired to follow in India's footsteps, as a natural leader of an impending free and resurgent Asia.

In the forties, as India headed towards political independence, Nehru had looked to Southeast Asia as a region whose history, fate and destiny were somewhat linked with India's. For centuries, trade and human migration traversed the Bay of Bengal. Complex networks sustained by commerce, culture and community criss-crossed the Indian Ocean, connecting maritime Southeast Asia and the Indian Subcontinent. As a consequence large parts of Southeast Asia came under profound Indian influences, and great civilizations like the Srivijaya Empire and Majapahit Empire flourished in the region. All that remained in the colonial period were the networks that strengthened after the Indian subcontinent and territories to its east were brought under the British sphere of influence, underpinned largely by trade and commerce.

The end of the Second World War brought major political changes in the modern world. Nehru believed that in the twilight of European imperialism and the emergence of Asian nationalism, the peoples of India and Southeast Asia would rediscover their own identities again. While Nehru scrupulously avoided creating the perception that a greater India would replace the British Empire east of Bengal, he was keen on promoting a united Asia occupying its rightful place in the world. During a visit to Burma (now Myanmar), Malaya and Singapore in 1946, Nehru mooted the idea of India playing host to a gathering of Asian nations to signal that Asia was on the threshold of a new era. A year later, in March 1947, Nehru opened the Asian Relations Conference in Delhi with the pronouncement that 'this conference [would] stand out as a landmark which [would] divide the past of Asia from the future'.[2] Nehru's vision for India and Asia captured the imagination of young Asian nationalists captivated by his charisma and the ideals he espoused.

The Asian Relations Conference was attended by representatives from twenty-eight countries, including Burma, Malaya and Indonesia, and was seen as a form of 'missionary outreach to the national struggles of large parts of Asia that remained colonized'. The largest individual contingents came from the still-colonized Southeast Asia.[3] In these parts, especially in Burma, Malaya and Indonesia, Nehru personified the new mood of Asia; his leadership of India's freedom movement, passionate commitment to anti-colonialism and vision of a new, free Asia inspired those agitating for independence from foreign rule. Nehru's stock rose further when he actively roused international support for the Indonesian nationalist revolution against the Dutch. As long as large parts of Southeast Asia were still under colonial rule and regarded India's experiences as a beacon of a future they could emulate, relations between India and Southeast Asia remained close. The Asian Relations Conference was perhaps emblematic of the special relationship India enjoyed with Southeast Asian states in the first decade following the end of the Second World War.

One could perhaps see this as an early expression of India's 'Look East' policy, with Nehru laying the foundation of an Asian community in which India would exercise an important influence. A united Asia, Nehru envisioned, would eventually replace the Atlantic community as the future nerve centre of the world. Such an intent was again expressed at the Bandung Conference in 1955. Twenty-nine Asian and African states gathered in Indonesia to discuss their political agendas and to insist that the opinions of Afro-Asian states must have a role in the new international order. They rejected Cold War definitions of world affairs as representing a continuation of imperialistic control by the great powers. The Asian Relations Conference and the Bandung Conference were high points in early attempts of newly emerging Asian states to create a free and neutral pan-Asian identity and presence in the international order. In this, there was clear convergence of interests between an emerging India and the Southeast Asia nation states in waiting. Non-alignment and freedom from foreign domination were commonly held ideals and Nehru's vision of an Asia uncommitted to either of the two power blocs appealed to like-minded Asian nationalists, most notably Aung San and Sukarno. But these ideals faded by the sixties, when Southeast Asian states, having attained independence to become nation states in their own right began articulating their own foreign policies in light of their respective national interests. With that, Indian interests and those of the new states of Southeast Asia began to diverge.

Geopolitics and the Cold War

In the sixties the international relations of Asian countries were inexorably shaped by the forces of the Cold War. Despite its avowed commitment to non-alignment in the early post-colonial years, India gradually distanced itself from the non-communist nations of Southeast Asia by shifting towards the Soviet Union. Nehru had long been an admirer of the Soviet economic system, and while not drawn to the concept of a one-party state, had an affinity with the socialist system of the Soviet Union. The once close relationship between India and Southeast Asia was further strained by the political distance that India consciously kept from the newly formed Association of Southeast Asian Nations (ASEAN). It saw the ASEAN grouping as a reincarnation of the Southeast Asia Treaty Organization (SEATO) and was suspicious of an American conspiracy to use Southeast Asian states to serve its Cold War designs in the region.[4] Irked by not being invited to join the regional grouping, India adopted a cool attitude towards ASEAN without openly criticizing it. Most importantly, India was not drawn to ASEAN because the latter was considered redundant to India's immediate security interest. ASEAN was formed at a time when the war in Vietnam was spreading to Cambodia, and non- and anti-communist Southeast Asian states saw in the regional grouping a means to contain the threat of communist insurgencies (and to keep China's influence at bay) in the region. India, for its part, saw no need to get close to ASEAN lest this be seen by Beijing as a hostile manoeuvre against China. While it was concerned with China's influence in some parts of the region, it did not want to be seen to be doing anything that might be construed as anti-China and therefore pro-Western. That would also complicate its growing relations with the Soviet Union. While ASEAN members felt that American presence was necessary to contain China, India was suspicious that ASEAN would become a mechanism to serve American interests in Southeast Asia. ASEAN's closeness to America and Japan—seen as a strategic economic triangle—did not make it easy for India's entry into the region. Indeed, it began questioning the objective of ASEAN's formation whenever security and defence issues were discussed in its forums. Gradually, the differing strategic interests between the ASEAN states and India drew them further apart.

By this time, Cold War considerations were beginning to have a major impact on India's policy in Asia. Wary of Soviet intentions in the region, pro-Western Southeast Asian countries like Thailand, Malaysia and Singapore viewed India's closeness to the Soviet Union with considerable unease. This complicated India's relations with ASEAN members as it failed to de-link its relations with the Soviet Union on the one hand and ASEAN states on the other.[5] Not unexpectedly, India's proposal for a regional security convention received a lukewarm response from the ASEAN states as it was regarded as a loosely modelled Soviet proposal for collective security.[6]

The divergence of interests further aggravated in the seventies. ASEAN countries saw in India's war with Pakistan in 1971— during which India depended on the Soviet Union to intervene in East Pakistan—a betrayal of its non-alignment policy as well as an outright violation of Pakistan's sovereignty. India–ASEAN relations were made worse with the signing of the Indo-Soviet Treaty. Member states were worried that the Moscow–New Delhi alliance would allow the Soviet Union to use its influential status in South Asia to advance its interests in Southeast Asia, despite India's assurances that the treaty was not a defence pact, but an agreement for peace and friendship. India was seen as practising double standards when it criticized American activities in Diego Garcia while backing Soviet presence in the Indian Ocean by claiming that it was 'reactive development'.

Throughout this period, the only Southeast Asian state to remain on good terms with India was Vietnam. By backing Vietnam, which was then locked in mortal conflict with the US, India demonstrated its obvious pro-Soviet tilt and got its own back against the Americans for supporting Pakistan in 1971. This worried ASEAN, which regarded Vietnam as the main source of the communist threat in the region. India saw no need to address ASEAN anxieties as it had, by that stage, decided its relations with the Soviet Union and Vietnam were more important than those with ASEAN. Its interaction with ASEAN during the Cold War era mostly took the form of bilateral relations with individual countries rather than with the association as a whole, and even then, bilateral trade agreements with the Philippines, Indonesia, Malaysia and Thailand were not significant in terms of economic benefits.[7] The incentives for India to get closer to ASEAN, and vice versa, were simply not there.

Matters reached a head in the eighties when Indian Prime Minister Indira Gandhi chose to recognize the Vietnamese-backed Heng Samrin regime in Cambodia, much to the consternation of the ASEAN states. The failure of India to establish any meaningful relationships with Southeast Asia despite its cultural and geographical affinity with that region,[8] stemmed largely from the dictates of regional geopolitics and the Cold War regime. It has been argued that India's relationship with ASEAN was considered secondary to its more fundamental security concern involving Pakistan and China, which was in turn intensified by the circumstances of the Cold War.[9] The situation was perhaps best summed up by an Indian analyst who commented that during the Cold War, India was regarded by the ASEAN countries as 'politically suspect, economically unimportant and, at times, even militarily threatening'.[10] However, the change in geopolitical realities following the end of the Cold War forced India to reassess relations with its neighbours in the east. A reorientation took place in India that gradually led to a 'renaissance in relations' with Southeast Asia.[11]

India's Economic Liberalization and the Look East Policy

In the early nineties, compelled by a severe economic crisis, India took decisive steps towards economic liberalization, leading to a strategic shift in its foreign policy that was subsequently articulated as the Look East policy.[12] This new eastward tilt was driven primarily by India's trade and investment needs, of which ASEAN became a primary platform. The Look East policy led to closer diplomatic ties with ASEAN: in March 1993, India was accorded sectoral dialogue status within ASEAN, and in 1995, India–ASEAN relations took a significant step forward when it was made a full dialogue partner. Following a period of 'benign neglect', growing convergence of security and economic interests in the post-Cold War period brought India and ASEAN closer again.

Changing geopolitics made it easier for the forging of closer ties. By the late eighties, India was no longer regarded by ASEAN as a potentially threatening maritime power. Cuts in defence spending, leading to the gradual reduction to its fleet of principal combatants, led to a shift in the Indian naval doctrine from 'sea control' to a more defensive 'sea denial' role.[13] This was accompanied by several confidence-building measures, which included the opening up of its facility at Port Blair to visits from regional military attachés, as well as initiating naval exercises separately with Indonesia, Singapore, Malaysia and Thailand. When ASEAN decided to institute the ASEAN Regional Forum (ARF) to serve as a conclave for annual dialogues with major powers with interest in Southeast Asia, there was little question that India would need to feature prominently in it at some stage. Through its eventual involvement in the ARF, India became part of regional deliberations representing the changing and expanding regional security architecture. It had broad agreement with the ARF's basic agenda, and, more importantly, over China and Myanmar, the two countries with which the interests and security concerns of India and the ASEAN countries overlapped.

An engaged India offered many strategic advantages to Southeast Asian countries. They were aware that unbridled rivalry between India and China would have potentially ominous consequences for the region. It was, therefore, important for ASEAN to get India to share a common approach of adopting a constructive engagement policy as the best way of dealing with China.[14] Similarly, in the case of Myanmar, India supported the ASEAN approach of 'constructive engagement', which represented a significant change from its erstwhile policy of no dialogue with it. India's longer-term perspective remained the restoration of democracy to Myanmar, but in the short term, it would promote economic links for countering China's influences in Myanmar.

Shared interests in pursuing economic development for the region as a whole drew India and ASEAN closer. India primarily looked to Southeast Asia for markets and sources for investments, and ASEAN, for its part, understood that sound economic and diplomatic relations with India would form the basis of long-term, secure bilateral relations. While India's trade with ASEAN improved significantly since 1991, the trading pattern varied, determined largely by the existing levels of economic complementarities between India and the individual ASEAN countries. Singapore and Malaysia dominated bilateral trade between India and ASEAN, accounting for over 80 per cent of India's imports from ASEAN countries, and absorbing more than 60 per cent of India's exports to ASEAN countries in the early nineties.[15] There was, however, hardly any bilateral trade between India and Brunei, whilst trade with Indonesia and the Philippines remained unsubstantial.[16]

There were other forms of economic complementarity. India became an important source of trained and skilled labour for the manpower needs of the economies of Singapore, Malaysia and Thailand. India, for its part, saw countries like Singapore as a bridge to the economies of the broader East Asian region. As Indian skilled manpower increasingly found their way into Southeast Asia, India began opening up as an important business destination, offering market potential, communications networks and skills availability at competitive prices.

There was a clear upswing in economic cooperation between India and ASEAN from 1991. But, despite early enthusiasm and some gains, the initial promise did not lead to the significant momentum of trade and investment that was anticipated. Concerns over political instability and confusion, as well as policy inconsistencies, and in some cases, reversals, made potential investors adopt a cautious, wait-and-see attitude.[17] Unfortunately, ASEAN continues to see India as bureaucratic and inherently protectionist, with an absence of political will, coupled with poor infrastructure and complicated land and labour policies. This meant India, despite its huge economy and tremendous promise, was not seen as an easy or attractive place to do business. Stifled by red tape and bureaucratic inertia, the frustrations faced by some of the regional consortia from Southeast

Asia on lack of progress in their Indian projects hardly encouraged new ventures.[18]

Close Ties through Converging Interests

The lack of momentum notwithstanding, successive Indian governments signalled their commitments to the Look East policy. Trade and investment continued to be prime movers of the relationship, but other factors soon came into play. First, Delhi had begun taking note of the potential dangers posed to regional security by the resurgence of Islamic fundamentalism and extremist groups in Southeast Asia. There were concerns that a destabilized Indonesia and rampant piracy activities in the Bay of Bengal area and the Straits of Malacca might threaten India's shipping lanes to the south and east of the subcontinent. In 2000, the Vajpayee government began articulating the importance of maritime security. Second, India has been concerned over the possibility of Pakistan spreading its influence in some ASEAN countries through likely linkages of terrorist groups (e.g. Lashkar-e-Taiba) with emerging extremist Islamist groups in the region. Third, India needed to keep up with China in its engagement with ASEAN. China was already part of the ASEAN+3 (China, Japan and Korea) cooperation framework. Economic and trade cooperation between China and ASEAN had grown rapidly. Not wishing to lag behind, the Vajpayee government began making similar offers to ASEAN countries, leading to the signing of a Comprehensive Economic Cooperation Agreement (CECA) with Singapore in 2005. This was preceded by a bilateral Free Trade Agreement (FTA) with Thailand in October 2003. Other initiatives like the Mekong–Ganga Cooperation (MGC) project launched in November 2000 to forge closer ties with India's eastern neighbours—Thailand, Myanmar, Vietnam, Laos and Cambodia— demonstrated India's interests in the region.

The change of government in 2004 did not affect India's orientation towards Southeast Asia. The Manmohan Singh-led United Progressive Alliance (UPA) coalition government continued with many of the economic reform initiatives undertaken by the Vajpayee government. For instance, the idea of an Asian economic community that was first mooted by Vajpayee in 2003 featured in the new government's foreign policy plans. Not wishing to be outmanoeuvred by China, and seeing that trade with East Asia had risen from USD 8 billion in 1990 to USD 67.6 billion in 2005, accounting for nearly 30 per cent of India's total external trade,[19] India remained keen to participate in the East Asian economic integration process. It was thus regarded as an important step in the right direction when India was invited to the East Asia Summit (EAS) in 2005. Thereafter, several new initiatives were announced: further pursuing an open skies policy that was proposed by Singapore; early operationalization of an India–ASEAN Science & Technology Fund to enhance collaborative R & D between India and ASEAN; developing annual training courses for ASEAN diplomats; and launching of special tourism campaigns in India and ASEAN.

India and ASEAN relations, based primarily on economic ties, grew gradually to encompass military and security cooperation. Membership in the EAS has accorded India the status of a legitimate player with a major role to play in the region's evolving security architecture. Through its membership of the ARF, India's engagement with ASEAN also paved the way for its involvement in other important regional organizations such as the EAS and the Asia–Europe Meeting (AEM). ASEAN countries came to see India 'as a potentially important economic partner that could provide a useful balance and a hedge [as well as a potential security provider] against . . . unilateralism by the big powers . . .'[20]

Regardless of the desire for closer ties, the degree of cooperation has varied widely among the grouping's member countries with a view that the full potential of India's partnership with ASEAN remains unrealized. Momentum had stalled and progress was lacklustre, particularly in the area of trade and India's eastward connectivity. Figures from 2015 revealed that India's trade with ASEAN amounted to only one-seventh of ASEAN's trade with China, and is, therefore, proportionally low.[21] This has led to the view that in the latter years of the Look East policy 'India's approach to ASEAN looked tired, if not stale'.[22]

In November 2014, Prime Minister Narendra Modi announced at the India–East Asia Summit in Myanmar that the Look East policy would henceforth become the 'Act East' policy. The change was meant to reinvigorate India's stagnating relations with ASEAN and expand India's engagement beyond the region to include the whole of East Asia to Australia and New Zealand in the south, and from neighbouring Bangladesh to Fiji and Pacific Island countries in the Far East.[23] Later in 2015 in Singapore, Modi reiterated his pledge to deepen India's focus on the countries to its east. He stressed the need to ensure freedom of navigation in Asia's waters and the need for cooperation in areas including oceans, cyberspace and space.[24]

One of the motivations behind the Act East policy can be attributed to India's concerns over China's growing ambitions in Asia. The policy can be regarded as a 'hedging strategy' (the key element in this strategy being the search for strategic partners to defuse a threat) rather than an outright challenge as India lacks the wherewithal to contest an assertive and sometimes belligerent China. ASEAN remains the main pillar in India's Act East policy. However, the efficacy of the policy remains hindered by the inability to translate ideas and policies into concrete actions and investments. Infrastructure projects in India's northeast is one such idea. If implemented successfully, these projects (e.g. the India–Myanmar–Thailand Trilateral Highway) would significantly improve connectivity between northeast India and the ASEAN countries.[25]

Acting East

India's relations with Southeast Asia have been marked by false starts and unfulfilled promises. More than half a century has passed since Nehru first attempted to build a regional identity that would galvanize the new and emerging states of India and Southeast Asia. Nehru's vision for Asia, built on idealism, hopes and aspirations, was nearly wrecked by geopolitical conditions created by the Cold War.

His non-alignment policy, which still exists as a statement of policy, was for the most part nothing more than a mirage. In the post-Cold War period, globalization and transnational challenges have made Asian regionalism possible again. In a world that is headed towards multi-polarity and global connectedness, India's non-alignment would have to mean an openness to seek convergence and cooperation, an open and flexible approach of inclusion and engagement. Since the beginning of the twenty-first century, India has taken a major step forward in the realization of its earlier vision for 'Pan-Asianism' through regional cooperation. India's place in the new Asia is predicated, since the nineties, on a pragmatic approach that is grounded in common economic and security interests.[26]

ASEAN will remain an important region to India for several reasons. Parts of Southeast Asia are socially and ecologically linked to northeast India, and this conduit offers India immense possibilities of an east-through-northeast approach. Several ASEAN countries have become important investment and joint venture destinations for Indian businesses, while at the same time being an important source of commodities to feed India's economic growth.

The rise of an economically powerful and stable India, with close ties to the US, and confident in its dealings with China, adds immeasurably to the stability of the region. Southeast Asia stands to be transformed by the rise of China and India, and this strategic relationship, if managed properly, is set to determine the future of the Asia-Pacific region.

VI

Normalizing the Unique: Explaining the Persistence of Caste

Dipankar Gupta

Why does caste lead to so much excitement? What is so unique about it?

Apparently, it is the only form of social hierarchy where those at the bottom agree to be there; or, at worst, are humbly reconciled to their lot. In fact, if one were to go by traditional interpretation, there is no contestation at any point over social placement anywhere in the caste system. That is because caste is premised on the presumption of different physicality, which ranges from the most pure to the most impure.

Accordingly, Brahmins and Untouchables are at either ends of this continuum, while other castes find their place somewhere in between. Through all this, let us not forget that the special fact about caste is the supposed acceptance of the hierarchy by everybody, including the most oppressed.[1] The view that poorer 'subaltern' castes participated in their own subjugation is what makes the caste system unique.

Even though the presentation of caste is fetching and attractive, contemporary India puts it under considerable pressure. If castes ordain ranking and if this is accepted by all, then how can caste competition be explained? This is particularly relevant when observing the passion with which politics is conducted in India. This is a major contradiction, which a traditional understanding of caste just cannot reconcile.

Caste competition, regardless of how it is seen, cannot allow for acceptance without protest of how bodily substances[2] are placed hierarchically. Therefore, in a nutshell, caste politics, including caste alliances, violate the essence of the pure hierarchy, as it is known. When castes compete against one another, how can there be a single hierarchy?

Yet, it is not as if, for all these reasons, castes have disappeared. What has changed is that castes no longer form a 'system', but are active as 'identities'. The phenomenon has morphed quite significantly, and has become one that we need to be sensitive to in order to understand how different castes manifest themselves today. When castes interacted as a 'system', people behaved in accordance with an ascribed rank, or what was ordained by birth. This hierarchy was manned and patrolled by the ruling caste of the region and even defined by them. This is why caste rankings differed from region to region; but, more importantly, the 'system' held.

This worked well for centuries with different Kshatriya castes heading the system, but came unstuck once the closed village economy collapsed. Almost all powerful castes, such as the Jats, Rajputs, Bhumihars, Thevars, Okkaligas, do not want to be Brahmins but covet the Kshatriya status. In India, there has been a gradual undermining of the rural way of life from the late nineteenth century onwards. What had remained unchanged in essence for centuries began shaking in the latter decades of colonial rule.

By the time Independence came and zamindari was abolished, the system began to wobble seriously. The rural economy was no longer closed, and as time went by, it was not overwhelmingly agrarian either. Today, over 60 per cent of India's Rural Net Domestic Product is non-farm in character, and only 13 per cent of its GDP is agricultural. There are very few big landowners, and the old landlords have all but disappeared. This has wrecked caste as a 'system' for there is no oligarch, or ruling patron, who could keep the various castes in place.

In time, the systemic aspect collapsed, but caste as an identity remained, and it is this that fuels competition and politics in India today. In fact, the collapse of caste as a system encouraged the emergence of caste as an identity. Now that caste functions as identities, there are open declarations of contesting origin myths that are as fantastical as the Rig Vedic Purusha Shukta.[3] The only difference is that many of these are borne by oral traditions and are not part of the great Hindu textual heritage. Here too, changes are occurring for many of these alternate origin myths are being written up at the pace with which its subscribers are getting literate.

The question then is whether the caste identities that are now sprouting up everywhere —were they brand new, or were they there earlier, but suppressed?

The more credible argument, which would fall in line with what has been said so far, is that the fear of punishment kept subaltern castes from asserting themselves. Now that times have changed and the old oligarch is no longer the source of power and patronage, it is much easier to come out in the open and shut the closet door behind.

It is hard to make the claim that in the past most people adhered to the ruling castes' versions of hierarchy and, therefore, remained obedient and servile. The present has taught us to suspect the traditional treatises on caste. Pressured by contemporary circumstances, we begin to appreciate caste as 'identity' and once we do that its uniqueness disappears. This is because people across the world fashion origin tales for themselves and are often willing to die for them. It has often been observed that members of a particular caste attach a great deal of 'patriotism' to belonging to it. Indeed, Brahmins may consider certain castes to be 'low', but that is not how these castes view themselves. In fact, there are several occasions when a Brahmin is seen as inauspicious and borderline 'impure'. This phenomenon was adequately captured by Celestin Bougle when he said that the principle of 'mutual repulsion' is active between castes.[4]

Having said all that, it can also be admitted that India is not the only country where birth defines a cultural identity. This is a human failing everywhere, an anthropological truth, as it were. The world is separated on the basis of language, religion and colour, and none of these markers are achievement-based, but determined by birth. Likewise, one is born into a caste and dies in it.[5]

People are not just divided into 'us' versus 'them'. Each identity has a certain pride of belonging. No matter which category people fall into, everybody believes that their character and heritage are the best of all. This is true for everyone, from our ancestors in the Stone Age to Hindus and Europeans alike.

Therefore, castes share many of these characteristics that are present in other forms of social stratification elsewhere in the world. In addition, contrary to the traditional view, generated by Purusha Shukta partisans, the castes that were taken to be low, actually never believed in their positioning. This completely robs castes of their unique attribute. Like people everywhere in the world, those who are considered to be low or impure by some standards have a different opinion about themselves. There is no caste that does not see itself as superior to all others. How ordinary and commonplace is this?

There are hierarchies everywhere—in Britain, France, the US and in African nations as well. Yet, nowhere can it be said that those who are politically and economically dominated actually acquiesce in their humiliation. Racism, in whatever form, whether in Europe, America or South Africa, did not result in Blacks saying that they deserve to be punished by Whites.

The colonized also always found reasons to explain away their defeats at the hands of outsiders to factors that did not question their heritage. The French, true to form, believed that the Prussians gave them a sound hiding in the late nineteenth century simply because their children went to better schools. Nationalism, in many cases, arose out of defeats in the battle field. The vanquished often attribute their defeats, not to their physical or intellectual shortcomings, but to traitors, named and unnamed.

Once again, all these features come alive in the making of caste identities as well. So what is so unusual about them? For instance, even those who were once called Untouchables, refuse to bow down to orthodox pressures. They too have their own origin stories to relate, and they are all grand. These castes, like Blacks in apartheid-driven South Africa, may concede that others are richer, more educated, and so on. But when it comes to the crunch, they will never accept the fact that their lower social status is on account of the inherent substances that make them. If 'Black is beautiful' gave voice to this view in America, the 'Dalit' heritage has done it for those who were once considered impure in Hindu India. If Black counterculture, from the margins of New Orleans, Harlem and Chicago, can be the carrier of pride, so can Dalit poetry and worship be for the once considered Untouchables. In which case, the established view that is put forward in sociological texts of lower castes participating in their own subjugation is false and untenable.

Interestingly, in none of the studies that assert that lower castes participate in their own subjugation, are the views of the subordinated people taken into account. What is overlooked is that India too has its own version of the 'Harlem culture' and this is best expressed in the way those who were once deemed as low castes have carved proud niches for themselves.

For example, one of the legends of leather workers relates an episode that purportedly happened long ago when three Brahmin brothers went out to bathe in the Ganges. On the way to the river they saw a cow trapped in quicksand and struggling for life. As the other two were weak and scared, it was the youngest brother who went out to rescue the cow but failed to pull it out alive. When he returned his older brothers turned on him and claimed that because he had touched a carcass, he would henceforth be called a 'leather worker'.[6]

Then there are ex-Untouchable legends that claim that they were once rulers and much loved by their subjects. In this happy world descended some evil forces, often with divine help, and cheated them of their land and power. Jyotiba Phule propounded a similar view, but went on to add that it is the culture of this community that is actually the origin, the *adi*, of Hindu civilization. In other words, true Hinduism rests with the culture of the adis, who were tricked by usurpers to the horror and anguish of their erstwhile subjects.

Communities like the Meradh, Kammara and Jajjagara, who are blacksmiths by occupation, also believe they were among the adis.

Other lower-caste-origin myths need not even be about Brahmins, rulers or kings; they deal directly with gods. The washer-men of Bengal believe that they were born of Shiva's divine intervention. Many, many years ago a washer-woman sent her son to collect Shiva's soiled clothes. The boy waited patiently, but as Shiva was so completely immersed in meditation, Parvati asked him to play around and then go back. After his meditation, when Shiva came to Parvati, she scolded him and said that a little boy was waiting outside to take his garments for a wash. When Shiva stepped out, there was no boy in sight. This horrified him for he feared that some devil or ogre had gobbled the boy up. How would he face the little one's mother now? So Shiva, by pure meditative skills, that only he was capable of, created another boy, a doppelganger of the one he thought had been picked up. However, he later came to know that the first boy got tired of waiting and went home. Now there was one boy too many and out of this creation of Shiva's, arose the caste of Chasadhoba of Bengal.

The Mochis of Maharashtra claim that their ancestor saved Shiva from a tiger and turned the beast outside in and made socks (or *mojas*) from his skin. This was then presented to Shiva and that is how they came to be known as 'Mochis'. The Valmikis trace their descent from the famous sage, while the members of one of its sub-castes claim that their ancestors were born of the Balaji creation myth.[7] The Nhavi, or barbers of Maharashtra, contend that they are superior to Brahmins as they emanated from the serpent, Sheshathat, that encircled Shiva's neck. Those who were once pejoratively known as Chandals believed that their ancestor was a Brahmin who was cheated into eating something impure by his enemies and thus got degraded. However, a time would come, and soon, when this treachery would be avenged.

Let us now move on to the Vaisya category. The Purusha Shukta legend places them at the third spot, just above the lowest-ranking Shudra. As observed earlier with the so-called Untouchable assertion of dignity, the Vaisyas have their own origin tales resplendent with honour and glory. There are other origin tales of north Indian merchants, or Baniyas, that also assert that they were once rulers and that too of significant kingdoms of ancient India such as Ayodhya, Kaushambi and Mathura. The Agarwal community traces its origin to King Agrasen. This claim became hugely respectable after Bharatendu Harishchandra, the renowned nineteenth century poet endorsed it. That Jaisalmer had a Baniya king in the early nineteenth century made merchant claims to kingship credible. Similar stories can be found in south India as well, especially among the Kaikkoolars, who are also known as Segunthar Mudaliyar. They trace their origin to Parvati and her original forebears, who even helped Shiva overcome his deadly enemy, Suurubatman.

All of this should explain two enduring truths. First: nobody wants to be trampled upon or accept the ideology of domination thrust upon them by a superior community or communities. Second: caste positions are seriously contested across the spectrum. It wasn't visible earlier because the 'system' was strongly held in place by the closed village economy that was ruled over by the rural oligarch. As that is no longer the case, the hidden aspects of 'identity' that remained submerged for fear among the non-privileged castes have since sprung to life.

This also suggests that whenever there was a social flux, caste hierarchies too underwent transformations. Once we are aware of this possibility, their occurrence in history can be spotted clearly. Kshatriyas like Marathas, Rajputs and Jats were associated with humble professions; they were pastoralists like the Jats. The founder of the great Mauryan Empire might well have been a non-Vedic person from the Morya tribe. There is a difference, however, between then and now. In the past, caste positions changed on account of bloody wars and that happened after decades, if not centuries, of tranquillity. Today, these disputes happen every day and signify a transition from medieval times.

Caste identities also express themselves in politics. There are many known caste alliances—such as between Kshatriyas,

Harijans, Adivasis and Muslims, whose acronym 'Kham' gained near conceptual status in the 1980s. Then there was the other grand alliance between the Ahirs, Jats, Gujars and Rajputs, known by the acronym 'Ajgar'. Both of these came and went because these alliances were not the result of like-minded views but were vehicles of convenience. These castes saw a certain advantage in banding together for a particular election, but once that was over, individual identities began to press for a breakaway.

The backward class movement that gained traction post the Mandal Commission recommendations faced a similar fate. While peasant castes (e.g. Jats, Gujars, Kurmis and Koeris) might appear homogeneous, they compete with each other due to identical interests of being rural communities with agricultural professions trying to break into the urban world. The common interest makes political sense for them to unite.

A discussion of caste alliances tends to impute a natural affinity between different communities, which is actually non-existent. What exists are transient interests that bring different identities to temporarily merge before parting ways. The tie that binds identities together in a political alliance is notoriously fickle; the moment the context changes so do friendships. For example in the 2017 Uttar Pradesh elections, the Jats, Yadavs and other peasant castes, who were once together, went their separate ways.

This process can also be found among the Scheduled Castes. The Bahujan Samaj Party, which was successful in Uttar Pradesh for several elections, has lost its charm and its loyal followers. One need only examine its performances in the 2002 and the 2007 elections and contrast them to the 2017 one to understand this process. Constituencies that went with the Bahujan Samaj Party in one election ditched it in the next, and so forth. In fact, this is true of all elections. In politics, caste alliances are temporary, what holds over a longer term is the internal sense of identity and belonging.

Castes, then, are not as unique as they are often made out to be in mainstream literature. They contest over positions of superiority, just as other status groups do. They have identity tales that elevate their backgrounds and breeding, just like other status groups. The only feature that separates them from others is the large number of different status groups in the caste order. Finally, caste Hindus are just like other individuals in the rest of the world. When it serves their interests, they abandon caste identities altogether and opt for more secular ones.

There is a clear empirical reason for this. Hindus may belong to different castes, may be attached to them too, but they have identities and interests that are not determined by their caste position. For instance, Jats did not vote for Jats in the 2017 UP elections and neither did the Paswans vote for the Paswans in Bihar in 2015. It is also fairly certain that a large number of Jatavs, traditionally Bahujan Samaj supporters, voted for the Bharatiya Janata Party during the UP elections in 2017. Such examples abound.

Finally, no one caste numerically dominates any constituency. The Yadavs are but 9 per cent of UP's population. Only 8 per cent of the population of west UP are Jats;[8] but it is mistakenly considered to be a Jat bastion. In such a situation—where in a constituency about five castes of equal numbers are present, what must a voter do? As nobody wants to waste a vote and there are usually only two major contenders, most people are forced to vote outside their castes.

It is disappointing for exotic hunters to know that Indians are actually ordinary, normal people, but with a difference—as with all other communities. The great advantage of discarding the exotic veil around castes is that it promotes analytical thinking in social science. Once that happens, universal theory comes alive and understanding across cultures grows.

VII

Towards Sustainable, Productive and Profitable Agriculture

Ashok Gulati and Gayathri Mohan

An Inconvenient Truth

With a population of 1.3 billion today, which is likely to overtake that of China by 2024, India has more than 17 per cent of world's population.[1] In comparison, India has about 2 per cent of world's overall area, about 11 per cent of arable land, and 4 per cent of global freshwater supplies. Given that an average household in India still spends about 45.5 per cent of its expenditure on food,[2] and with per capita incomes likely to rise by about 6 per cent per annum in the coming decade or so, demand pressures for food, feed and fibre are going to rise rapidly. With increasing urbanization and industrialization, pressures on land and water are going to increase even more.

Given these challenges, there is need to increase continuously land and water productivities for sustainable and productive agriculture. Unfortunately, the focus of policymakers and scientists has been largely on land productivity, and issues concerning water productivity are often relegated to the background. But water would be a bigger binding constraint than land in India's agriculture and overall development. In a global ranking of water availability, India is already categorized as a water-stressed country with per capita annual availability of less than 1700 cubic meters (cu. m).[3] In 2011, India's per capita water availability stood at 1544 cu. m and it is continuously falling over time (CWC, 2013, 2015).[4] Water needs to be used more judiciously through better technologies and farming practices and its pricing should also reflect its scarcity. Only then can one hope to have a sustainable agriculture that is both productive and profitable.

Agriculture and Water

Almost 78 per cent of freshwater supplies in India are used for irrigation in agriculture.[5] The typical method of irrigation in India is 'flood irrigation', i.e. flooding the field, be it through pumping of groundwater or using canal waters. The water-use efficiency under 'flood irrigation' hovers around 65 per cent, i.e. roughly 35 per cent of water applied for irrigation either evaporates, leaches through or goes to waste. And in case of canal waters, there is an added conveyance loss of about 30–35 per cent, which makes the water-use efficiency of canal waters as low as one-third. Thus, crops based on canal irrigation use only one-third of water supplied from the dams. These methods of irrigation need overhauling if India has to make best use of its scarce water resources for sustainable agriculture.

Currently, India has roughly 47 per cent of its cropped area irrigated, while the rest is rain fed.[6] If India has to raise agricultural productivity and bring stability in farm production, it must increase its irrigation cover and use water supplies more productively. In this context, it is interesting to note the recent slogans that Prime Minister Narendra Modi has rightly given, 'har khet ko pani' (water to every field), and 'more crop, per drop'. The slogans are matched by increased funding for water in the last two Union budgets, be it for major or medium irrigation schemes through the Long Term Irrigation Fund (Rs 40,000 crore) with NABARD, the Micro Irrigation Fund (Rs 5000 crore) or the Pradhan Mantri Krishi Sinchayee Yojana.[7] All these are steps in the right direction to augment water supplies and promote better use of water.

The ultimate irrigation potential in the country is about 139.9 million hectares (m ha) at current levels of technology. If rivers are interlinked, it can go even up to 175 m ha.[8] This needs to be seen in the backdrop of the current Gross Cropped Area (GCA),[9] which is around 195–200 m ha, and the current irrigated area at about 90 m ha.

The issue of sustainable agriculture against the backdrop of water supplies and irrigation methods can be seen clearly by focusing on two crops: rice and sugarcane. Both crops are water guzzlers. One kilogram of rice grown in states like Punjab and Haryana needs almost 5000 litres of water; and a kg of sugar produced in Maharashtra needs about 2000 litres of water. In Punjab, the water table has been depleting at the rate of 70 cm per year during 2008–12[10] primarily due to paddy cultivation, which shows how Punjab is heading towards unsustainable agriculture. And in Maharashtra, sugarcane, which occupies only 4 per cent of the cropped area of the state, takes away almost two-thirds of irrigation water, leading to extreme inequality in the distribution of water and a cause of much distress in certain pockets.

Paddy Cultivation in Punjab: How Far Is It Sustainable?

Punjab, the seat of the green revolution success, has the highest gross irrigated area ratio in India. Almost 98.5 per cent of its GCA is irrigated (2013–14) with around 80 per cent irrigation from ground water. The data from the Central Ground Water Board (CGWB) reveals that of 138 blocks in Punjab, 110 are over-exploited. Ironically, almost 36 per cent of Punjab's GCA is under paddy, which requires more than 200 cm of water for irrigation, much of which has to be sourced from underground.[11] As the water table is receding at an alarming rate, tube wells are being dug deeper for drawing water from even 300–400 feet at several places. That raises the pumping costs, but electricity is supplied at a highly subsidized price, with the marginal cost almost zero. With almost the entire paddy under irrigated cover, Punjab has the highest paddy yields in the country with more than 70 per cent of the produce procured by the Central government for feeding a large Public Distribution System (PDS).[12] Thus, Punjab with its largest contribution of wheat and rice to the central pool has been 'feeding the country's poor'. But it is at a huge cost to the state's ecology, especially due to paddy cultivation. During the kharif season, Punjab becomes a large lake of paddy fields, spreading malaria, and at the time of harvest, paddy straw is burnt in the fields causing clouds of smoke all over. These social costs are not captured in any robust analysis of sustainable agriculture practices in Punjab.

Although West Bengal, Uttar Pradesh and Punjab were the top three states in terms of area and production of rice in 2015–16, compared in terms of productivity/ha, Punjab stands first and Uttar Pradesh and West Bengal are at the fifth and the fourth positions respectively.[13] Some of the key reasons for lower productivity in these states are their relatively low irrigation cover, low fertilizer usage and low procurement of rice. As a result of highest productivity of rice on per ha basis,[14] and robust procurement system, the profitability of farmers in rice cultivation over their paid out costs (cost A2) is the highest in Punjab (Figure 2). High profits keep farmers locked in paddy cultivation despite high social costs—the depleting water table, the burning of paddy straw, etc.

Figure 2: Profitability in Paddy Cultivation over Paid Out Costs (Cost A2) across Major Paddy Growing States (Triennium Average Ending 2014–15)

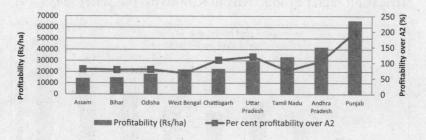

Source: Commission for Agriculture Costs and Prices (CACP), 2017–18.[15]

From the sustainability point of view, one needs to analyse the issues differently for a better understanding of the problems, especially water-related ones. First, land productivity across states should be compared only for irrigated rice to make it comparable among states.

Such a comparison shows Tamil Nadu topping the list (Figure 3a). Second, and most importantly, one should estimate rice productivity per unit of irrigation water, say per lakh litres of irrigation water. Such an analysis can throw greater light on the issue of sustainable agriculture. The results of this analysis are stunning. Punjab, instead of being at the top, slips to the bottom amongst major rice-growing states. Paddy in Punjab, from this view point, is certainly not a wise choice. West Bengal can produce almost 42 kg of rice from one lakh litres of irrigated water, while Punjab can produce only 19 kg from the same quantity of water. More precisely, Punjab consumes almost two times more water than West Bengal and almost three times more water than Bihar for producing the same amount of rice (Figure 3b). Bihar has the highest productivity of rice per unit of irrigation water (56 kg of rice per lakh litre of irrigation water). This is commendable. But unfortunately, states with high productivity rankings on per unit of water basis (Bihar, Assam, and West Bengal) do not have an efficient procurement system for rice and their farmers often face prices for paddy way below the corresponding minimum support prices (MSPs) obtained by farmers from Punjab. The net result of such a policy environment is that their profitability remains much lower.

Figure 3: Comparison of Irrigated Land Productivity and Irrigation Water Productivity of Rice across the States (2013–14)

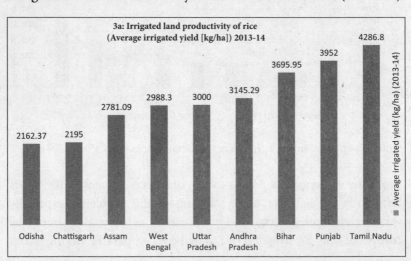

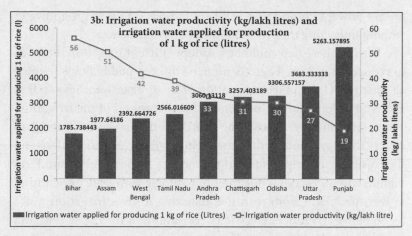

Source: National Sample Survey Office (NSSO), 2013–14; Authors' calculation using data from CACP, 2013–14.[16]

In the light of this new analysis, is Punjab suitable for cultivating rice? Should one promote rice there despite having its highest land productivity but lowest water productivity? The answer is definitely no.

But how does one shift Punjab towards sustainable agriculture? The government as well as the farmers know that paddy cultivation is not good for the future generations as the water table is depleting fast. But it is the high profitability that acts as a deterrent. The state's farmers are ready to switch to other crops provided the profitability is not less than that of paddy.

As a first step, Punjab passed the Punjab Preservation of Subsoil Water Act, 2009.[17] The Act is directed towards delayed sowing and transplanting of the paddy crop with a view to saving the depleting water table. But it has not been able to turn Punjab away from paddy or even arrest the depleting water table. More focused steps are necessary for a significant turnround. The first should be to reorient the policy of free electricity for agriculture and shift towards Direct Benefit Transfer (DBT), i.e. putting that much money directly into the accounts of the farmers. It can be tweaked so that large farmers get a bit less than small farmers on a per ha basis. The pricing of electricity can be on a full cost recovery basis with metered power. This will encourage farmers to save power bills and that will help indirectly to save groundwater without impacting the profitability of paddy farmers.

The next best step could be to adopt efficient irrigation methods to reduce water loss. There is no need to keep paddy fields flooded all the time. One can irrigate paddy every three or four days so that standing water is fully used before the next round of the irrigation. This itself can save almost one-fourth of the irrigation water and electricity use. Pilot studies are being carried out to understand the feasibility of drip irrigation technology in rice cultivation. Drip manufacturers carrying out the pilot studies with state agricultural universities claim from recorded data that it saves irrigation water by 66 per cent, reduces electricity consumption by 52 per cent and increase yield by 50 per cent.[18]

The Johl Committee had recommended crop diversification in Punjab way back in 1986. A recent study on Punjab by the Indian Council for Research on International Economic Relations (ICRIER)[19] also suggests diversification away from paddy to maize (corn), livestock, and fruits and vegetables. Maize uses one-fifth of the water needed for paddy irrigation and can save 80 per cent of the power subsidy of the state on a per ha basis when farmers shift from paddy to maize. The saving can be used to promote maize-based value chains, such as incentivizing feed mills,[20] silage units, and starch factories[21] based on corn. But farmers must be assured of at least the same profitability as in paddy, if not more. For this, if necessary, the state government must intervene in maize markets for some time, in the greater interest of protecting the state's depleting water table. The way forward is to identify blocks where the water table is worst affected, and encourage farmers to grow maize and procure it, if needed, and discourage procurement of paddy in those blocks. Punjab currently has less than 3 per cent area under fruits and vegetables compared to 8 per cent across the country. It can encourage farmers towards fruits and vegetables duly supported by cold chains and processing units. The process has to be demand driven, i.e. first identify the markets and then usher in change in the production systems. Only then can Punjab farmers raise their incomes and make agriculture sustainable and productive.

Sugarcane in Maharashtra and the Issue of Sustainable Agriculture

Sugarcane in Maharashtra is an interesting case of an unsustainable cropping pattern. Maharashtra has only 19 per cent of its GCA under irrigation.[22] The water-guzzling sugarcane crop, which occupies only 4 per cent of the GCA, alone consumes almost two-thirds of the irrigation water in the state. This irony became more critical when the trend continued even in the midst of an acute water scarcity when parts of the state, especially Latur district of Marathwada region, were quenching its thirst using water shuttled through life-saver trains called 'Jaldoot express'. Thus, it becomes imperative to understand the sustainability of growing sugarcane in Maharashtra.

Marathwada is in the sugarcane-growing belt of Maharashtra with almost 23 per cent share of the state's sugarcane area.[23] The sugarcane crop consumes almost three times more irrigation water than cotton, the major crop of the state. Latur district, one of the worst water scarcity affected regions in the 2014–15 and 2015–16 drought, recorded the highest share of sugarcane area (20 per cent in 2015–16) in the Marathwada region.

In the countrywide scenario of sugarcane, Uttar Pradesh (UP) ranks first in terms of area (44 per cent) and production (38 per cent), followed by Maharashtra, with a share of 19 per cent in area and 22 per cent in sugarcane production.[24] The other major sugarcane states are Andhra Pradesh (AP), Karnataka, Tamil Nadu (TN) and Bihar. The land productivity (production per unit area) of sugarcane across these states is displayed in Figure 4. Among these states, Tamil Nadu has the highest land productivity (103 t/ha). Uttar Pradesh (61 t/ha) and Bihar (52 t/ha) are far below Karnataka (89 t/ha), Maharashtra (80 t/ha) and AP (76 t/ha). These values, however, indicate that the traditional sugarcane-growing subtropical belt comprising UP and Bihar is less suitable for cultivation of the crop, whereas the tropical belt comprising AP, Maharashtra, Tamil Nadu and Karnataka are more productive producers of the water-guzzler crop. Incidentally, the recovery ratio of sugar from sugarcane is also higher in AP, Maharashtra and Karnataka compared with Uttar Pradesh and Bihar. All these justify a thriving sugar industry in the tropical belts. But such a conclusion would be biased if one does not look at the water balance in the state, and also adjusts for the duration of the crop.

The results of sugarcane productivity per cubic metre (cu. m) of irrigation water (as estimated earlier for rice, per lakh litres) across major sugarcane-growing states reveal a very different and interesting picture. Wide variation exists in the duration of crop and sugar recovery rates across these states. For example, the average duration of the crop in Uttar Pradesh is around 9.6 months while in Maharashtra it is 13.5 months (Appendix 2). The number of standard irrigation requirements for the sugarcane crop per hectare in Maharashtra, AP, Karnataka and Tamil Nadu are about 26, 27, 34, 40 respectively while those in Uttar Pradesh (7.6) and Bihar (5) are much less.[25] Maharashtra has the highest sugar recovery rate of 11.3 per cent while Bihar and Tamil Nadu are at 9 per cent each. The different rates reflect the variation when sugar productivity (sugar being the final product of sugarcane) and efficiency per unit area is compared. The land productivity of sugarcane across the states without adjusting for these parameters is thus not comparable. Hence, there is a need to adjust the production per unit area with respect to duration, water intake and recovery rate to enable any meaningful comparison. In Figure 4, the normalized land productivity of sugarcane across states after adjusting with crop duration is given along with the unadjusted land productivity for comparison.

Further, in Figure 4, the irrigation water productivity of sugarcane across the states is displayed and compared with the land productivity and adjusted land productivity of sugarcane across states. The irrigation water productivity, which is the land productivity after adjusting for water intake, shows that Bihar and Uttar Pradesh have almost 2.5 to 4 times more productivity than Maharashtra, AP, Tamil Nadu and Karnataka with respect to irrigation water applied. Among the states, Bihar has the highest irrigation water productivity (13.9 kg/cu. m) while the lowest is observed for Tamil Nadu and Karnataka (3.5 kg/cu. m) and this ranking is seen to be in exact contradiction to the land productivity values of the states.

The sugar productivity after adjusting the land productivity of sugarcane by crop duration, water intake and recovery rate shows that Bihar (1.25 kg/cu. m) and Uttar Pradesh (1.00 kg/cu. m) are at par and more efficient than Maharashtra, Andhra Pradesh, Tamil Nadu and Karnataka (where productivity is less than one-third that of the sub-tropical states). Thus, for production of 1 kg of sugar three to four times more irrigation water need to be applied in the subtropical belts of Tamil Nadu, Karnataka, Andhra Pradesh and Maharashtra when compared to the tropical belts of Uttar Pradesh and Bihar (Figure 5).

Thus, it is established that the traditional subtropical sugarcane belt is more efficient in terms of sugarcane and sugar productivity than its tropical counterpart, when time duration of the crop and recovery rates are adjusted and productivity is calculated on per unit of irrigation water requirement.

Figure 4: Comparison of Sugarcane Land Productivity, Normalized Land Productivity and Irrigation Water Productivity across the Major Sugarcane-Growing States

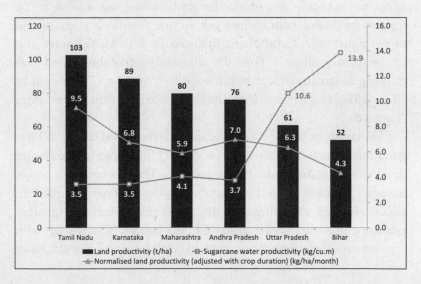

Figure 5: Irrigation Water Productivity of Sugar and Irrigation Water Applied for Production of 1 kg of Sugar (TE 2014-15)

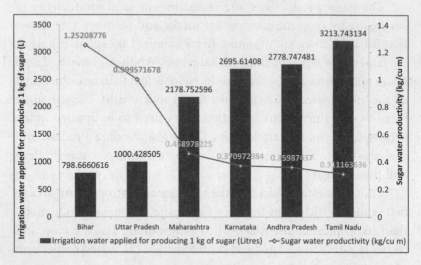

Source: Authors' calculation using data given in CACP (2015–16) and Directorate of Economics and Statistics.[26]

The profitability of sugarcane across the states before and after adjusting for the crop duration also reveals similar results. Before adjusting the crop duration, the profitability was found to be highest for Maharashtra while per month profitability was found to be highest for Tamil Nadu followed by UP. Maharashtra was in the third position.[27] Thus the adjusted profitability shows that growing sugarcane in UP, bestowed with irrigation (77 per cent of GCA, 2013–14),[28] is more profitable compared with Maharashtra (Figure 6).

Maharashtra has prospered with sugarcane cultivation and has good infrastructure in terms of processing industries, research and development institutions. The farmers and the economy as a whole have not warmed up to the idea of changing the cropping pattern, which requires exploring options for better water management practices like the micro-irrigation technology. Compared with conventional surface irrigation methods with low water-use efficiency of 30–65 per cent, the drip irrigation system exhibits almost 90 per cent efficiency, by bringing down water loss during application. The drip technology in sugarcane can save water by around 28 per cent over flood irrigation method (considering application efficiency alone) which is what is required for irrigating approximately one hectare of cotton crop. Thus, the water saved by using drip irrigation technology can be used for bringing additional land under irrigation for other principal crops of the region resulting in a multiplier effect in increasing farmer incomes.

Figure 6: Profitability and Adjusted Profitability of Sugarcane across Major Sugarcane-Growing States in India (TE 2013–14)

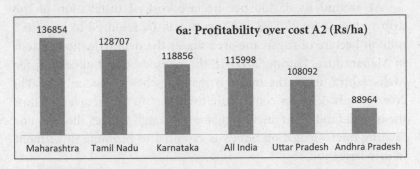

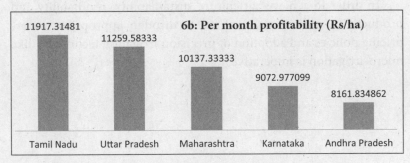

Source: Authors' calculation based on data from CACP (2016–17).[29]

The adoption of the drip irrigation system is found to be economically feasible in the majority of cases even in the absence of subsidy.

However, owing to the high initial investment cost associated with the installation of the technology, subsidies become imperative for its adoption by small and marginal farmers. So far, only 22 per cent of sugarcane area has been brought under the drip irrigation system.[30] Recently, the chief minister of Maharashtra announced that most of the area under sugarcane must be put under drip irrigation by 2019 to save water for other crops as well as for drinking purposes in water-scarce regions like Marathwada.[31] The Maharashtra government aims to bring an additional 3.05 lakh hectare of the sugarcane crop under drip irrigation in the next two years through a pilot project that is to be implemented with loans from NABARD, and based on the results, make drip irrigation mandatory for the remaining area after 2019.

At around Rs 85,400 per hectare cost of installation of the drip system, a total of Rs 6832 crore will be required to bring 0.8 million hectare of sugarcane area under the drip irrigation system in Maharashtra. During 2017–18 the revised budget allocation for Maharashtra under the micro-irrigation scheme was only Rs 380 crore[32] (only 5.56 per cent of the total cost to be incurred). Thus, the overall funding in micro-irrigation through budget allocation or floating micro-irrigation bonds is essential to promote investment in drip irrigation.

In order to achieve agriculture sustainability, profitability and productivity, judicious use of water through appropriate water-pricing policies and adoption of precision irrigation technology like micro-irrigation is imperative.

VIII

The Rise and Fall of Indian Planning

Pronab Sen

For the past seventy years since Independence, India has followed a path of planned development, which has by and large served it well. National planning came into prominence in the fifties and sixties with India's decision to adopt planning as the centrepiece of its development strategy, and its sequential adoption by many developing countries as they emerged from colonialism.[1] This period witnessed tremendous activity in academic research on planning models and methodologies not only in developing, but also in developed countries.

National planning came under attack in the late-seventies from international multilateral agencies (the World Bank and IMF) as well as the academic community. By the early eighties, national planning was in full retreat and was retained by just a few countries such as India. However, in the late nineties, national planning began to make a comeback, although with a changed nomenclature. Ironically, this process was led by the World Bank itself that required all countries seeking its assistance to prepare a 'Poverty Reduction Strategy Paper' (PRSP), which was nothing but national plans under a different rubric.

Unfortunately, during the intervening two decades, planning had disappeared from the academic radar leaving little capacity for preparing PRSPs except in a few countries like India. Nevertheless, planning has re-established its importance in country after country since then. In reverse irony, India, which was the mother lode of national planning outside the communist world, brought planning to an abrupt end with the dissolution of the Planning Commission in 2014.

This essay seeks to place economic planning in India both in its historical context and also in terms of the process leading to its end. There has been a tendency in recent years to treat the development strategy followed by India as an undifferentiated continuum, with little substantive variation from plan to plan. Nothing is further from the truth. Indian development strategies have evolved from one plan to another in response to the objective conditions of the economy and to the challenges of the moment. Some of these changes have been strikingly bold and original, others more modest; but change there has been.

The Golden Years

The first Five Year Plan was not really a plan at all, but an agenda for the reconstruction of a badly damaged country following the Partition. The Second Five Year Plan set the stage for formal planning. Its politically mandated objective was to increase the growth rate of GDP to the maximum feasible given the limitation of resources. The principal constraint was the availability of savings, and existing growth theories and models held little hope for any dramatic improvement over an extended period of time. The decision to convert the savings rate from a constraint to an additional objective bore the imprimatur of Professor P.C. Mahalanobis, who was not a politician but a technocrat. The emphasis on establishment of heavy industries through public investment, both as a means of rapid industrialization and raising the low savings rate, was certainly original in its conception.[2] It reflects the confidence that the political leadership of the time, led by Jawaharlal Nehru, had in the analysis and judgement of technocrats in choosing a path largely untrodden. The phased reduction of the savings constraint and the need for maximizing short-run growth required planning over multiple time horizons leading to the perspective plan (i.e. long-term planning) being set for fifteen years, while the operative plan was for five years, and annual plans were to concretize resource allocations.

The Third Plan, conceived during a period of emerging balance of payments problems and falling international prices of primary products, led to a rethinking of the strategy. A new constraint—foreign exchange—was emerging and had to be considered in addition to domestic savings. There were two possible ways to address this issue: (a) increased emphasis on exports; or (b) reducing imports through domestic production. The first would require derailment of the strategy to increase savings and the long-run productive potential of the economy. Thus, the Third Plan introduced the concept of 'import substitution' as a strategy for industrialization and growth. The genesis of this strategy was both political and technocratic. While gelling well with the political desire for national self-reliance, it was consistent with the 'export pessimism' of mainline economics of the time. Whatever be the merits of this strategy in hindsight,[3] it received considerable attention, and even acclaim from academics and practising policymakers, and was widely emulated by other developing countries.[4]

There were two other notable institutional developments during this period. The first was recognition of the need to decentralize planning that was mandated by the federal nature of India's Constitution. Indian states were to undertake state-level plans within the broad framework and resource allocation of the national plan. Technical support was provided by the Centre to the states for this purpose. Second, the import-substitution strategy required the government to intervene in the pattern of industrialization beyond the role of the public sector envisaged in the Second Plan. Detailed sectoral planning using input–output models to determine optimal industry-wise capacity creation by the private sector was institutionalized at this time.

The Fourth Plan came after one of the most difficult periods of Indian economic history. The period from 1965 to 1967 witnessed one of the worst droughts and consequent famines in large parts of north India. At the same time, all aid was cut off to India by donor countries on account of the Indo-Pakistan War of 1965, including food. This traumatic experience brought food security to the forefront of policy imperatives, which was further buttressed by the observation that sustained industrialization was not possible without adequate provision of wage-goods.[5] Thus, a third constraint was introduced into growth theory—the wage-goods constraint. The necessary efforts to address the agricultural constraint meant greater involvement of the Centre in agricultural development—a state subject under the Constitution. This Plan was also characterized by the introduction of another concept that became popular in the international discourse much later—environmental sustainability.

The Fifth Plan too was path-breaking in that it recognized that growth and industrialization by themselves would not necessarily improve the living conditions of the poor—a recognition which only recently finds echo in the development position of the World Bank. The strategic thinking in this instance was purely politically driven by one of the most potent slogans of independent India—*Garibi Hatao*[6]—coined by Indira Gandhi. The concepts of 'minimum needs' and directed anti-poverty programmes were innovations of this recognition. However, this also involved the Centre treading further into the domain of the states. The Fifth Plan also marked a point of departure from the Mahalanobis model and adoption of the Harrod–Domar model. This was a clear pointer to the view that was emerging at that time that savings may no longer be the main constraint to long-run growth.[7] In effect, therefore, it could be moved back to being a constraint instead of an objective.[8]

Disenchantment and Demoralization

The Sixth Plan represented a shift towards a more 'technocratic' planning approach, where the plan targets became more 'realistic' than 'visionary', as they were in the preceding four plans. This persisted for the next three plans as well. It also marks the beginning of disenchantment with planning within the political leadership.

Nevertheless, this plan, for the first time, explicitly recognized the success of the Mahalanobis heavy industrialization strategy in raising the national savings rate. That had created a situation where the savings constraint was no longer binding and excess capacities were becoming evident in certain industries. This especially applied to steel and petroleum products in which India had moved from being a large importer to a net exporter. A shift in the pattern of industrialization, with lower emphasis on heavy industries and more on infrastructure, began here. But in the absence of a compelling vision, this plan was, at best, an exercise in incrementalism.

The Seventh Plan represented the culmination of this shift in perspective. It may be termed as the 'infrastructure' plan. The government was slowly withdrawing from leading the economy. There was a re-evaluation of the import-substitution strategy and a shift towards a more liberal trading regime. The strategic change was not decided by technocrats but by the political leadership, especially Prime Minister Rajiv Gandhi, who did not believe in planning and made it known to all.[9] However, the technocrats were to convert the politically dictated strategy to an operational blueprint. In hindsight, a demoralized Planning Commission did a half-hearted job and, in particular, did not clearly address the potential risks of the new strategy.

The Eighth Plan was overtaken by the foreign exchange crisis of 1991 triggered by the Gulf War, and the economic reforms that came in its wake. The dramatic events and policy initiatives of the two-year plan holiday period between 1990 and 1992 demanded a full reappraisal of the planning methodology. The Eighth Plan represents the first efforts at planning for a market-oriented economy. Although the shift in planning did not entirely take place, the economy performed unexpectedly well, recording an average annual growth rate of 6.7 per cent.[10] However, the Planning Commission could claim little credit for this performance.

The growth momentum could not be maintained in the Ninth Plan, even though the planning methodology had adjusted to reflect the new conditions. It recognized that private investment was central to attaining Plan targets and was driven by the functioning of the financial sector of the country. For the first time in Indian planning, the financial sector became an integral part of the Plan. This added a fourth constraint —the financial constraint—which is quite distinct from the savings constraint. It recognizes that weaknesses in the financial sector can potentially prevent the economy from absorbing investible resources available.

The other critical point about the Ninth Plan is that again, for the first time in the Indian planning history, it recognized the possibility that demand rather than investible resources could be the main constraint to growth and, as a consequence, fiscal policy needed to be brought into the planning framework rather than being left entirely to the finance ministry.[11] The warning was not heeded by the economic administration in the country. Pressures of fiscal rectitude following implementation of the Fifth Pay Commission award led to a sharp reduction in public investment for the Centre and states, precipitating a cyclical economic downturn. Agricultural failure in three out of the five years exacerbated the problem with tight monetary measures for checking inflation adding to fiscal pressures.

Recovery and Relapse

The Tenth Plan marked the return of visionary planning to India after a long period of incrementalism. It sought to double national per capita income and create a hundred million jobs in the next ten years. These targets were largely motivated by the emerging demographic pattern. The single biggest challenge to Indian planners and policymakers at least for the next two decades would be to provide employment to a labour force growing faster than ever before. Demographic projections indicated that although there might be a reduction in the rate of population growth, the growth

rate of the working-age population had peaked during the Ninth
Plan period at about 2.4 per cent per annum and would decline only
gradually thereafter. The growth rate of the labour force, however,
was likely to be slower at 1.8 per cent per annum, but this needed to
be seen against the past record in creation of work opportunities.
During the eighties and early nineties, the average rate of growth of
employment—a proxy for work opportunities—had been around 2
per cent per year, but dropped sharply to around 1 per cent during
the latter part of the nineties. Therefore, if the immediate past trends
in work creation continued into the future, the country faced the
possibility of adding about 2.5 million people to its unemployed
each year. Such a situation was clearly insupportable.[12]

It was further realized that creation of work opportunities in
the macro sense in itself may not solve unemployment and poverty.
Since the growth of the labour force was regionally uneven, the spatial
pattern of creation of work opportunities became extremely relevant.
It would have been naïve to believe that there were no barriers or costs
to large-scale internal migration. This confluence was a planning
issue, which could not be left entirely to markets. It was noted that
there would always be a tendency for private investment to move
to developed regions, which would accentuate regional disparities.
Unless public intervention, particularly in infrastructure, could
redress the initial imbalance, matters would become progressively
worse.[13] Therefore, the Tenth Plan emphasized regional balance and
for the first time had a separate plan document on states.[14]

The Eleventh Plan too was visionary in a different way: it
introduced the concept of 'inclusive growth'.[15] Along with concerns
on employment and infrastructure,[16] it focused on human resources,
especially health and skill-development. The prescience of this
became evident during the course of the Plan. As the economy
accelerated to a 9 per cent growth trajectory, skill shortages emerged
in almost all sectors other than agriculture. By the middle of the
Plan it was clear that skills, and not investible resources, had become
the binding constraint on the economy, and would remain so for
the foreseeable future. On the other hand, underemployment of

the unskilled or semi-skilled labour continued to pose challenges. Thus, increasing alternative work opportunities in rural areas was a key element of the Plan.[17] But the objectives also led to a sizeable increase in the Centre's involvement in state matters. The Plan was also overtaken by global events. The global financial crisis of 2008–09 and the severe drought of 2009 took their toll. Although the economy recovered fairly rapidly, the growth momentum had been damaged. In addition, the success of the Tenth and the early years of the Eleventh Plan in raising the growth rate of the economy and incomes of the rural poor led to a sharp increase in demand for non-cereal foods. Since the supply response was inadequate, food inflation accelerated and continued to remain in double digits.

Therefore, the Twelfth Plan was not framed under favourable circumstances. The global economy was slow in recovering and the Indian economy too had lost its momentum. Corporate investment, which had led the high growth performance of the Tenth and Eleventh Plans, was floundering for several reasons, including tight monetary policy and regulatory bottlenecks. By now it was clear that the Indian economy was substantially integrated with the global economy and its growth path could no longer be viewed independently of international developments. The Plan, therefore, was less about new initiatives and more about bringing coherence in the development policy environment. Its basic premises remained more or less the same as that of its predecessor with focus on the measures necessary to improve the impact of initiatives.

The Path to the End

The national planning experience in India is most instructive in terms of the processes that were employed and their impact on the resentment that built up across a range of stakeholders. The Second and Third Plans had very little by way of consultations, but that did not really affect ownership or accountability since there was a very high level of decentralization. The plans scrupulously stayed away from areas in the domain of the states. They were also not overly prescriptive with regard to the domains of most Central ministries other than laying down the broad contours of policy. In view of the limited coverage of these plans, both the information and the feedback needs were relatively modest and could be obtained without any great information flow from the subordinate units.

The downside of this hands-off approach was that since each state was left to its own devices without any real central guiding principle, they formulated their own plans independent of each other. The net result was a wide array of development experiences across the states of the country, leading to increasing divergence between them. The second problem was that there was no rational basis for the Centre to determine the amount of central funds to be allocated to each state for their development needs. This led to a certain degree of resentment among states that accused the Centre of allocating funds on a political basis rather than on any objective economic or development criteria. This was despite the fact that the Centre and almost all states were governed by the same political party until the early seventies. Matters worsened subsequently as more states came under other parties.

This arms-length arrangement began to change from the Fourth Plan and gained momentum from the Fifth. In the forty years since, the encroachment of the Centre into domains of the states has increased progressively from agriculture to social protection (anti-poverty programmes) to a wide variety of social services. As a consequence, the national plan increased steadily in both scope and level of detail.[18] Correspondingly, the planning process too became increasingly elaborate and complex. In particular, formal political consultations became necessary. This was carried out through meetings with state governments usually led by the chief ministers. The main consultation was on 'the Approach Paper to the Plan'. The Approach Paper and the final plan document were placed before the National Development Council (NDC)—headed by the prime minister and including the Union Cabinet and all state chief ministers—for approval, at which time the political leadership in principle could demand changes in these documents.

This procedure could have elicited a fair degree of buy-in, provided that the follow-up processes were better. As things stood, state-level consultations were meticulously documented, but no feedback was ever provided on which suggestions were accepted and which were not, along with appropriate justification. States, quite rightly, felt the consultation was merely a façade for the Centre to do as it pleased. The NDC meetings were even more pro forma with the states convinced that their views did not count. The decentralization process progressively worsened over the years and steadily eroded the degree of buy-in, first among states and then even among the ministries. Its effects on accountability were even worse. Originally, the Centre transferred a block grant to states for development purposes, which was used by the latter to fund programmes designed and implemented by them.[19] Later, carve-outs were made from the total state allocations for specific purposes of national importance, with the design and implementation left to the discretion of the state governments. Up to this point, there was considerable ownership of the Plan by the states despite reservations on consultation. This began changing from the Fifth Plan with Central ministries becoming more involved in matters belonging to the domain of the states through Centrally Sponsored Schemes (CSS) implemented by the states but partially funded by the Centre.[20]

Initially, the CSS were designed by the Central ministries. The unified designs were then imposed on all participating states. States resented the imposition and had little accountability for failure of the CSS. To make matters worse, the CSS reduced funds available for states from the Central allocations, as well as the amount available from their own funds. This was yet another blow to ownership by the states and a source of even greater resentment. Given the complexity that was introduced by the CSS, which at their peak numbered more than 350, the state governments, usually led by their chief ministers, had to come to the Planning Commission to finalize the state plans. This was quite rightly considered humiliating by state politicians and gave rise to a deep-seated anger amongst them.

During this period, the Planning Commission did not interfere with the design and implementation of the CSS, except to undertake cost-benefit appraisal of the proposed project. This approach ensured that there was full ownership and accountability of the schemes, at least in the Central ministries. Later, however, the Planning Commission also began interfering with the design of the CSS. This was the kiss of death, since it removed both ownership and accountability among not only the states but also the Central ministries. To a large extent, the eventual demise of the Planning Commission was probably the outcome of this over-reach, since it led to widespread resentment in all other tiers of government.

Rise of the Phoenix

One of the earlier acts of Prime Minister Narendra Modi, who carried his resentment as a state chief minister to New Delhi, was to announce the dissolution of the Planning Commission and its replacement with a new entity—the NITI Aayog.[21] The intent was made amply clear—old-style Central planning was out; a new-style reforms agenda was in. With this step, India, supposedly the world's last surviving bastion of Central planning, would join the rest of the world in embracing a market-led process of growth and development. It was, however, quite clear even at the outset that the NITI Aayog would eventually have to be mandated to develop a formal strategic plan for the country, even though the nomenclature may be changed.[22]

The NITI Aayog has been entrusted with developing a fifteen-year vision, a seven-year strategy and a three-year implementation framework. Although the term 'plan' is scrupulously avoided, it is quite obvious that planning is back. This is a good thing. After all, the principal function of planning is to evolve a shared commitment to a common vision and an integrated strategy among all stakeholders. No development strategy can be successful unless each component of the system works towards a common purpose with the full realization of the role that it has to play within an overall structure of responsibilities.[23] The NITI Aayog mandate meets this requirement, but the devil is in the details.

IX

Will India Ever Be a Great Power?

Sumit Ganguly

Since its emergence as an independent state from the collapse of the British Indian Empire, many of India's policymakers have harboured the hope that the country will eventually achieve the status of a great power. This chapter will first provide a brief historical overview of India's quest for a great power status, and then take stock of the country's current domestic institutional capabilities. Finally, it will conclude with a brief discussion of India's prospects as a great power.

Nehru's Quest

There is little or no question that the country's first prime minister, Jawaharlal Nehru, entertained this aspiration. Nehru, of course, did not seek this pathway through the acquisition of military capabilities but instead focused on building the sinews of heavy industry at home and through the pursuit of an ideational world order abroad.

His emphasis on industrialization stemmed from his admiration of the Soviet Union's success with forced-draught industrialization albeit without its highly repressive features. The pursuit of a global order based on multilateralism and a rejection of power politics can be traced to two different sources. At one level there is little or no question that Nehru was convinced that a new global order, one that eschewed the use of force, promoted decolonization and reduced global inequalities, was a moral imperative. At another level, it can also be traced to a concern about the opportunity costs involved in diverting the scarce resources of a poor country to military expenditures. Furthermore, he had genuine fears about the possibility of Bonapartism—a hardly unreasonable misgiving given the fate of so many states that emerged from the end of colonialism, including Pakistan.

Nehru's emphasis on industrialization laid the foundations for a modern Indian economy.[1] However, it abjectly failed to promote significant economic growth or dramatically reduce poverty. His internationalist focus, especially under the aegis of the Non-Aligned Movement (NAM), did raise India's profile in global affairs. More to the point, the country played a significant role in promoting international peacekeeping, in placing nuclear disarmament on the global agenda and in promoting decolonization. None of these were trivial achievements given India's lack of material power.

Sadly, the significance of material capabilities was underscored when the country faced a military onslaught from the People's Republic of China (PRC) in 1962 and confronted a complete rout. Few, if any members of the NAM, came to India's assistance. The great powers, which had been subject to India's stinging criticisms at various international forums on a range of issues, expressed no great sympathy for India's plight. For example, both the United Kingdom and the United States only provided modest amounts of military assistance. Worse still, they exerted pressure on India to settle the Kashmir dispute with Pakistan on terms favourable to India's adversary.

India after Nehru

In the aftermath of the 1962 war and Nehru's death, India's great power aspirations were effectively set aside. The most important change that the war engendered was the much-needed modernization of the Indian military. However, even as this process was belatedly under way, the country had to cope with another war of aggression as Pakistan launched a second war in 1965 over the disputed state of Kashmir. Nehru's successor, Prime Minister Lal Bahadur Shastri, ably coped with the crisis. He also took the decision, shortly after the 1964 Chinese nuclear test, to authorize the Subterranean Nuclear Explosions Project (SNEP) that eventually culminated in the first Indian nuclear test of 1974. However, Shastri was not in office long enough to pursue any other significant initiatives at home or abroad. Those tasks fell to Nehru's daughter, Indira Gandhi, who inherited his mantle of leadership following Shastri's demise in 1966.

It is possible that Indira Gandhi shared her father's vision of establishing India as a great power. However, more pressing domestic issues, including the possibility of a looming famine in 1966, consumed most of her energies in the initial years in office.[2] Subsequently, especially after orchestrating a dramatic military victory over Pakistan in 1971 she did try to raise India's global profile. To that end, India became one of the most vocal exponents of the New International Economic Order (NIEO). This effort, which was launched at the United Nations General Assembly (UNGA), sought to bring about a radical redistribution of global resources and to restructure the global economy for addressing extant North–South disparities.[3] In the end, despite its grandiloquent goals, it accomplished little. Indeed its effects had perverse consequences for both growth and equity in the global south and certainly did little to enhance India's stature in international affairs.

Indeed, during much of her tenure and that of her son and successor, Rajiv Gandhi, India could neither address critical problems of domestic poverty nor assert itself as a significant global presence. At home, the country witnessed mostly anaemic economic growth and abroad, its role was largely confined to grand rhetorical flourishes. Its failure to address domestic poverty, its limited significance in the global economic order and its lack of substantial military capabilities effectively reduced its status to that of a marginal actor in global affairs. India's policymakers may have chafed at the country's limited role in international politics but they lacked the wherewithal to make a meaningful difference.

Confronting the Cold War's End

The abrupt end of the Cold War and the simultaneous collapse of the Soviet Union amounted to a dramatic exogenous shock to both India's economy and polity. From an economic standpoint, India's model of a mixed economy reliant on massive state intervention suffered a body blow with the Soviet collapse. The strategy of economic growth that the Soviet Union had pursued and that India had emulated to some degree was effectively discredited. The Soviet collapse also meant the loss of India's most invaluable strategic partner. To compound matters, other factors, including the loss of substantial remittances from the Persian Gulf as well as a series of debt payments that became due, converged to create an unprecedented fiscal crisis for the country. These twin shocks, strategic and economic, induced India's policymakers to undertake a fundamental reappraisal of the country's economic and foreign policy.

In the realm of economic policymaking, the country abandoned its commitment to substantial state intervention, opened its markets and drastically reduced regulations. Within a year thereof, the economy not only recovered but began posting unprecedented rates of economic growth. Within the decade, the country had not only embarked upon a pathway of steady economic growth but had also made a significant dent on poverty. It also overcame its residual reservations about the utility of force in international politics. To that end it carried out a series of five nuclear tests in May 1998 ending a long span of strategic ambiguity.[4] Despite widespread international diplomatic disapprobation and a raft of bilateral and multilateral sanctions, the country was able to cope with the fallout from the tests. Its economy was robust enough to withstand the sanctions and its diplomatic corps sufficiently dexterous to cope with the political condemnation.

Ironically, the crossing of the nuclear Rubicon, combined with significant economic growth, actually catapulted the country into an altogether new realm in the global arena. With two key elements of material power harnessed, India could now assert itself in a hitherto unprecedented fashion in the global sphere. Not surprisingly, it increasingly started to lay claim to a permanent seat in the United Nations Security Council (UNSC). It also became an active member of the G-20, helped create the India–Brazil–South Africa forum (IBSA) and embraced the Brazil–Russia–India–China–South Africa (BRICS) organization. All of these developments, both at home and abroad, boded well for India's hopes of achieving a great power status.

Institutional Challenges and Limits

Despite these obvious achievements, there are a number of factors, mostly domestic, that can hobble its quest. These need to be discussed in some detail. The first impediment can stem from what was one of India's greatest strengths: the quality and efficacy of its political institutions. Indeed as early as the late sixties, the noted American political scientist Samuel Huntington had highlighted the significance of its institutions as an indicator of the country's political development.[5] Unfortunately, as Huntington had warned, political development cannot be assumed to be a linear process. Institutions can both develop and decay. Owing to a complex array of factors, virtually every political institution has witnessed a decline both in its probity and efficacy.

India now faces an interesting paradox. A host of countries in the global South are poorly institutionalized. A great deal of decision-making is simply based upon the personal vagaries and proclivities of leaders. Such a problem does not plague India. It has an extraordinary range of institutions that run the gamut from a working Parliament to a mostly independent judiciary. However, over the past several decades all of them have witnessed varying levels of decay. Their internal norms have frayed, their efficacy is at question and their autonomy increasingly at risk. Unless this process of deterioration is arrested, it is far from clear how the existing institutions can address the plethora of problems that currently besiege the country.

Just one or two examples should help illuminate the problem. There is little or no question that the higher echelons of the Indian judiciary have contributed to important developments in modern jurisprudence. For example, through the creation of the system of Public Interest Litigation (PIL) it has extended the reach of the law to many who had hitherto lacked the resources to approach the bench. However, there are widespread concerns about delays in disposing cases by the judiciary, particularly at the lower level. The large number of pending cases[6] delays delivery of justice and adds to the woes of the aggrieved by imposing financial stress. Judicial delays also affect commercial transactions and investment decisions with investors apprehending possibilities of protracted litigations in case of disputes.

Another related area also demonstrates the limits of India's existing institutions. This is the realm of policing. Admittedly, in the country's federal system, the efficacy of the police does vary considerably across the country. That said, some aggregate statistics underscore the dimensions of a nationwide problem of under-policing. According to a Human Rights Watch report of 2009, India had one civil policeman for 1037 residents against an Asia-wide average of one per 558 residents and a global average of one per 333.[7] Another recent article revealed that in India's most populous state, Uttar Pradesh, as many as 50 per cent of police posts remained vacant. The same story indicated that on a nationwide basis as many as 24 per cent of police posts remained vacant.[8]

These statistics, of course, only underscore one facet of the myriad problems of policing in India. Beyond this issue of under-policing, the police in the vast majority of states are under-resourced, overworked and frequently venal. Worse still, a disproportionate number of them are assigned to the task of protecting India's administrative and especially political elites.[9] Though there have been no end of calls for police reform and various commissions have been formed to that end, they have had little or no effect on the actual conduct of policing in the country.

To compound matters, the police, with marked exceptions, have proven wholly inadequate to the task of quelling the resurgence of a neo-Maoist insurgency, the Naxalites, across vast swaths of the country. Prime Minister Manmohan Singh, while in office, had publicly stated that the renewal of the Naxalite insurgency was the single greatest threat to the country's internal security. The statement was hardly hyperbolic as Maoist violence has wracked as many as seven states across the country.[10] Worse still, despite state strategies of both repression and co-opting, they have been able to inflict spectacular strikes on police and paramilitary forces. If a state cannot perform one of the most fundamental Weberian tasks— maintain a monopoly over the legitimate use of force—it is hard to see how it can emerge as a great power.

The institutional deficits that the Indian state confronts are not confined to entities dealing with domestic issues. They also afflict areas of foreign and defence policymaking. For example, there is little or no question that India has a highly professional and thoroughly dedicated foreign service. However, as a number of commentators have argued, its size is quite inapt for a country of India's size. With a sanctioned strength of 912 in 2016, it had a mere 770 full-fledged officers.[11] This made it comparable to that of the Singaporean Foreign Service that handles the foreign affairs of a country of five million.[12] Despite multiple plans to expand the foreign service, the results of such efforts have been most uninspiring. It is indeed a testament to the service, that despite its small size, it has been able to cope with the growing complexity of India's foreign relations. Of course, a counterfactual thought experiment might raise an uncomfortable question: what opportunities have been lost or squandered owing to the limited size of the service?

Despite the structural limits that plague the service, it is widely believed that it is mostly an efficacious institution. This judgement, however, cannot be proffered about various other governmental bureaucracies charged with safeguarding particular aspects of

India's national security. Few major defence projects in India have been completed on time. The ones completed have also often been noted to have design flaws. As a result, the armed forces have had to bear with poor-quality weapons and equipment. Indigenization of defence manufacturing has fallen short of its objectives with dependence on foreign prototypes and components continuing, as in the case of Light Combat Aircraft (LCA), which is reliant on an imported engine.[13] Serious efforts to improve the situation in the foreseeable future are yet to be noted.

Conclusions

This overview has made clear that India's quest for a great power status is long standing. For decades the effort was mostly chimerical as the country simply lacked the material wherewithal to achieve that standing. Seventy years later, it has some of the capabilities that might enable it to pursue that goal. It has one of the fastest growing economies in the world; it has managed to make a significant dent on endemic poverty; it is a de facto nuclear weapons state with a growing arsenal; and it has a military with increasing reach. All of these attributes should boost its search for great power standing.

Yet, as this analysis has demonstrated, it also suffers from a number of chronic institutional shortcomings that can hobble its efforts. These inadequacies are not subject to quick or easy redress. They have evolved over extended time spans and will require major reform efforts. Given the resistance of most institutions to drastic changes it is hard to see such reforms emanating from within. Significant exogenous shocks may induce these institutions to undertake the drastic changes that are necessary to enhance their capabilities and efficacy.

There is indeed reason to believe, based upon the country's post-Independence trajectory, that major institutional reforms or policy shifts have been carried out only in the wake of significant endogenous or exogenous shocks. For example, the much-needed modernization of the Indian armed forces only took place in the aftermath of the 1962 military debacle. Similarly, the market-friendly reforms that were undertaken in the early nineties stemmed from an acute and unprecedented fiscal crisis. Unfortunately, after the initial impetus to pursue reforms the country has often witnessed a renewal of institutional inertia or policy stagnation. Consequently, while shocks have certainly played a vital role in boosting institutional and policy changes, their effects seem to wear off over time. India's political culture of incremental change seems to prevail over attempts to induce drastic alternations. Given this uneven record, it is hard to envisage a future where the Indian state might harness the requisite motivation to propel itself to tackle various endemic problems that stand in the path towards a great power status. Indeed, it is tempting to conclude that the likelihood that India will achieve that status remains quite uncertain.[14]

X

Non-Governmental Organizations in India: Contribution, Challenges and Future Prospects

Poonam Muttreja

India has a long and rich tradition of social action by civil society organizations rooted in the principles of *dāan* (charity) and *seva* (help).[1] Both these principles have shaped India's development across various dimensions, ranging from food security, environmental sustainability, education and healthcare to advocating transparency in governance, promoting communal harmony and representing the rights of minorities, women and children. Much of private voluntary activism to start with was driven by India's dominant religions. A significant shift occurred when Mahatma Gandhi gave it a new orientation by linking activism with political change and social transformation. The seventies witnessed another major change in India's voluntary action movement when young sociopolitical activists re-conceptualized the role of non-governmental organizations (NGOs).[2] From 'do-gooding' by offering relief to poor 'beneficiaries', the new NGOs started underscoring the rights and entitlements of citizens as enshrined in the Constitution, and holding the state and political establishment accountable for delivering on the promise of development.

NGOs engaged in private and voluntary social action have a very visible and active presence in India. The reach of these organizations extends from metropolitan cities to rural and remote tribal areas, rivalling and often exceeding the reach of the state. The contributions and significance of civil society organizations are perhaps best captured through the sustained trust that Indians place in them. According to the 2017 Edelman Trust Barometer (2017), Indians' trust in NGOs was 71 per cent—up from 64 per cent in 2016.[3] India comes out as an outlier given the global trend of declining trust in institutions.

Private social action in India today presents a rich tapestry of diverse ideologies and approaches. Civil society organizations differ from one another in their missions, goals, structures and modalities of working. This heterogeneity makes it conceptually difficult to define precisely, classify and categorize civil society organizations. As a result, even the estimates of the number of NGOs in India differ considerably. According to a study conducted by PRIA, there were close to 1.5 million civil society organizations in India in 2001. In 2016, the Government of India, in a submission to the Supreme Court, placed the figure at 3.1 million NGOs.[4] While it is likely that the number of registered NGOs has gone up over the fifteen-year period, the phenomenal increase can also be attributed to the absence of an appropriate regulatory framework that defines, registers and monitors NGOs.

This essay briefly reviews the experience and contribution of Indian NGOs, and identifies the challenges they are likely to face in the years to come. It argues that collaboration between the State and NGOs is critical to ensuring large-scale sustainable social development. This is possible only if a well-defined regulatory framework is put in place, the adversarial relations between NGOs and the state are smoothened, and the trust deficit is bridged.

The Space for NGOs

Seventy years since Independence, the Indian state has not been able to substantially deliver on its promises of alleviating poverty, relieving inequalities, ending discrimination, providing access to quality services and ensuring equal opportunities to all. With the advent of economic liberalization, the market was believed to be the great equalizer whereby benefits of development would trickle down to the last person. However, this has not happened. Economic inequalities persist and in some instances, casualization and feminization of labour have made earnings even more insecure and precarious.

The rise of NGOs, to a large extent, reflects the failure of the Indian state and markets to usher in equitable development and economic redistribution. The rapid expansion of NGOs, since the eighties, overlaps with the ushering in of neoliberal policies and the retreat of the state from social welfare.[5] NGOs have grown and helped people living in the most marginal and backward regions. They have sought to address the everyday problems in the lives of ordinary people, lent a sympathetic ear, and carried their voices, demands and complaints to decision-makers in the government. By representing minorities, challenging discrimination, and demanding state action for equitable access to economic and social benefits, NGOs have consistently worked towards advancing India's social development.

In doing so, disagreements with the political establishment are unavoidable as NGOs hold the state accountable to the people, especially the poor. NGOs act as a watchdog, checking totalitarian tendencies and upholding India's democratic principles. For instance, during the political emergency declared by Prime Minister Indira Gandhi between 1975 and 1977, NGOs were at the forefront of protests, defying the curtailment of freedom of speech and expression, and criticizing government's overreach and authoritarianism. Various scholars have traced the origins of NGOs' adversarial relations with the state to this political phase.[6] They argued that the Foreign Contributions Regulation Act (FCRA) introduced in 1976 ostensibly to check threats of the 'foreign hand' was primarily meant to delegitimize protests and intimidate those critical of the government. While the Emergency is now many decades behind us, state–NGO relations continue to face threats from the state, and FCRA regulations have become even more draconian and controlling of civil society actions.[7]

Contribution of Indian NGOs

NGOs in India have been at the forefront of drawing public attention to socioeconomic and environmental problems, and helping formulate policies to address them. Some have fought for human rights, others have worked to preserve arts, crafts, livelihoods, and cultural heritage, and yet others have developed alternative models for delivering basic services, including health and education to the poor and marginalized communities. For instance, the Centre for Science and Environment (CSE), a non-profit organization founded in 1980, has devoted its attention to the fight for environmental protection. CSE, for example, worked alongside the Chipko Movement[8] to highlight how environmental degradation impacted the health, lives and livelihood of India's poor and rural residents.[9] It was also instrumental in identifying strategies that could prevent pollution and redress environmental degradation, like the implementation of CNG-run public vehicles in Delhi.

Indian NGOs have been forging issue-based movements that have gained political significance and yielded new regulations. Engagement of governments with NGOs and similar movements have been very positive in this regard. For example, the genesis of the Right to Information Act of 2005 and the Mahatma Gandhi National Rural Employment Guarantee Act of 2005 can be traced to effective advocacy for the rights to information and employment by the Rajasthan-based NGO Mazdoor Kisan Shakti Sangathan (MKSS). At the same time, there are several issues such as finding solutions to Delhi's air pollution and the failure to check corruption through the 'jan lokpal',[10] where progress has been slow.

NGOs have also been at the forefront of expounding local solutions to protect people's skills and livelihoods. After Independence, for instance, the government's push for industrial development led to the neglect of local arts and crafts. To address the crisis, Dastkar, a Delhi-based NGO, was founded in 1981 to promote and revive India's arts and crafts, and to address the plight of artisans. Dastkar believed that if Indian artisans were not cared for, they would suffer, and the country would lose its rich heritage of local arts and crafts. Today, Dastkar's fairs (bazaars) are an annual feature with more than 350 groups participating, exhibiting and selling their crafts. Following the success of Dastkar melas, crafts exhibitions are now supported by the Central and state governments. Dilli Haat, designed as a permanent crafts exhibition, is a popular tourist destination, and annual events like the Taj Mahotsav in Agra (Uttar Pradesh) and the Surajkund Mela in Haryana are held all over India.

NGOs have developed alternative models for delivering services to ensure better reach of public services that are more cost-effective, efficient, and free of corruption. For example, the state-run Public Distribution System (PDS) provides subsidized food products (grains, sugar, cooking oil and other products) to poor people through fair price shops. While well-intentioned, the PDS has been severely and consistently criticized for food wastage, corruption and providing spoiled and substandard produce.[11] The MKSS set up its own fair price shops in the state to challenge the widely held view that state-run food bureaucracies are necessarily inefficient and that they should be disbanded and replaced by market-based solutions. The shops operated by MKSS have functioned successfully, without being bogged down by corruption and leakages, and have provided an different model that can be emulated by the government to shape up its own PDS. These initiatives underline the indispensability of NGOs to India's social development and highlight the critical importance of collaboration between the state and NGOs.

Persisting Challenges

Despite appreciable contributions, Indian NGOs continue to face numerous problems. Three in particular, that are interconnected, pose serious challenges.

The first has to do with the influx of foreign funds. Starting with the mid-eighties and more so after the opening up of the Indian economy in the early nineties, NGOs began to attract financial support from international donor agencies for their research, outreach and interventions. However, over the years, critics argue that while donor support has enabled some cutting-edge research and action, such financial support has bred chronic donor dependence, affecting the work culture and autonomy of NGOs. Although the availability of funds has attracted committed and bright young individuals to work with NGOs, voluntary social activism has been transformed for some into a career-oriented path for development professionals, which has often undermined the need to address the local needs and priorities. It has also led to the neglect of issues, such as family planning, that are not deemed attractive enough to attract donor funds.[12] Many grassroots groups working with a rights-based approach, such as ending childhood violence and advancing tribal rights, have also found it difficult to mobilize financial resources.

Second, financial support from international donor agencies has often been viewed by governments as an enabler for political criticism. This is largely because of a tenuous regulatory framework for NGOs. Indeed, the absence of a well-defined regulatory framework that monitors NGOs in India has contributed to mounting distrust between the state and NGOs.

Successive governments, for instance, led by different political parties, have failed to delete some of the requirements that make NGOs vulnerable. On the contrary, certain provisions of the FCRA continue to be invoked against NGOs that challenge state actions.[13] For example, bank accounts of NGOs protesting against the Kudankulam Nuclear Power Plant were frozen on the grounds that they were using foreign funds to fuel protests and cases were registered under the FCRA.[14] This has unfortunately attracted considerable international criticism. India has been pulled up in the international fora by countries like the US and Germany that have criticized the FCRA as 'arbitrary' and lacking transparency.[15]

Concerned with the arbitrary use of state authority to control them, NGOs and activists have come together (through Voluntary Action Network India [VANI] and other networks of civil society organizations). These activists and NGOs have demanded that FCRA be replaced by consistent and well-defined regulations that are transparent, fair and systematically applied to all recipients of foreign funds, including political parties. The persistence of this ambiguous regulatory framework has led to tensions between NGOs and the state.

The third problem has to do with the failure to scale-up successful NGO-led interventions across the country. NGO-led initiatives have been successful at the local and state level, but attempts to replicate them on a national scale have failed.[16] While the inability to scale up pilots to a pan-Indian level has much to do with financial and network constraints, it highlights the limited capacities of NGOs to influence state policies and programmes. It also points to the limitations of NGOs in effecting positive social change on a large scale.

Adversarial relations with the state compound this problem. The state possesses resources, executive authority, infrastructure and reach to replicate and scale up nationwide pilot projects initiated by NGOs. However, collaborations between NGOs and the state have been few and far between owing largely to lack of trust on both sides about intentions and actions.

There are, however, positive examples where such collaborations have improved public policies and delivery of services. For instance, the Population Foundation of India (PFI) has consistently worked alongside governments to spread awareness about government-led healthcare programmes and to ensure better healthcare delivery. The PFI continues to collaborate with the Ministry of Health and Family Welfare in providing technical assistance for scaling up the implementation of Community Action for Health (CAH). A key strategy of the National Health Mission (NHM), CAH adopts a bottom-up approach to ensure that the health needs and rights of the community are fulfilled. Being implemented in eighteen states, CAH covers 202,162 villages in 2129 blocks across 353 districts.[17]

Looking Forward

Clearly there exists both the need and scope for collaboration between the state and NGOs. For this to happen, it is important to review laws and formulate a regulatory framework that will allow NGOs to function independently and efficiently. Doing so will help weed out corrupt and dubious NGOs and ease tensions between the political establishment and NGOs. It will also allow for greater collaboration between both to pursue research and expand opportunities for adaptation of work being done by community-based NGOs. An urgent review of FCRA and other regulations that preserve the political autonomy of NGOs while monitoring their finances is the need of the hour. The Government of India has displayed its intentions to do so. India's former Union minister and current vice-president, Venkaiah Naidu, has gone on record to say: 'The registration laws, Foreign Contribution Regulation Act, provisions in the income tax laws—all these need to be periodically reviewed and revised in order to enable the sector to function independently and impartially.'[18]

However, transparency in funding cannot be expected of one entity without reciprocity from the other. It is in this context that it becomes imperative for India's political parties to disclose their finances and open their records to public scrutiny. Public disclosure of inflow and outflow of funds in political parties is likely to check partisan patronage, wherever it exists. Such transparency will also help dispel the belief among some that political parties in the government support NGOs that are ideologically aligned with them and target those that are opposed to them.

NGOs will need to resolve two other issues relating to resource mobilization. As foreign funding becomes scarce, Indian NGOs will have to rely increasingly on the government, the private sector under corporate social responsibility, and Indian philanthropies. All three potential funders have considerable introspection to do. Funding from the government should come with no strings attached. NGOs should be able to transparently report not only all financial data but also their successes and failures. The corporate sector needs to rethink its role beyond narrow commercial interests and address issues of genuine national concern. Finally, Indian philanthropists will have to realize that helping the poor can be as rewarding, if not more, than funding temples and religious activities.

The human resource issue is another matter of concern. Voluntarism, political autonomy and commitment to social justice constituted the ethos of India's NGO sector soon after Independence. Today, this sense of public service is missing in many professionals. This does not augur well for a nation that has to clear a huge backlog of human poverty and also address many new challenges. Civil society organizations need to play a more active role to instil in young people a greater respect for the Constitution, a better sense of equity and social justice, and a respect for human lives and dignity.

India faces many human development challenges. Ensuring more effective collaboration between NGOs and the state can certainly accelerate the pace of progress as India ensures greater freedom, equality and justice for all.

XI

Indian Industry: Prospects and Challenges

Rajiv Kumar

India's industrial development since Independence has charted its own rather unique path. Industrialization began in the early nineteenth century when the first textile mill was established at Fort Gloster near Calcutta (Kolkata) in 1814, followed by many such mills in Bombay (Mumbai) and Ahmedabad. Industrialization came of age with the commencement of steelmaking by the Tatas in Jamshedpur in 1907. This put India among the early 'industrializers' outside Europe and North America. But India's industrialization was unable to benefit from either this early start or the distinct advantage of catering to a large and growing domestic market and emerging markets in neighbouring Asia.

Several factors, both external and self-inflicted, led to the 'arrested development' of the industrial and manufacturing sector in India. These were in broad chronological order: the colonial administration's anti-colony bias;[1] upheaval and partition of India during Independence; central planning and Soviet-style heavy industrialization;[2] dysfunctional regulation over capacity expansion and technology upgradation;[3] growth-retarding inverted protectionism (with higher import duties on inputs compared to finished products); and export pessimism.[4] These policy-driven shifts and swings have led to underperformance by Indian industry, in terms of its share in the Indian economy, aggregate employment and stagnant share in external markets.

The liberalization of 1991 generated strong optimism on the much-needed expansion of the manufacturing and industrial sectors. This optimism has been unfortunately disproven. The liberalization led to the take-off of IT and IT-enabled services (ITES) but hardly impacted manufacturing and industry, with their shares in GDP stagnating between 16 to 28 per cent during the post-liberalization period (Appendix 2). The services sector took up the decline in the share of agriculture by raising its share from 45.2 to 53 per cent during this period (Figure 7A) with IT revenues increasing from USD 2 billion in 1994–95 to USD 3.1 billion in 2004–05 and further to USD 119 billion in 2014–15.[5]

Apparently, India side-stepped the second phase of the Rostowian development path[6] with the secondary sector being replaced by the tertiary sector as the driver of growth and absorber of surplus labour from agriculture. The shift occurred even when India's per capita incomes were low enough to have generated growth from industry as opposed to services. The contrast is stark compared to China's manufacturing share in GDP ranging between 32.2 and 30 per cent during 1991–2015. The next section discusses the relative stagnation of the industrial and manufacturing sectors during the twenty-five years following liberalization.

Successive governments since prime minister Vajpayee's in 1998 have refused to accept the slow growth in manufacturing. India's political leadership across party lines have emphasized accelerated manufacturing sector growth as the key for achieving high GDP growth and full employment, facilitating its transition from a low to an upper middle income economy. The emphasis on manufacturing, as pronounced by successive prime ministers, is summarily reflected in the objective of raising the share of manufacturing in GDP from 16 per cent to 25 per cent and employing as many as 100 million workers or approximately 20 per cent of the total workforce. This target is repeated on multiple occasions despite the growing evidence that given the trends in global trade and technology flows, the share of manufacturing in GDP of emerging economies is likely to plateau at a much lower level than those of advanced economies and by China.[7]

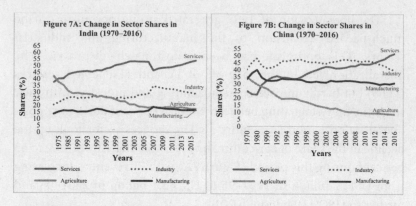

Figure 7A: Change in Sector Shares in India (1970–2016)

Figure 7B: Change in Sector Shares in China (1970–2016)

Source: World Development Indicators Database, World Bank, Ministry of Statistics and Programme Implementation, Government of India, and National Bureau of Statistics of China.

The critical question facing Indian policymakers is whether it is feasible to achieve the ambitious target for manufacturing given that automation, robotization, digital networking, including 'Internet of Things' and advanced machine interface, are reducing labour intensity in and employment potential of the manufacturing and industrial sectors. The consequential 're-shoring' of manufacturing capacities back to advanced economies, which had earlier relocated these industries to emerging economies with lower wage costs, has manifold implications for Indian industry, as discussed later, along with some major emerging trends in industrial automation often referred to as 'Industry 4.0'.

The last section in this article argues that emerging trends in automation and re-shoring should not propel Indian policies to become protectionist for shielding Indian manufacturing. This would be a Luddite response destined to fail in meeting the manufacturing sector's growth and employment generation targets. Such an inward-looking and protectionist strategy would further shrink the Indian manufacturing sector for two strong reasons. First, as a founding member of the World Trade Organization (WTO) and having joined several bilateral and regional free trade agreements, India will be forced to increase tariff and non-tariff barriers to protect its producers from imports. Indeed, a reversal from existing levels of globalization is not feasible and the domestic manufacturing unable to compete with imports will shrivel further.

Second, in a self-reinforcing manner, complete reliance on domestic demand will not permit adoption of frontline technologies and production processes that generate economies of scale and lower costs, necessary for making Indian manufacturing globally competitive. This would spell the slow but certain demise of the Indian manufacturing industry. The last section provides an alternative policy direction for making Indian manufacturing globally competitive and better equipped for meeting its ambitious objectives.

Stylized Features of the Indian Manufacturing Sector

An overview of the manufacturing sector reveals the following:

- The share of manufacturing in GDP has been around 15 per cent since 1965. Notwithstanding an increase to around 19 per cent in 2007, it declined to around 16 per cent in 2015 (Appendix 2).
- The above share is significantly lower than that of China, which while being as high as 40 per cent in 1980, has consistently been around 33 per cent. Again, in contrast to India, manufacturing made up for a lower share of agriculture, as well as the labour displaced by the latter (Appendix 3).
- Sub-sectoral composition of manufacturing output in India has been somewhat lopsided and not in line with other emerging economies.[8] Relatively labour-intensive industries like light engineering, garments and leather goods have grown much slower than capital-intensive chemical and petrochemical industries. This has been policy-induced and prevented India from exploiting its comparative or low wages.
- The rather perverse composition of Indian manufacturing is due to dysfunctional government procedures and licencing requirements that critically constrained the growth of

manufacturing. For instance, in 2016, India was thirty-ninth and 130th in the global competitiveness business environment indices. These rankings, much worse earlier, did not permit expansion of manufacturing. Services with less dependence on licencing and regulations performed much better since 1991.

- The lopsided growth of manufacturing industries prevented India from capturing global markets through labour-intensive exports. The share of Indian manufactured exports in global manufactured exports increased from 0.5 per cent to 1.5 per cent during 1991–2015. In contrast, China's manufactured exports increased their share from around 2 per cent to more than 18 per cent in 2015 as a result of higher focus on labour-intensive industries.

- The share of manufactured exports in India's total exports has remained relatively unchanged at around 70 per cent between 1990 and 2015.

- Regionally, manufacturing has remained inequitable despite the liberalization of 1991 and further reforms. Maharashtra, Gujarat, Tamil Nadu and Karnataka account for more than 50 per cent of the manufacturing output since 1970–71. The share of the weakest ten states in manufacturing has increased from 10 per cent in 1970–71 to only 15 per cent in 2014–15.[9]

- Overall, the industrial sector's share in total employment increased from 15.4 per cent in 1999 to 24.8 per cent in 2012. But manufacturing's share in employment over eighteen years (1993 to 2010) remained stagnant at around 11 per cent. India seems to have reached the plateau in the manufacturing sector's share in employment far earlier in its development journey.

The twin questions facing us are: Can India reverse the trend of low share of employment through focused policy intervention? And does India represent the emerging global trend of manufacturing's contribution to GDP and employment plateauing at substantially lower per capita income levels than those in advanced economies or East Asian 'tiger economies', including China?

Current Trends in Global Technology and Production Networks

The global economy is experiencing the 'Fourth Industrial Revolution'. Industry 4.0 has demonstrated the ability to replace not only routine but also complex and intelligent human intervention in both manufacturing and services. Industry 4.0 has resulted in some remarkable changes.

- Energy is becoming cheaper and cleaner with countries committing to 100 per cent energy from renewables. Smart grids are likely to dispense large generating plants on the one hand and establish a time-of-the-day energy market on the other.
- The onset of 3D printing might replace serpentine assembly lines for several industries by final assembly or manufacturing in closest proximity to the consumer.
- E-commerce has already disrupted wholesale and retail trade. More transformative changes in the pipeline would alter the logistics needs of manufacturing, and manufacturing itself. Mass customization will be on offer widely.
- Robotization, greater use of sensors and artificial intelligence (AI), backed by 'big data', has radically altered factor proportions in manufacturing. Labour is being rapidly replaced by 'interfacing machines' reducing the labour intensity of traditional labour-intensive industries (e.g. textiles, leather, garments)— once considered impenetrable by AI and robots.
- Industry 4.0 is resulting in 're-shoring of industries' with labour-intensive industries being attracted back to advanced economy locations to operate in close proximity to demand centres. This will transform the character of global production networks and the comparative advantage of emerging market economies like India.
- Competitive advantage in global manufacturing will henceforth be determined almost entirely by the countries' ability to establish world-class infrastructure and acquire high-quality, knowledge-intensive human resources that can adapt to changing technology.
- The days of sequential catching up from initially starting with hugely labour-intensive manufacturing operations to semi-

assemblies and subsequently to high technology and design-intensive manufacturing may be behind us.

Challenges and Prospects for Indian Manufacturing: Some Recommendations

It is far too optimistic to expect that the Indian manufacturing sector will succeed in contributing a quarter of GDP or generate 100 million jobs over the next two decades or more. The sheer pace of sustained acceleration required to achieve these targets is staggering. With the annual GDP growth expected to be in the range of 7–9 per cent in real terms, manufacturing must grow by 10–12 per cent in real terms, or more than 15 per cent in nominal terms, for its share to start rising. In the past, there have been only seven years when manufacturing attained high, double-digit growth (Figure 8). With barely 11–13 per cent of the workforce engaged in the formal manufacturing sector given the stagnation in jobs and job losses in recent years, it would be a real challenge to generate sufficiently large opportunities for employing 20 per cent or 100 million additional workers in the manufacturing sector.

Figure 8: Annual Growth Rates of the Manufacturing Sector in India (1970–2016)

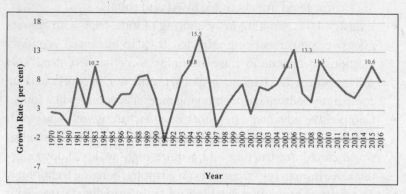

Source: World Development Indicators Database, World Bank, and Ministry of Statistics and Programme Implementation, Government of India.

The employment challenge is compounded by the strengthening of Industry 4.0 trends lowering labour intensities across the board. Rising automation and robotization has been severe on employment of unskilled and even semi-skilled workers in manufacturing. Manufacturing will henceforth see the emergence of production processes that integrate software and hardware in machines and require highly-skilled workers to be sufficiently flexible for adapting to evolving technologies.

The emerging trends have given rise to strong 'manufacturing pessimism' in emerging economies, including India. This is perhaps needed to balance the optimism of those who conceive of manufacturing growth in India as replicating the Chinese experience of the last three decades. That is simply not possible. Conditions in domestic labour markets, which prevent wages in India from matching those in countries with semi-authoritarian regimes, increasing use of hybrid and automated technologies, and growing pressure from global competition based on mass customization and rapid product innovation, rule India out of the phase of becoming an exporter of mass-produced, low-quality and labour-intensively manufactured products. An alternative strategy needs to be devised for accelerating the manufacturing sector growth.

Unfortunately, in the current and evolving global scenarios, there are no easy fixes to increasing the share of manufacturing or for it to generate a large number of new jobs. Both the government and industry must recognize that they will have to work closely together for Indian manufacturing to achieve global competitiveness, which is a sine qua non for ramping up domestic manufacturing capacity.

India must try and achieve greater integration of its manufacturing capacities with regional and global production networks for increasing the share of intra-industrial trade in its total trade. This has two important policy implications. One, the prevailing infrastructure deficit, putting Indian manufacturing at a significant disadvantage vis-a-vis its competitors and discouraging foreign investors from choosing India as an export hub, must be eliminated at the earliest. The government will have to take the lead in this as physical infrastructure is a public good where social returns greatly outweigh private returns. Two, foreign trade procedures must be streamlined and made seamless for encouraging intra-industry trade, which accounts for more than two-thirds of global trade flows. Intra-industry trade, in which emerging economies manufacture and export relatively low technology components and sub-assemblies, perhaps, remains an area where India can see greater labour absorption and expansion of manufacturing capacities.

The brunt of component manufacturing and exports should be borne by SMEs, many numbers of which are 'informal'. These must be formalized and provided access to commercial bank credit at reasonable terms; made attractive to foreign joint venture partners; and given access to information about global markets and technology trends. This requires a major shift in the focus of industrial policy by making it focused on SMEs. The formalization and, more importantly, modernization of the tier two and three of private-sector firms, predominantly unlisted and working as proprietary and partnership companies, could see an exponential growth in domestic manufacturing capacities in the coming years. The focus on intra-industry trade and the 'next 500' companies offers a good bet for accelerating manufacturing growth and employment generation in India.

Greater attention must be devoted to strengthening the sources of the knowledge economy. This implies greater attention to R & D, especially directed towards product innovation. Total R & D expenditure in India is woefully low at barely 1 per cent of GDP, compared to more than 3 per cent in Japan and the United States and 4 per cent in Korea. The Indian private corporate sector hardly contributes to this abysmally low R & D expenditure. This must change. Government policy should aim to provide sustained incentives for product innovation as opposed to process or cost-reducing form of 'incremental innovation' that presently dominates corporate R & D expenditure. Strengthening of the intellectual property regime; greater collaboration amongst public and private corporate R & D activities; and lowering of policy-induced barriers for scaling up operations could be possible policy responses for addressing this perceptible weakness in Indian manufacturing, especially in view of the immense breakthrough opportunities offered by the ongoing fourth global technology revolution.

A special effort is necessary to push back global protectionist tendencies being echoed domestically. India must participate more forcefully in the G-20 platform for protecting the multilateral liberal global trading regime that has delivered the longest and most robust rise in living standards of global population in the post-Second World War period. The perception in some quarters that a liberal order determining global trade, technology and financial flows is detrimental to Indian manufacturing is misplaced. That would stunt Indian manufacturing capacities and capabilities as domestic firms will neither achieve economies of scale for becoming globally competitive nor acquire critical new technologies essential for increasing shares in the global market. The inevitable result will be slow and certain shrinking of domestic manufacturing, which will be unable to withstand import competition.

Instead, policy should be directed to urgently address critical constraints making Indian manufacturing globally uncompetitive. Greater focus should be on productivity-enhancing policy measures at reasonable price points. This includes addressing infrastructure deficits, including transport (roads, railways, ports and airports); electricity availability and its quality; and logistics. Notwithstanding some improvements over the past two decades, significant gaps remain, especially as one moves away from metros and state capitals.

There is a critical need to improve the level of trust between the government and business. This lack of mutual trust results in over-regulation and excessive compliance burdens on private businesses, and leads to extensive rent-seeking opportunities. The prevailing environment of mistrust and over-compliance explains the inability of many SMEs to scale up operations and become globally competitive. This is neatly summed up in the terse remark that conditions in India spawned companies that are not born as regular start-ups that grow over time but as 'midgets' that remain stunted and globally uncompetitive.

The private sector can and must play its due role in building the trust-based relationship with the government, which is a sine qua non for achieving global competitiveness, pushing innovative growth strategies and successfully integrating with global and regional production networks. For starters, as Prime Minister Narendra Modi has suggested, the Institute of Chartered Accountants as the established self-regulating and self-certifying institution should enforce corporate governance and financial accountability as required under existing statutes.

Apex industry organizations like the Confederation of Indian Industry (CII), Federation of Indian Chambers of Commerce and Industry (FICCI) and the Associated Chambers of Commerce and Industry of India (ASSOCHAM) and indeed the principal regional ones as well, must disqualify members charged with misdemeanours and evasion of statutory compliances. This process of self-regulation has been effective in several countries and helps in improving prospects of collaboration between public and private sector and attracting FDI, which may then have greater confidence in forming joint-ventures with Indian companies.

The issue of reducing mutual mistrust and laying the basis for greater collaboration and partnership between the government and business has not received adequate attention either in policymaking or in academic enquiries. It is a critical driver of India's manufacturing prospects and deserves greater focus going forward. These improvements can lead to the emergence of a true 'India Inc. coalition', which is presently confined to rhetoric. Creation of an effective India Inc. coalition is one of the principal conditions for expanding India's share in global manufacturing and for its firms to achieve sustained global competitiveness.

XII

Land: Finite, Fragmented, Fragile, Fraught

Sanjoy Chakravorty

There is little doubt that land is India's most important resource, and because of the rising demands on this finite and increasingly fragmented resource by a growing and urbanizing population, it is also the source of some of the most intense conflicts in the nation. Land is a fraught subject. Much of the recent attention to the subject has been focused on land acquisition. However, it can be argued that equally important and deep structural issues arise from the low income generated by agricultural land, the fragility of some land due to climate change and agricultural intensification, and the extraordinary land market that has emerged in the new millennium and created arguably the highest land prices in the world.

No one is immune from the need for land. This is especially because, just like us, 1.3 billion other Indians also need land. Half the labour force (and population) still derives some or all of its income from working on land. They, and much of the remaining half, the working and struggling classes, spend most of their lives and their savings, such as they are, looking for land and housing. The upper middle class uses the land and housing market as the primary location for parking its savings (investments); criminals focus most of their activities on land and housing (which are far more lucrative than the old standards—the smuggling and sex trades); and the political class derives much of the considerable (black) money needed to run parties and elections from the land market. At the same time, the old struggles of domination and alienation between majorities and minorities, the powerful and the marginalized, have not only not gone away, but may also have intensified. These are expressed through innumerable caste and tribal conflicts over land in various parts of the nation, most sharply in what is euphemistically called the 'Maoist' insurgency, but what truly is an Adivasi uprising for control of their traditional lands.[1]

These manifold and vital issues cannot be covered in this brief essay. One reason for being selective is the fact that despite its significance as a major element in India's political economy, there is relatively little research on the subject, especially in the last three decades after the death of 'land reform' as a serious policy issue (discussed later). Some of the most interesting and consequential matters—such as criminality and corruption on land among agents from the underworld and politics (embodied, more and more often, in the same person, the 'real estate politician')—have not even been researched. It is the tiger in the room—everyone knows it is there, but is too scared to acknowledge it. Moreover, capable scholars tend to find that land as a research subject (like public administration and urban planning) provides less attractive career opportunities. Thus, despite land being the most constant subject on the minds of most Indians, it has hardly received serious analytical attention.

The remainder of this essay focuses on three subjects among the many that are important. First, it presents some basic information on land in India: how much there is, how much is cultivated, and most important, how fragmented it is. Second, land policies in India are discussed, focusing on 'land reform' in the first decades after Independence and 'land acquisition' in the last decade. Third, it outlines the basic condition of the land market, with some general information about prices. It argues that land prices in India have exploded in the new millennium and now are possibly the highest in the world. The essay ends with a brief discussion on the consequences of this new land market.

Distribution

India's total land area is about 812 million acres.[2] To put it in context, one acre (43,560 sq. ft.) is roughly the size of a soccer field, or sixteen tennis courts, or twenty-nine apartments of 1500 sq. ft. each. Of the total, in 2007–08, about 348 million acres (or 43 per cent) was under cultivation. The remaining land was forested, steep, urban, fallow, under water, or in use for transportation or other infrastructure. The most productive land is irrigated land.[3] About 154 million acres or about 44 per cent of India's cultivated land area is irrigated. Much of this is also land on which more than one crop is grown annually. These 'multi-crop' lands cover about 136 million acres or about 39 per cent of the land under cultivation.

According to the most recent agricultural census of 2010–11, the agricultural land in the country (not all of it is cultivated) covers about 395 million acres divided into 138 million discrete land parcels; an average of 2.86 acres per holding. This is the lowest average ever recorded. Data from previous agricultural censuses show that the average landholding size was 5.63 acres in 1970–71 (in the first census), 4.55 acres in 1980–81, 3.83 acres in 1990–91, and 3.04 acres in 2005–06. In the forty years that the agricultural census has been undertaken, the average landholding size has decreased by about half.

To put it in context, while not the lowest in the world, the average size of agricultural landholding in India is among the lowest (Bangladesh, for instance, is lower). It is worth noting that the nationwide average of 2.9 acres masks the reality that small holdings (92 million of the 138 million land holdings) averaged just 1 acre per holding. In several major states, the average landholding size was less than 2.5 acres (which is roughly 1 hectare): Kerala (0.5 acres), Bihar (1 acre), Uttar Pradesh and West Bengal (1.9 acres each), and Tamil Nadu (2 acres); together, these states cover close to one-quarter of all the agricultural land in the country.

In contrast, the average landholding size in France is 110 acres; in the US, it is about 450 acres, and even more than that in much of South America. Largely as a result of this abysmally low size of landholding, income from cultivation is also low. According to the most recent National Sample Survey (NSS) assessment (70th round, 2012–13), the average monthly per capita income from cultivation for agricultural households was merely Rs 687 (or about Rs 41,000 per year for a household of five). This—the fragmentation of agricultural land—is the root cause of poverty in India.[4] This point cannot be emphasized enough.

Data from the agricultural censuses show that there has been a massive growth in the number of marginal farms[5] (tripled in forty years) and an equivalent decline in the area covered by farms larger than 10 acres (down to one-third in forty years). The condition is unambiguous and unrelenting: agricultural land in India continues to fragment into increasingly unsustainable sizes as a result of the continuing growth of the agricultural population, the intergenerational subdivisions of already-small holdings, the inability to move enough of the population into salaried jobs in the formal sector (instead of casual labour) or business or other non-farm occupations, and the inability of the urban sector to absorb low-skill rural labour (caused principally by the slow growth of urban jobs, the failure to create a labour-intensive manufacturing base, and the appalling quality of life for the urban poor).

Policy

The current politics and policy on land are squarely focused on land acquisition, whereas in the initial years and decades after Independence, the politics and policy were focused on land reform. Land was the primary source of revenue during the colonial rule—more under the pre-1857 Company Raj and less under the later Crown Raj. Land revenue was the primary reason for colonization; not, contrary to popular belief, trade or British industrialization. The revenue was extracted by a variety of agents of expropriation, like zamindars and 'kings'. After the First World War, there was, for the first time in Indian history, a rapidly rising population and consequent land fragmentation (this was the beginning of the demographic transition in India and its population explosion), expanded tenancy rights that led to exchange rights, a feudal ownership structure with numerous intermediaries and subinfeudation, and informal credit markets run by usurious local moneylenders. After Independence, a few years post the devastating Bengal famine in 1943, four-fifths of the labour force worked in agriculture, under conditions of widespread poverty, exploitation, illiteracy, and landlessness.

Land reform was one of the most important items on the large and difficult agenda of the newly independent nation. The First, Fourth, and Seventeenth amendments to the Constitution created the legal basis for key land reforms. The abolishment of intermediaries (zamindars, inamdars) was the first reform attempted and its success led to some decrease in inequality in landownership in the first decade after Independence. Tenancy reform had mixed outcomes—it was successful under communist administrations (in Kerala and West Bengal), but far less so under other regimes, especially Congress regimes. Land ceiling reform was generally unsuccessful and very possibly counterproductive (producing outcomes opposite to those desired). All the land reforms together led to the redistribution of less than six per cent of cultivable land. Inequality in landownership remained virtually unchanged from the sixties and may have increased markedly in the last two decades. One must agree with the conclusions of numerous observers of land reforms in India that other than eliminating the zamindari system they failed. To be fair, it is difficult to see how successful they could have been with redistribution even with more sincere efforts given the extreme scarcity and fragmentation of land.

It may well be that the more important policy/action by the independent Indian state on land was acquisition rather than reform. No new law was created for it. The existing colonial Land Acquisition Act of 1894 was retained, unchanged. This act was vital for enabling the massive industrialization and modernization programme of the Nehruvian state. Over the seventy years after Independence, much agricultural land was acquired for infrastructure and industry. The state took land it deemed necessary for development, using the language of public purpose—for dams, defence, irrigation, factories, townships, power, roads, rails, etc.—this time in the national interest, as opposed to the colonizer's interest. The geography of modern India was created by the Land Acquisition Act of 1894.

I have written that 'the independent Indian state's policies on land were fundamentally contradictory. It gave (or redistributed) land with one hand, and took (or acquired) land with the other. It took more than it gave, and the giving stopped long ago, whereas the taking intensified in recent years.'[6]

No entity has kept track of how much land was acquired or how many people were affected. In the absence of any official data, independent scholars have reconstructed the impacts from sources like government gazettes. Their findings can be treated as reasonably reliable estimates.[7] It is possible that as much as 50 million acres, or about six per cent of all the land in the country, was acquired or converted from common use after 1947. It is likely that as many as 50 million people were displaced or adversely affected. The land-losers were paid very little compensation (sometimes none at all) and few were resettled or rehabilitated. Many others, perhaps more in number than the land-losers, were displaced without compensation because they did not own the land. The socially marginalized groups were the worst affected: Dalits, because they lived in but often did not own land in project-affected areas, and Adivasis, because much of their land was community-held rather than privately owned (and could be taken lawfully without compensation).

There is little doubt that the land- and livelihood-losers 'effectively subsidized India's development, or, to be more accurate, its winners—that is, the populations that got power and roads and water . . . This regressive redistribution system lasted well into the 2000s. It was politically sustainable for many reasons, not least because the direct winners outnumbered and were more powerful than the direct losers. Even if the worst accounts of land takings are exaggerated, even if the highest numbers of affected people are overblown, this would have to be considered a deeply inequitable and significant state failure by today's standards.'[8]

This regressive system existed for almost six decades without much resistance. No political party emerged to champion the rights of the displaced. However, in the last ten years, the system broke down. There were well-known cases of very troubled and violent acquisition processes (in Nandigram, Singur, Kalinganagar, land for Posco, Vedanta, and the Yamuna Expressway, for example), plus hundreds of small and large cases of land acquisition processes faced resistance, many in the new economic spaces that were enabled by the Special Economic Zones (SEZ) Act of 2005. The seeds of the resistance may have been sown by the Narmada Bachao Andolan, a social movement that began in the mid-eighties to resist the displacement created by the Sardar Sarovar Dam Project in Gujarat and Madhya Pradesh. But the seeds were able to bloom because of fundamental changes in India's information system with new media and information agents acting in an environment of increasing political competition. Land acquisition became a wedge issue in Indian politics. And there was a new land market.

Resistance to land acquisition became so widespread that some called it India's 'biggest problem'. It became a major issue in state-level politics. In West Bengal, the thirty-four-year rule of the communists was upended by Mamata Banerjee and the Trinamool Congress over this issue. It could have been one of the reasons behind the defeat of the Mayawati-led Bahujan Samaj Party (BSP) government in the Uttar Pradesh assembly elections in 2012. So important was this issue that the Congress-led UPA government made the subject and the new land acquisition law framed in terms of the rights of land-losers just before the elections, a major plank of their re-election campaign in 2014.[9] The law has five important elements: (a) increased compensation—market prices are doubled in urban and quadrupled in rural areas; (b) expanded coverage—non-owners facing livelihood loss are compensated; (c) rehabilitation and resettlement—compulsory above certain thresholds with minimum set standards; (d) informed consent of land-losers—using referenda, specifically when the acquisition has any private sector involvement; and (e) a new process—involving social impact assessments and a new multilayered bureaucracy. All major parties voted for the new law, including the BJP.

But within months of coming to power in the 2014 Lok Sabha elections, the BJP tried to amend the law, specifically by diluting the 'informed consent' and 'social impact assessment' elements. This was done initially through ordinances and later by making an unsuccessful attempt to change the law in the Parliament. The main goal surely was to make land acquisition easier in what appears to be the BJP's primary development thrust—the creation of industrial corridors near and between key cities. In their view, this is where the investment action is concentrated, and this is how urbanization and the economy are likely to grow. It would be a mistake, however, to see the failure of the BJP amendment as the end of the legal story. This is a long-running epic and India is nowhere near the end of the story.

Market

In the meantime, while the resistance to land acquisition was growing, fundamental changes were taking place in India's land markets. Land prices more than quintupled between 2000 and 2013 (and stabilized after that in many places), so much so that India now has arguably the highest land prices in the world. The global peak prices—as in central Hong Kong, Shinjuku and Shibuya in Tokyo, or midtown Manhattan in New York—are not reached in India yet, though south-central Mumbai comes very close (at around Rs 250 crore/acre). But everywhere else—from near-suburban, to far-suburban, to peri-metropolitan, to midsized and small towns, to prosperous well-connected rural regions, to struggling poorly-connected rural regions—land prices in India appear to be unmatched anywhere (with the possible exception of China, which does not, however, have an individualized agricultural land market like India).

In peri-urban regions (around all the megacities and most major cities) and prosperous rural regions in states like Punjab and Haryana, farmland prices are easily one crore rupees per acre; often they are much higher. Almost nowhere in the country is it possible to find farmland that costs less than Rs 10 lakh per acre today. To put these prices in context, consider that the price of farmland in the US state of Kansas is about USD 1300 (less than Rs 1 lakh) per acre. This is what highly productive land should cost if the price were based only on productivity. Therefore, one must conclude that the price of farmland in India is a dozen to a hundred times more (or higher) than can be justified by agricultural productivity.

Part of the explanation for this unprecedented rise comes from a mismatch between supply and demand. The supply is more or less fixed, whereas the demand from all parties (industrial users, the service sector, farmers, homebuyers) is increasing. There is a lot more money in the system. Home mortgage loans alone grew forty-fold (in nominal terms) in 2001–13, bringing millions more homebuyers into the market, not to mention the unquantified growth in NRI, black, and criminal money in the system. Land was always an important status good; its status value has probably increased further with scarcity. In addition, rising income and wealth inequality has enabled India's upper- and proto-upper-class families to drive up prices for everyone else. This is a new condition, and seems to be not a bubble but a structural transformation (that has lasted for close to two decades through a global economic recession and a radical demonetization).

This new land market has very serious implications for growth, development and justice. It provides opportunities for urban revenue generation in ways and volumes that simply never existed (but appear to be largely mishandled so far). Important policy initiatives like 'Make in India' and 'Smart Cities', and major budget allocations on road, rail and irrigation will both influence and be influenced by these land markets. Acquisition prices under the new law are likely to reach levels that are simply unaffordable in all but distant rural regions, which means that the new law will either have to be rewritten or land use change will have to happen without acquisition. These prices have already constrained the supply of some public goods (like housing and open space) and will squeeze them even more. Finally, the land and property markets are now the pillars of the Indian economy: new housing creates demand (for consumer durables) that spurs manufacturing, creates jobs (construction is the single largest urban job sector), and serves as the principal instrument for savings (and status-seeking). It is vital to understand the extent to which India's development trajectory is tied to the land market.

XIII

Healthcare in India: Looking back, looking ahead

A.K. Shiva Kumar

India's most notable achievement over the past twenty-five years has been the country's impressive economic growth record. After 1991, its per capita income grew nearly two-and-a-half times faster in real terms compared to the preceding three-and-a-half decades.[1] By 2014, India's contribution to global economic growth (in Purchase Power Parity terms) stood at 14.4 per cent, and its share in the world GDP was around 7 per cent.[2] Medium- and long-term prospects of further economic expansion remain bright.

India's performance in health, however, has not kept pace with the country's remarkable economic expansion.[3] Policies have failed to effectively convert economic growth into better health for its people. In 1990, for instance, India's life expectancy at birth (sixty-six years) was lower than that of Sri Lanka and the Maldives, but higher than the rest of the neighbouring South Asian countries. Today, India's life expectancy at birth (sixty-eight years) is still lower than that of Sri Lanka (seventy-five years) and the Maldives (seventy-seven years), but has fallen behind that of Bangladesh (seventy-two years), Nepal and Bhutan (both seventy years). This is in spite of India's per capita gross national income in 2015 (PPP USD 6030) being significantly higher than that of Bangladesh (PPP USD 3560) and Nepal (PPP USD 2500). And over the period 1990–2014, India's

GDP per capita grew, on average, by 5 per cent every year—much faster than the corresponding rates of 3.6 per cent for Bangladesh and 2.6 per cent for Nepal.[4]

This is not to undermine in any way India's achievements in health over the past seventy years. Life expectancy at birth has more than doubled since Independence—from thirty-two years in 1950–51 to sixty-eight years in 2015. In 2015, the infant mortality rate was thirty-seven per 1000 live births—down from 139 in 1976. From 556 in 1990, India's Maternal Mortality Ratio (MMR) fell to 167 per 100,000 births by 2011–13. The spread of HIV/AIDS has been successfully contained. The World Health Organization (WHO) officially declared India polio-free in March 2014 and free of maternal and neonatal tetanus in August 2015.

Despite these gains, India's health burden is still huge. Non-communicable diseases contribute to 60 per cent of the entire disease burden, while communicable diseases contribute 28 per cent and injuries 12 per cent.[5] A large burden of infectious diseases, reproductive and child health problems, and nutritional deficiencies coexists with a number of chronic diseases. The increasing Multi-Drug Resistant tuberculosis, the resistant strains of malaria, and the rise of viral encephalitis, dengue and chikungunya, particularly in urban areas, are matters of concern. In addition, occupational health needs of both the formal and informal sector, adolescent health, mental health, geriatric care and palliative care remain neglected. Unchecked pollution, unplanned urbanization, insufficient access to safe drinking water, inadequate food security and poor sanitation pose additional health burdens on India's population.

Unhealthy Healthcare: The Key Factors

Health outcomes in India are also far from equitable. Caste, class, gender and geography continue to account for large differences in morbidity, mortality and nutritional status. The neglect of women's health in particular is striking. For instance, in 2015–16, over half (53 per cent) of the women aged fifteen to forty-nine years were anaemic. Much of this neglect stems from the subordinate position of women and the strong anti-female biases that characterize Indian society. Men continue to outnumber women in India. Even more disturbing has been the decline in the female-to-male ratio among children aged zero–six years from 927 in 2001 to 914 in 2011, signalling the widespread prevalence of anti-female biases and discrimination against girls and women, including daughter aversion in Indian society.

Clearly, the healthcare system, as it has evolved in India, over the past seventy years has not been able to effectively meet the health needs of the people. There are many reasons why this is so.

One, nearly every country in the world that has achieved anything like universal health coverage has done it through the public assurance of primary healthcare. The basis of almost every successful health transition in the history of the world from Britain to Japan, China to Brazil, South Korea to Costa Rica has been the support of basic public health facilities.[6]

Unfortunately, the public sector in health has not grown to play a vital role in providing healthcare in India. The public sector has expanded enormously since Independence to include thousands of health sub-centres, primary healthcare centres, and community hospitals. However, the reach of the public sector even for primary healthcare remains grossly inadequate. For instance, in 2015–16, less than two-thirds (63 per cent) of children aged twelve to twenty-three months were fully immunized, and only 21 per cent of mothers had received full antenatal care.

The reasons for the underperformance of the public sector in health are not difficult to guess. Most public sector facilities tend to be under-staffed, under-resourced, over-crowded and poorly managed. Rural areas are especially poorly served. Location at a distance, inconvenient timings, poor quality of services, high absenteeism, inadequate supervision and the callous attitude of healthcare providers tend to discourage people from accessing public facilities even for outpatient care.

The extremely low level of public spending on health is a cause of and an exacerbating factor in the challenges of health inequity, inadequate availability and reach, unequal access, and poor-quality and costly healthcare services. In 2011, at USD 19 per capita, India's public expenditure on health was half of that of Sri Lanka's (USD 39) and significantly lower than that of China (USD 153) and Thailand (USD 166). A consequence of the low levels of public spending on health has been the high, private, out-of-pocket expenditures in India—69 per cent in 2011—among the highest in the world and much higher than in Thailand (22 per cent), China (44 per cent) and Sri Lanka (58 per cent).[7] Such an unusually high burden of private health expenditure has been pushing over 63 million persons into poverty every year due to healthcare costs.[8]

A second reason for poor health outcomes is the extraordinary dependence of Indians on the private sector. Given the shortage of public sector facilities, most Indians have had no option but to access healthcare from a rapidly expanding private sector that has remained, by and large, unregulated. From 8 per cent in 1947, the private sector now accounts for 93 per cent of all hospitals, 64 per cent of all beds, and 80–85 per cent of all doctors. Between 2002 and 2010, the private sector contributed to 70 per cent of the increase in total hospital beds across the country.[9]

Unfortunately, people get very low value for money in both the public and private sectors. Poor-quality services, wastage, corruption, and weak management characterize many of the public healthcare institutions. The most commonly cited reason why people do not avail of public services is that they are not satisfied with medical treatment by a government doctor or facility. Other reasons include distance and non-availability of facilities and services. As a result, though treatment is almost free (except for some minor user fees), in 2014, more than 70 per cent of outpatient care (72 per cent in the rural areas and 79 per cent in the urban areas) and more than 60 per cent of inpatient care (58 per cent in rural areas and 68 per cent in urban areas) was in the private sector.[10] But there is hardly any assurance of proper care. Many health centres and hospitals in the private and non-profit sector offer good quality healthcare services. However, with the virtual absence of effective regulation and oversight by the state, the quality of healthcare is mixed at best and the costs are often unreasonably high. In the virtual absence and enforcement of national regulations for provider standards and treatment protocols for healthcare, many private medical facilities over-diagnose, over-treat and maltreat. Many also dispense substandard and counterfeit medicines, prescribe unnecessary drugs and tests, avail of kick-backs for referrals, and manipulate hospital admissions and length of stay.[11]

It is well known that private markets in healthcare are grossly inefficient given the large informational asymmetry (where the profit-oriented doctor can 'cheat' the patient by prescribing unnecessary medicines or unwanted treatment). Further inefficiencies are also generated by the 'public goods' nature of healthcare stemming from the interdependences involved.

Third, Indian policymakers do not seem to realize private healthcare, even if properly subsidized, or private health insurance, subsidized by the state, can simply not meet the challenge of universal health coverage. Both the Central and state governments have introduced a number of publicly financed health insurance schemes to improve access to hospitalization services and to offer financial protection to households from high medical expenses. For instance, by 2014, close to 370 million (almost one-fourth of the population) enjoyed coverage under the Government of India's Rashtriya Swasthya Bima Yojana (RSBY),[12] which was launched in 2008. Nearly two-thirds belonged to families below the poverty line (BPL category). Those above the poverty line, and most in the informal sector (that employs close to 90 per cent of the workforce) are forced to rely on commercial health insurance markets.

There are serious incentive-incompatibility problems with commercial insurance as interests of providers, consumers and insurance companies do not align to maximize returns to consumers. Typically, insurance companies deny use, medical practitioners induce demand or encourage overuse, and patients themselves misuse the facility (commonly referred to as the 'moral hazard' problem). For instance, because inpatient treatment is 'free' and covered by health insurance schemes only if the patient is hospitalized for at least twenty-four hours, do insurance companies settle the bills, even when such a stay is not warranted. Furthermore, evidence suggests that quite apart from the problems of oversight to check malpractice and a high level of induced demand and inappropriate care, conventional insurance schemes siphon away large sums for tertiary care; they do not incentivize preventive and promotive care; and they do little to help with cost-containment.

Many of these shortcomings are observed in the Indian health insurance markets as well. Governments admit of low awareness among the RSBY beneficiaries about entitlements, denial of services by private hospitals for many categories of illnesses, and oversupply of some services. They also acknowledge that some hospitals, insurance companies and administrators resort to collusion and various fraudulent measures. For instance, in July 2015, the Competition Commission of India imposed a fine of Rs 6.71 billion on four public sector insurance firms after finding them guilty of involvement in anti-competitive practices in bidding for the Kerala government's Rashtriya Swasthya Bima Yojna (RSBY).[13] Furthermore, in May 2016, the Bihar Human Rights Commission directed the state government to pay a compensation of around Rs 150 million to 703 victims whose uteri were removed purportedly to gain incentive money under the RSBY.[14] There have also been reports of major increase in certain operations like hysterectomies (surgical removal of uterus) due to coverage under the health insurance schemes.

Fourth, governments have not been able to put in place appropriate regulatory frameworks for ensuring the provision of high-quality healthcare services to people in both public and private sectors. For instance, in the case of institutional births (i.e. births in a hospital or healthcare centre), standard protocols are often not followed during labour and the postpartum (occurring immediately after birth) period. Poor quality of care has also been directly responsible for sterilization-related deaths. There are gaps in access to safe abortion services too, as well as in the care for sick neonates (a baby from birth to four weeks). Many self-declared 'doctors' practise without any qualifications. Informal care providers, with no formal medical training or registration with government for medical practice, are estimated to represent 55 per cent of all providers and are also frequently the first point of contact, especially in rural areas.[15]

Looking ahead

The country's GDP is expected to grow, on average, by around 8 per cent per annum over the next fifteen years. By 2030, GDP is projected to more than triple to USD 7.25 trillion. Real per capita GDP is expected to triple by 2031–32.[16] Translating economic expansion into better healthcare is one of the major challenges facing India over the coming decades.

This can happen only if, as a nation, India embraces the idea of Universal Health Coverage (UHC). UHC embodies specific health and social goals: it is the aspiration that all people can obtain the quality health services they need (equity in service use) without fear of financial hardship (financial protection).

Adopting UHC has five major implications. First, the commitment to Universal Health Coverage would require 'to stop believing, against all empirical evidence, that India's transition from poor health to good health could be easily achieved through private healthcare and insurance.'[17] Commitment to expanding government-provided health services should become a priority. Second, entitlement to healthcare should be independent of the specific financial contributions made by individuals. In other words, every individual, regardless of their ability to pay, should be entitled to a package of essential healthcare services. Third, healthcare should be cashless at the point of service delivery. User charges and fees for any kind for use of healthcare services should be done away with. Government should ensure availability of essential medicines and diagnostics free of cost. Fourth, general taxation should be used as the principal source of healthcare financing—complemented, to the very limited extent possible given India's large workforce in the unorganized sector, by additional mandatory deductions for healthcare from salaried individuals and taxpayers. Finally, the government should make a firm commitment to step up public expenditures on health.

The recently announced National Health Policy 2017 (NHP 2017) embraces some of the UHC principles. It calls for increasing health expenditures by the government as a percentage of GDP from the existing 1.15 per cent to 2.5 per cent by 2025; increasing state sector health spending to more than 8 per cent of their budget by 2020; and ensuring a 25 per cent decrease in the proportion of households facing catastrophic health expenditure from the current levels by 2025. Two other features of the NHP 2017 are noteworthy. One, it calls for allocating a major proportion (up to two-thirds or more) of resources to primary care followed by secondary and tertiary care. And two, it also calls for viewing public hospitals as part of a tax-financed single-payer healthcare system, where the care is pre-paid and cost-efficient.

Three constraints, however, need to be addressed for meeting the financial targets specified under the NHP 2017. First, without significantly expanding the tax base, India is unlikely to generate the kind of resources needed not only for health, but also for education, water and sanitation, nutrition, infrastructure and other priorities. Expenditure on social sectors has hovered between 6 and 7 per cent, and public expenditure on health at around 1.2 per cent of GDP for over two decades. For public expenditures on health to be stepped up, India will have to increase its tax-to-GDP ratio, which now between 16 and 17 per cent is significantly lower than that of China (19–20 per cent) and Brazil (35–36 per cent). In a nation of over 1.25 billion people, 36.5 million individuals filed their tax returns for the assessment year 2014–15.[18] In addition, the state needs to ensure that benefits of public spending reach the poor. According to the Economic Survey 2015–16,[19] an estimated Rs 100 billion spent on subsidies continues to go to the well-off, not to the most deserving; and tax benefits have not reached the middle class, but the mega rich.

The second constraint to address is the limited competence and capacity of human resources, especially at lower levels of governance. Health being a state subject under the Constitution of India, state governments are primarily responsible for the funding and delivery of health services. As acknowledged by the Economic Survey 2016–17,[20] with increasing devolution of responsibility to state governments, capacity constraints at lower levels pose serious implementation challenges. For instance, even if national regulation of healthcare is introduced, the lack of capacity at the level of state governments, and particularly in districts, will pose serious challenges to effective implementation.

Above all, it is important for India to firmly, and not half-heartedly, embrace the concept of Universal Health Coverage. This calls for a new political commitment and a determination to make UHC succeed. Policymakers and politicians seem mesmerized by targets of economic growth. They do not seem to realize that if India's growth has to be sustained, good health has to be assured to all Indians.

XIV

Jobs in India

Amitendu Palit

It's hardly surprising that for a country with a population of 1.3 billion, which is nearly 18 per cent of the global population of 7.6 billion,[1] employment will be one of the foremost public policy concerns. The concern has aggravated as India has added almost a billion people to itself since 1947. Over the last couple of decades, the quality of the concern has changed dramatically with India beginning to realize the long-term implications of labour-saving technological innovations displacing existing jobs and bringing down creation of new ones to a trickle. Dwindling jobs and livelihood prospects have serious social, economic and political ramifications for a country itching to maximize its demographic dividend.

The concern over the country creating less and less jobs and fast losing the existing ones was highlighted by none other than India's 13th President, Pranab Mukherjee. Less than eight months before stepping down from office in July 2017, Mukherjee drew attention to the problem in as blunt a manner as possible:

We must turn our evolving demographic configuration into strength. For that, adequate job creation is a priority. The job creation figures of 1.35 lakh in 2015, which is the lowest in seven years, are not encouraging. With machines fast replacing men, we have to look at a paradigm shift. We have to prepare our youth, who are buzzing with innovative ideas, to turn into entrepreneurs. We also have to enable our students-turned innovators-turned entrepreneurs to be able to successfully harness the market.[2]

As a lower-middle-income country still grappling with the challenge of lifting a substantial part of its population from poverty, inability to create jobs and the consequent lack of sufficient livelihood opportunities can aggravate poverty, more so since India's population continues to increase. With India fast catching up with China as the world's most populous country,[3] the ominous possibility of more and more young people entering the workforce to find themselves jobless is indeed real. Rising unemployment, apart from impacting poverty, will increase social tensions and unrest. This is evident from the increasing number of communities demanding reservations in public sector employment such as the Jats in Haryana and the Patels in Gujarat.

The problem of low growth in jobs is compounded by the loss of jobs to automation. This heavily complicates long-term employment policymaking in an economy aiming to capitalize the demographic dividend of a large young population. The demographic dividend from a steady supply of young labour to various sectors of the economy, who, in turn, would save, consume both wage and non-wage goods, and invest productively in sustaining various sectors— thereby creating virtuous forces of economic growth on both supply and demand sides—would remain unrealized if the jobs deficit constrains youth employment. Greater absorption of young people by the economy would increase consumption of both wage and non-wage goods and also increase savings and investment. But if the jobs deficit does not allow such absorption, then the demographic dividend would remain unrealized. This would imply failure of labour-intensive industrialization in a labour-surplus emerging market economy creating obstacles for national economic aspirations and development plans. The dual challenge of reversing lower job growth and preventing job losses emerges as probably the most significant public policy imperative in modern India. The

grimness of the situation becomes more stark given the fact that jobs
need to be 'productive' and 'decent' by ensuring they fulfil individual
and national aspirations.

Structural Transition Not Employment-Intensive

India's structural transformation over the last seven decades has
resulted in services contributing more than 60 per cent of its national
output. Both manufacturing and agriculture now have shares of less
than 20 per cent in the national economy.[4] The higher contribution
of services to the national economy has been accompanied by lower
shares of agriculture and manufacturing, with the combined share of
the latter reducing from 43 per cent in 1991–92 to 32 per cent at present.

While many service industries, led by IT and including finance,
hospitality, education, health, real estate, retail, entertainment,
transport, communication, have generated new jobs, they have
not been as much as the economy requires given the rising
population and youth bulge. Indeed, agriculture and manufacturing,
notwithstanding their lower contributions to GDP, continue to be
providers of livelihood for many, particularly agriculture, which
accounts for almost half of the total workforce employed in the
country, and is the main provider of rural jobs for both men and
women.[5] This is in contrast to services (as represented by the tertiary
sector in employment surveys conducted by the National Sample
Survey Organization) that is now the largest provider of jobs for
both men and women in urban areas, underscoring the urban bias
that services have had in generating employment. The latter bias
has created multiple employment opportunities for urban women
in services like the construction industry, retail trade, IT-based
call centres, business process outsourcing (BPO) establishments,
hospitality establishments, financial enterprises and educational
institutions. However, these opportunities should not obliterate
the fact that services have failed to generate jobs in rural areas
that continue to depend critically on agriculture, and partially
manufacturing, for employment. The nature of jobs created by the

'new' urban services are also those that require skills greatly different from those of most rural workers, making the latter unsuitable for the former.

Expanding further on the relationship between structural transformation of the economy and low job growth, the inability of services to generate jobs commensurate with its contribution to the national economy has given rise to 'jobless growth'. The phrase describes a situation where notwithstanding high economic growth, the economy is unable to create jobs and provide employment. While many service industries in India have created jobs, comparatively, growth in services has been less job-intensive than their similar growth in other emerging markets like China, Russia and Brazil. The share of services in India's employment increased by 4.7 per cent during 2001–14,[6] while those in the latter three economies increased by 34.3 per cent, 7.2 per cent and 17.2 per cent respectively.[7] This is regardless of services growth in India being among the highest in the four countries. Whether the disconnect between rate of growth in services and its ability to employ is due to specific characters of the service industries, or on account of other specific structural issues in the economy impacting labour force participation rates and employment is debatable. But there is little doubt over the structural transformation of the Indian economy resulting in jobless growth, which portends critical prospects for future employment generation.

The crisis of employment in India must also be looked at in the context of significant changes taking place in the labour market, including in the Labour Force Participation Rate (LFPR).[8] The Labour Bureau's estimates point to the LFPR for 2015–16 having declined to 50.3 per cent from 52.5 per cent in 2013–14.[9] Assuming a population of 1.2 billion, the reduction reflects a drop of more than 20 million in new entrants to the labour force. A lower LFPR is accompanied with higher unemployment with proportionally greater increase in rural unemployment, which, upon further disaggregation, reveals greater unemployment for rural women. The trend is representative of greater employment for urban women in services along with a reduction in employment opportunities for rural women. Lower LFPR follows lesser participation of women in the labour force, which can be attributed to various sociocultural factors (e.g. household responsibilities, difficulties in taking up work outside home). At the same time, for urban women in particular, greater pursuit of education is also a factor delaying their entries in the labour force. Nonetheless, female unemployment is an area of concern for the economy given that it is characterized by underemployment. This pertains to conditions where many of the persons who are reported as 'employed' or 'workers' in official publications do not get work for the entire duration of their stay in the labour force. And even those who get some work or another for the entire duration may be getting it for only a small fraction of the time that they are available for work. This apart, some may be working on jobs, which do not allow them to fully utilize their abilities, or from which they earn very low incomes.[10]

Automation and Displacement

The complexities of structural changes in India's labour market and the employment prospects for millions of Indians have been aggravated by the rapid advent of labour-saving technologies, such as artificial intelligence and robotics. In this respect, India's predicament is similar to that of countries in other parts of the world—developed and developing alike—and for policymakers, in all of which, automation is complicating the challenge of generating jobs and preserving employment. There is little doubt that policymakers across the world have been short-sighted in anticipating the impact of economic globalization and technological advancement on jobs. While the former, through fragmentation of production and relocation of its various stages in different countries based on comparative advantages of skills and wages, did generate jobs in several parts of the world through outsourcing, the latter has begun chipping away at existing jobs by shifting human functions to automation. The deleterious consequence of economic globalization and technological advancement on traditional jobs has been best described by celebrated physicist Stephen Hawking: 'The automation of factories has already decimated jobs in traditional manufacturing, and the rise of artificial intelligence is likely to extend this job destruction deep into the middle classes, with only the most caring, creative or supervisory roles remaining.'[11] Taken forward, the impact of 'job destruction' is grave from not only an economic perspective, but also in terms of the sociopolitical impact it would have on economies and societies, particularly those like India that are saddled with the limitation of weak governance.

Businesses have responded to automation by downsizing labour-intensive operations. In India, the effect is being experienced across multiple industries and sectors that have typically been major employment providers. The IT industry is a relevant example of the impact of automation on India's labour market. Hailed widely as one of the prodigious outcomes of industrial deregulation and economic liberalization since the early nineties, IT is one of those service industries that has generated jobs at various levels of skills for both men and women. Various studies and experts are repeatedly pointing to the employment contraction that the industry is suffering from and would experience in future. The views range from the industry losing 25,000–50,000 of new jobs each year currently being created along with displacement of middle-level managerial jobs[12] to loss of more than 600,000 low-skill jobs in the foreseeable future.[13]

These projections of job losses highlight the fact that a large number of existing jobs are getting redundant as human skills hardly fetch value in an environment where technological improvement is the key driver of productivity as opposed to more hands-on the jobs. The development has implications for the supply-side dynamics of the labour market, in the sense of new skilled entrants to the workforce, particularly the large number of engineering graduates, not being suitable for the new jobs. Globally, advances in automation have been accompanied by increasing redundancy of multiple skills—India's IT/BPO sectors are major examples. Greater digitalization of functions, apart from displacing jobs, has generated demand for new skills consistent with, and required by, digitally run and managed industrial processes. The most hard-hit as a result have been clerical and low technology-intensive skills. Demand for these skills from the IT sector enabled a large number of urban youth, including women, to get employed since the final years of the last century. Now, however, the situation is markedly different with even graduate degrees in engineering (BTech) becoming increasingly irrelevant for companies as the latter focus on more specialized skills.[14]

It is important to note the adverse 'substitution effect' that technological innovations like industrial robots and artificial intelligence have on the market. It is also not difficult to see why employers do not want to back off from inducting more of this in their businesses. Greater use of digital operations is firmly justified on the ground of efficiency notwithstanding the fact that the impact of these changes on employment is profound, particularly at a time when globally shares of wages in national incomes are either declining or remaining stagnant. Till some years ago, despite noting the advent of jobless growth, Indian policymakers and labour-market experts were content on rationalizing it as the traditional failure of the Indian economy to develop labour-intensive manufacturing and shift surplus agricultural labour to industry. Now, however, it is clear that even if manufacturing in India expands to contribute a much larger share of GDP than what it does now, it will be difficult to achieve high economic growth that is labour-intensive, given the advent of automation, which is fast replacing jobs from modern manufacturing. This phenomenon of premature deindustrialization is a major threat for developing countries and emerging market particularly populous nations like India.

The evidence about premature deindustrialization and the growing inability of manufacturing industries to create jobs is best exemplified by India's automobile industry. Beginning with the Maruti 800 in the eighties—the quintessential small car for the Indian middle class manufactured indigenously through Indo-Japanese collaboration—India's automobile industry has become a global hub for assembling passenger and commercial vehicles with almost all major automobile assemblers (e.g. Toyota, Honda, Suzuki, Ford, Hyundai, General Motors) working out of India. The industry has generated considerable employment across different categories of functions and skills, including engineering, marketing and financial. For an industry that has been at the forefront of automation and cutting-edge technological innovation to reduce costs and improve operational efficiency, the advent of automation has led to major operational shifts in its functioning and sharply slashed its employment absorption capacity.[15] The adverse substitution effect of labour-saving technological changes is also evident in industries and sectors connected to automobiles, such as transport services and engineering with large corporations like Larsen & Toubro shedding thousands of jobs for digitalizing operations and cutting costs.

In a rather chilling portrayal of the prospects awaiting labour markets of emerging economies, the World Bank projects two-thirds of all jobs in the developing world to be vulnerable to automation.[16] As the world's most populous developing countries, China and India risk losing 77 per cent and 68 per cent respectively of their current jobs to automation (Table 2). The impact of automation on jobs in these countries would be felt across skills and organizations in both these countries as labour-saving innovations hasten. In addition to China and India, developing countries with comparative advantages in moderately skilled labour-intensive production like Ethiopia, Nepal, Cambodia, Bangladesh and Guatemala are also at significant risks of job losses from automation.

Table 2: Countries and Their Jobs at Risk Due to Automation (per cent)

Country	Unadjusted	Adjusted
Ethiopia	84	43
Nepal	79	41
Cambodia	78	40
China	77	55

Country	Unadjusted	Adjusted
Bangladesh	76	47
Guatemala	75	46
El Salvador	75	46
Angola	73	53
Albania	72	52
Thailand	72	51
India	68	42
Romania	68	49
Ecuador	68	49
Costa Rica	68	49
Macedonia	68	49

Note: Unadjusted and adjusted projections differ in terms of the latter being adjusted for slower pace of technology adoption; the former estimates do not account for such adjustment.

Source: a) World Bank (2016), Figure 2.24, chapter 2, p. 129, and b) http://www.businessinsider.com/countries-where-robots-will-take-jobs-2016-3?IR=T&r=US&IR=T/#15-macedonia-1.

The expected impact of automation on the labour market makes it evident that for an economy like India, it will affect not only low-skill, manual, blue-collar jobs, but also many of those that require more sophisticated skills. While on the one hand this vindicates the onset of premature deindustrialization, on the other, it creates new supply-side challenges, especially for skilling new entrants to the workforce, along with those displaced. Progressive irrelevance of several skills and shrinking 'employability' augments the challenge of managing job prospects for Indian policymakers, given an economy rapidly adding large numbers of young people to its workforce.

Looking Ahead

Over the next couple of decades, India is widely expected to become one of the world's largest economies and at the core of a new global economic order dominated by large emerging markets that include itself along with China, Brazil and Russia. These optimistic expectations about India's economic prowess might not be accompanied by sustained improvement of the living standards of its people unless it can address the looming deficit of jobs. Unlike in the past, idle labour can no longer be absorbed, except for short cyclical bursts, through expansionary development programmes for building infrastructure and enhancing supply of public goods. Sooner or later, these programmes and projects would also be forced to reorganize into more automated managements entailing lesser employment and fewer jobs.

India is not the only country affected by adverse employment prospects. But it is in a league of its own with respect to the complex implications of the jobs deficit given the fragility it nurses in its society and polity. Already, one can hear rumbles among the political class arguing for reservations in jobs in the private sector for addressing the deficit. Apart from fetching short-term political gains, such steps would only accentuate socioeconomic divisions further. India can barely afford such catastrophes if it is to emerge as a leading economic power. All stakeholders need to engage constructively in a productive discourse to see what could be the best options for creating more livelihoods in India.

XV

Challenges Facing Higher Education in India

Sumita Dawra

India has one of the world's largest youth dividends, with about 140 million individuals in the eighteen to twenty-three year age group eligible for higher education (2011 GoI census). If this youth is not equipped with formal education and employable skills, India faces the risk of rendering them a liability rather than an asset for the nation. As a large proportion of this youth is increasingly going overseas to pursue higher education, so the nation now faces the policy dilemma of how to reform domestic higher education systems to compete with foreign universities and retain this domestic human capital. Towards this end, initiatives are being taken to overcome the various academic, administrative, financial, logistical and outreach challenges that the sector faces. Hence, the focus of the government is on equipping higher education institutes with trained and motivated faculty, industry-relevant curricula, merit-based leadership, centres of excellence, better budgeting practices, alternative sources of funding, and partnership with foreign universities and industry. Setting benchmarks through the National Institute Ranking Framework (NIRF) and policy reform to integrate multiple regulatory bodies into the Higher Education Empowerment Regulation Agency (HEERA) will also go a long way towards creating global standards in higher education. To summarize, in order to transform its higher education sector India needs to overcome the following challenges:

encouraging research and innovation, attracting government and private investment, bridging the gaps between innovation policy and mentorship, and facilitating a quantum jump in the quality of higher education through curriculum upgrading, all of which need to be addressed by policymakers and practitioners.

Large Higher Education Sector

India's higher education sector is one of the largest in the world, with a total enrolment estimated at 34.6 million. There are twenty-eight colleges on average for every 100,000 eligible people (i.e. in the age group of eighteen to twenty-three). With 799 universities, 39,071 colleges and 11,923 standalone institutions, not to mention an estimated 1.5 million teachers, India's higher education network is indeed impressive. Gross Enrolment Ratio (GER) in the eighteen to twenty-three age group stands at about 25 per cent, with almost 80 per cent of students enrolled in undergraduate programmes.[1]

System Bypasses Large Number of Eligible Youth

However, despite strides made in setting up a massive number of higher education institutions, including premier national institutes, the improvement over the years in GER and the increasing participation of the private sector in higher education, the fact remains that a large number of youth in the country are outside the fold of the higher education system. Of the nearly 140 million young eligible population in the eighteen to twenty-three age group (2011 census), large numbers are excluded from the higher education system. This is not to say that they are undergoing vocational skill training either.

Funding Constraints, Infrastructure Gaps and Huge Variations in Funding

Funding is low and budgetary allocation for higher education at 3.6 per cent against the global average of 6 per cent leaves much to be desired. Most universities find it a challenge to fund basic infrastructure, such as big classrooms, laboratory facilities, journals and computers, leave alone building smart campuses with Internet access for all students. Similarly, funds availability remains a challenge with either no funds or delays in release of monies. This results in the universities not being able to operate and maintain facilities such as research labs or libraries in a timely fashion, and impacts the development of research and educational standards. Also, all over the country, there are huge variations in the availability of infrastructure and funding amongst the higher educational institutions. Premier institutions such as the Indian Institutes of Technology (IITs), Indian Institutes of Management (IIMs), Indian Institutes of Information Technology (IIITs), Indian Institute of Science (IISc) and so on have developed multiple sources of income through research consultancies, research grants, industry research contracts, alumni and CSR funding, which allow them more liberal funding than most other institutions.[2] At the same time, many universities in the state sector pay millions of rupees as pensions to retired faculty, but do not utilize the services of many of these retired faculty members who would be willing to take up teaching assignments on an outsourced basis, which would help fill huge gaps in faculty vacancies.

Unable to Self-Finance Beyond a Point

Universities receive grants from the University Grants Commission (UGC), state-budgeted funding and also regular fees from affiliated colleges on various accounts, such as examination fees. In view of increasing demands for funds from educational institutions and constraints on the state's ability to fund the universities beyond a point, higher educational institutions are being encouraged to raise their own funds. However, few have got down to formulating the means to do so, through focused executive education programmes, for instance, or evolving PPP models for infrastructure development, industry collaboration for research or establishing centres of excellence by accessing funding under corporate social responsibility (CSR) and so on.

Indian universities can learn a lot in this regard through examples from the US. Since public funding to higher education institutes has declined significantly over the years, universities have adopted alternative sources of funding such as investments in endowment funds and online courses. This makes it possible for universities to raise their own funds and be self-sufficient. At the University of California at Berkeley only 13 per cent of the total budget comes from the state; till a few decades ago the share of state funds in their total budget used to 50 per cent.[3]

Quality of Education

Despite the size of the higher education system in India, the quality of education leaves much to be desired. There is no Indian institution of higher education (and this includes the heavily funded IITs) in the top 100 ranked institutes in the world. There are thirty Indian higher education institutes featuring in the top 1000 of the Times Higher Education Ranking, with the Indian Institute of Science being the topmost ranked Indian institute in the bracket 201–50. If we look at China, it has fared much better with sixty of its universities featuring in the top 1000 and its highest ranked institute, Peking University, at rank twenty-seven.[4] While one recognizes that there are variations in quality, with premier institutes setting the benchmarks for the country, most institutes face challenges in terms of quality and motivation levels of teaching faculty and interference from local politicians. The people at the helm of affairs in these universities are not sometimes occupying their positions strictly on merit but on several extraneous factors.

Students' gross employability ratio after graduation is woefully low at 7 per cent,[5] while career counselling centres, attempts to institutionalize student internships with industry, or building a choice-based credit system (CBCS) and a semester system, which gives flexibility to students to pursue job-oriented courses, or gives credits for skills, is still not emphasized by most state governments. Curricula need to be updated to match the skill requirements of industry, markets and the service sector. For instance, the syllabus in information technology courses is not up to date with requirements of artificial intelligence, robotics, Internet of Things (IoT), automation, and so on.

In addition to the poor quality of teachers and infrastructure in many of the privately-run institutions, they simultaneously also tend to have poor oversight over their functioning. Review committees are often aware of private institutions failing to meet benchmark standards in their legal precondition assessment as required by regulatory bodies. Yet, there are instances of individual members of these committees being lured to lean in with their clearances for such institutions. Further, there are allegations of corruption in many universities, where PhD candidates are treated differently depending on how well the faculty guide is 'taken care of'.

Leadership in Higher Education Institutions

Leadership qualities are seen lacking among the heads of many of the state-run institutions, and team building between colleagues for the holistic development of the institution remains a challenge for leaders who may feel insecure when surrounded by their academic equals or perhaps superiors. Besides, the transfer system among government college faculty remains a draconian measure to bring them in line, and they are shifted from one institution to another every few years, preventing any loyalty and attachment to any one particular institution. Even as teachers race to complete syllabi, there is an acute shortage of faculty, with vacant teaching posts estimated at 40 per cent of the total sanctioned faculty strength of colleges and universities.[6] While massive online teaching courses are currently being encouraged, developing e-content and bringing students to use the Massive Open Online Courses (MOOCs), with creative use of flipped classrooms, they remain a challenge for both teachers and students.

Yet, all is not dismal as a high quality of education is imparted in premier institutes such as the IITs, the IISc, the IIIT, the IIMs, and the NIT, with some of the reputed universities also beginning to appear in international rankings.

Gaps in Innovation and Mentoring

In a world of innovations and start-ups, there are gaping holes in policymaking to build an integrated, institutionalized system of encouraging and incentivizing innovative ideas, providing mentorship through sustained involvement of industry and safeguarding IPRs. The leaders who run the institutions of higher education have enough autonomy to reform curricula, to go in for CBCS and the semester system, take up platforms of e-learning through building relevant parameters for faculty review, introduce peer review of teachers and other reforms. Yet, they stand guilty of not doing enough to deliver a qualitative system of higher education due to lack of mechanisms holding them accountable and answerable. There are, however, efforts being made to put in place such accountability measures. In Andhra Pradesh, several Key Performance Indicators (KPIs) have been identified for higher education institutes, the data for which are updated monthly on the CM dashboard. The ongoing process of evaluation of performance through these indicators means that the university leaders are held accountable to improve their KPIs. While efforts are being made to better streamline the process, a step in the direction to establish accountability for university leaders has already been taken.

Attracting Investments into Higher Education

Smart classrooms, which link institutes of excellence within the country and abroad, have become an important requirement for a system groaning under the scarcity of qualitative faculty. A limited number of quality institutions and teachers, and the absence of diverse course content has been resulting in large outflows of Indian students and is unlikely to stop unless India is able to transform its higher education.

Two quick ways of doing so are by inviting private and foreign investments into the higher education sector. State universities can explore opportunities for collaboration through joint programmes, dual degree programmes, collaborative research and other forms of partnerships to combine strengths from both institutions while at the same time sharing best practices to enhance the quality of state universities. Options like inviting foreign universities to set up branch campuses or research institutes here can also be exercised. This often raises questions of the impact on state universities and access for the less privileged students. Such anxieties, however, cannot be allowed to hinder progress towards higher education reform.

Andhra Pradesh Attracting Private Investments in Higher Education

Similar questions were raised when the Andhra Pradesh Private Universities Act was notified in January 2016. Care was taken by the state government to simultaneously strengthen state universities through means such as a government order to fill up long-standing faculty vacancies, propagation of online education, industry-relevant curriculum upgradation and introduction of choice-based credit and semester systems. At the same time, four state universities applied for and received the prestigious Times Higher Education (THE) and Quacquarelli Symonds (QS) world university rankings for the first time, boosting their brand value.

Premier national institutions of higher education sanctioned by the Government of India at the time of the state's bifurcation in 2014 were expeditiously established with effect from the academic year 2015–16. Consequently, IIM at Visakhapatnam, IIT at Tirupati, NIT at West Godavari, IIIT at Kurnool and Indian Institutes of Science Education and Research (IISER) at Tirupati became functional. This established the state's credibility in the implementation of a vision in higher education to transform itself into an education hub and benefit its youth.

In this environment that strengthened the public sector institutes of higher learning, the ball was set rolling to simultaneously attract private investments into higher education. This was initiated with a new act hailed as the most progressive private universities act in the country. The legislation allows for a lot of autonomy for Greenfield private universities, while defining strict timelines for the government to complete the process of permissions to private investors. Within ten months of the enactment, eight Greenfield university proposals were accepted, which are expected to bring in investments of USD 14 million over the next eight to ten years. The initiative will also encourage best practices through a network of academic and industry partnerships, infrastructure of global standards and autonomy to the universities, while ensuring accountability through a higher education regulatory authority. To ensure access for less privileged students, the authority shall ensure that the fee charged by the private universities is reasonable. Also, it is open for private universities and the state government to offer scholarships to meritorious students from less privileged backgrounds.

More examples emerge in India of the coexistence of private and state universities. Gujarat passed the Private Universities Act in 2009. Earlier this year, the Gujarat state assembly passed bills that have allowed four new private universities and two new government universities to come up in the state.[7] The case study from Andhra Pradesh, where the Private Universities Act was passed in 2016, too, demonstrates how private and state universities can coexist and thrive. In addition, applying the twin strategies of resource-sharing of faculty, lab and research facilities, besides utilizing the large number of retired faculty members, would yield mutually beneficial results, and improve the supply side of the higher education sector.

Foreign Universities in India

Legislation regarding foreign universities that enables a 'win-win' situation for both Indian and foreign universities can see the emergence of higher education as a strong service sector segment that will attract larger numbers of students from Asia and Africa. This will result in forex earnings, more jobs in teaching and benefits to local economies. The Bay Area with Stanford and Berkeley and Boston city with Harvard and MIT in the US demonstrate the effect world-class universities can have on local economies. However, there has been a lot of resistance to foreign investment in higher education in India for fear that it will benefit only a small elite section. At the same time, the requirement for universities to be 'not for profit' institutions limits the scope for foreign investment in the country.[8]

As such, the question of keeping education affordable should not trouble the public as state universities can continue to be strengthened, and attracting offshore campuses of premier international universities to India will only provide boost to a possible 'Study in India' campaign, and to the economy at large.

Identifying Key Universities to Develop as World-Class Institutes

The time has come to identify key universities in India, facilitate generous funding (perhaps through CSR) and enable them to establish themselves as world-class universities. Such universities should also be allowed greater levels of foreign collaboration than possible under present regulations. This would ensure these universities emerge as institutions of high repute with strong links to socioeconomic research, serve the needs of local economic development, and design academic disciplines to benefit local area needs.

In this context, the Indian Institutes of Science Education and Research (IISERs) come to mind, which seek to utilize scientific research with the social sciences and humanities, to find solutions to socioeconomic issues. However, each university and college, and institute of higher education needs to adopt a similar approach, make themselves more relevant to local economies and foster innovations for local issues. That will create a unique body of research and innovations in these institutes, make them more relevant to the economy and help them strengthen funding as well, while improving the quality of teaching and learning and their own rankings.

Challenges in the Current Scenario

The current scenario in the higher education sector shows an improvement in GER, an impressive increase in the number of higher education institutions (at the rate of 9.6 per cent per annum during the Eleventh Plan Period) and increasing private sector participation (at the rate of 10 per cent during the Eleventh Plan Period).[9] However, the challenge remains to take GER from its current levels of 24 per cent to 50 per cent by 2050. This will require a massive increase in investments in infrastructure, faculty recruitment, training of faculty, reforms in curriculum, and so on.

Other positive trends are seen in the increase in accredited institutions to 67 per cent as an impact of funding under the national programme of Rashtriya Uchchattar Shiksha Abhiyan (RUSA). Universities and professional colleges in India are being supported under the National Mission on Education for enhanced connectivity, content and access devices to educational institutions. Almost 400 universities and more than 18,000 colleges have received broadband connectivity under the programme.

Various programmes have been launched to strengthen research and development activity in higher education institutions. Grants to improve infrastructure, fellowships for doctoral and post-doctoral work, schemes for faculty development and promotion of research have been taken up by the regulatory body of the University Grants Commission. The Government of India also launched the GIAN programme for engagement of an international pool of academicians with institutes of learning in India to augment existing resources and raise the quality of teaching inputs. Initiatives have been taken under a newly developed National Institute Ranking Framework (NIRF) for infusing a competitive spirit among institutions of higher education while identifying weaknesses in the institutions, with a view to bring transparency and accountability in the system. A National Digital

Library has been developed to increase the reach of books to millions of students for learning on the Internet. In addition to the above initiatives, the Government of India has also launched SWAYAM, which is a portal for free online education. Programmes like IMPRINT are aimed at addressing challenges in teaching science and technology.

Reforms for Qualitative Improvement in Higher Education

Reforms in the quality of education require interventions like reducing the number of affiliated colleges with each university, giving more autonomy to colleges, improving research and citations in universities and colleges, and building partnerships with private institutions that enable easy sharing of resources, whether pertaining to faculty or research-related infrastructure. Besides, financing models for universities will have to be fixed and regulated for access to greater funding from governments, multilateral bodies or industry. RUSA support may actually be focused more on institutions in remote areas that need the support rather than those that qualify on parameters of quality.

Further, public institutions need to focus on improving the standards of education imparted. This can be achieved through curriculum upgradation, adoption of CBCS and the semester system, regular teacher trainings, leadership and motivation workshops for teachers, foreign collaborations in research and teaching, adoption of massive online teaching with links to academic inputs from premier institutions within the country and abroad, getting industry experts to teach in universities and colleges, encouraging non-resident Indian (NRI) academicians to take up semester-wise teaching in India as visiting faculty or through online courses, encouraging visiting professors from foreign universities and so on.

Internationalization of Higher Education

Emphasis on internationalization of higher education through a curriculum that matches the best global standards, flexible faculty exchange programmes, collaborations with foreign universities, attracting foreign students to courses that are relevant, and setting up dedicated hostels, with good standards of accommodation and food, for foreign students would go a long way. For building new knowledge in Indian institutions, regular and relevant upgrading of curricula is extremely important as is targeting skills being demanded by an increasingly changing industrial and technological scenario. Encouraging institutes and students to involve themselves in local problems and build innovative solutions will encourage industry to come forward to support research and innovation in these institutes.

Good Governance in Higher Education

India needs to raise the educational standards right from schools, improve governance and introduce a professional approach in educational systems. It needs to have a national-level, data management system for enrolments and monitoring of results, outputs and outcomes. There is a recent policy announcement on integration of regulatory bodies like All India Council for Technical Education (AICTE) and UGC into a single regulatory body, doing away with multiple agencies, and giving clarity to new institutions in higher education. HEERA is a legislation that is awaited for establishing an independent body setting global standards for the sector.

XVI

Few Hits, Many Misses: India's Mixed Record in the International Sporting Arena since 1947[1]

Ronojoy Sen

One of India's most prominent sports administrators once said that sport is against the Indian 'ethos' and the nation's 'entire cultural tradition'.[2] While this comment was possibly borne out of acute disappointment with the country's poor performance in sports, the fact is that India has had a vibrant sporting tradition, arguably going back several centuries. Long before the British introduced various Western sports into India, there were wrestling matches being organized in the Vijaynagar kingdom and polo being played by the Mughals. This essay documents India's sporting performance across four periods. First, the immediate aftermath of Indian Independence and the 1948 Olympics in London. Second, the first two decades after Independence. Third, the seventies when India won some famous victories in cricket. And finally, from 1983, when India won the Cricket World Cup, to the contemporary period.

The Aftermath of Independence: Glory at the London Games

The 1948 London Games was India's first as an independent nation. Though India had sent an eighty-strong contingent, expectations were not too high except from the hockey team, which had won three gold medals on the trot from 1928 to 1936. The 1948 team was completely different from the one that had won in the 1936 Berlin Olympics with all the greats from the pre-war era, including Dhyan Chand, having retired. The team was captained by Kishan Lal with the brilliant K.D. Singh 'Babu' as the vice-captain. An India–Pakistan contest in the hockey final was narrowly avoided as Great Britain beat Pakistan in the semi-final to set up a gold medal match with India.

At the final held at Wembley Stadium before some 10,000 spectators on 12 August 1948—just three days before India's Independence Day—neither the persistent wet weather nor a ground made muddier by the play-off for third place played before the final, which was protested by the Indian officials—could stop the Indian team. As a correspondent reported, despite 'the heavy, muddy turf and the light rain', the Indians 'outclassed the British team with their superb ball control, accurate passing and intelligent positional play'.[3] Balbir Singh, who scored twice in the final, recounts that Kishan Lal and Babu both played barefoot to tackle the slippery surface with the Indians winning handily 4–0. In the crowd was the staunch anti-imperialist and close ally of Jawaharlal Nehru, V.K. Krishna Menon, independent India's first high commissioner to Britain, to whom the Indian victory must have seemed especially sweet. He was among those who ran onto the ground to congratulate the Indian team; later he hosted an official reception for the team at India House.

India's barefoot footballers made quite an impression despite getting knocked out in the first round of the 1948 Olympic Games. While Indians had been playing barefoot for decades, this was the first time that the Indian football team was playing with naked feet in an international tournament. As a veteran sports commentator pointed out, 'There was a certain Indianness about it, which was as unique [as] the rope trick or shall we say Ranji's leg glance.'[4] However, for the rest of the world it was a most unusual sight. And this was evident in the reaction in London and the several legends that grew up around the Indian team. When at a reception in Buckingham

Palace, Princess Margaret reportedly asked India's star footballer Sailen Manna if he was afraid to play barefoot, he replied that it was 'easier to keep the ball under control'.[5] Another story was that King George VI made Manna roll up his trousers to check if his legs were made of steel.

If India had resumed its pre-Second World War hockey supremacy as an independent nation and caught the attention of the world in football in 1948, the results on the cricket pitch were disappointing. India's first Test series after Independence was against Australia in 1947–48, where it lost four of the five Tests to Don Bradman's 'Invincibles'. The Indian team was, however, hailed by the Australian press as a beacon of hope for the newly independent and recently partitioned country. An Australian newspaper wrote that the Indian cricketers may 'well prove the magic elixir to banish national and inter-racial bitterness'.[6] Besides Hindus, the team to Australia consisted of two Muslims, a Christian, a Sikh and a Parsi. The Indian captain, Lala Amarnath, had proclaimed, 'We come from all over India, and when we play cricket we look on ourselves as playing for all of India.'[7]

The First Two Decades: Excellence in Hockey and Football

During the first two decades after Independence, India did rather well in sports. Oddly enough, cricket was the exception with the high point being India's victory over Pakistan in 1952 in the first-ever Test series played between both the countries. Though the series was played in good spirits, some of the tensions and acrimony that were to accompany these contests reared their head when the Hindu Mahasabha threatened to disrupt one of the matches.

India won the Olympic gold medal in hockey in 1952 and 1956, beating Pakistan for the first time in 1956 in Melbourne. Although India lost to Pakistan in the 1960 hockey finals, it regained the gold by defeating Pakistan in 1964. The mood in the Indian camp before the 1956 Olympic finals was best described by Balbir Singh: 'I could not sleep that night, and after tossing about restlessly for a while, I went out for a stroll. It was quite late in the night when someone called out my name.'[8] Also up at that late hour was Ashwini Kumar, who took Balbir back to his room and gave him a pill to soothe his nerves. Only then could Balbir go to sleep. On the morning of the match, the Indian camp was very jittery as was evident from an incident on the team bus. Just as the bus was about to leave for the stadium an official sneezed, considered to be a bad omen by some in India. Ashwini Kumar immediately asked Balbir to get off the bus, go back to his room, and lie down for five minutes and then return. The match itself was a close one with India winning by a solitary goal scored by R.S. Gentle in the second half. Balbir, who already had two gold medals, admits that the Melbourne victory stood out since it was against Pakistan. His sentiments were unsurprising considering Balbir was from Punjab, which had borne the brunt of Partition violence in 1947.

The sixties were the golden years of Indian football. The pinnacle of Indian football was perhaps reached at the 1962 Asian Games in Jakarta, where India won its second football gold medal but against a much stronger field than in the 1951 Asiad. The Indian team led by Chuni Goswami, and with stars like P.K. Banerjee and Jarnail Singh, beat Japan and South Korea, both future Asian soccer powers, to win the gold. The final against South Korea was played before a hostile crowd, which was incensed by India's protests on barring Israel and Taiwan from participating in the Games.

One of the goal scorers in the final, the turbaned Jarnail Singh, later recalled that on the way to the stadium he sat on the floor of the team bus to avoid getting the Indian team noticed.[9] Goswami writes in his autobiography that the words 'Indian team' were erased from the bus that ferried the players from the Games village to the stadium on the day of the finals.[10] Of the situation inside the stadium, an Indian official reported: 'A very large section of the crowd of a hundred thousand persistently booed the team. Not satisfied it continued to boo when the victory ceremony to present the Gold medals to our team was performed.'[11] The legendary coach of the football team, S.A. Rahim, used the adverse circumstances to India's advantage. Before the game he made the entire team hold hands and sing the national anthem. He repeated this routine during half-time to pep up the team in the face of the relentless hostility of the crowd.[12]

There were some stirring individual sporting performances in this period. While Milkha Singh's fourth-place finish at the Rome Olympics might be the most debated non-medal track and field finish in Olympic history, K.D. Jadhav won a bronze in wrestling in 1952, which remained the only individual Olympic medal for India till 1996. In tennis, Ramanathan Krishnan charmed the world with his elegant style. Though he did not win any of the majors, he did achieve in 1959 the highest-ever seeding by an Indian player—number three—in the world rankings. In the 1952 Games, Indian women for the first time participated in the Olympics with athletes Nilima Ghose and Mary D'Souza representing India. Rita Davar was runner-up in the junior women's event at Wimbledon the same year and in the 1954 Manila Asiad, the Indian women's relay team won gold.

The story of Indian sport in the fifties and the sixties would be incomplete without a mention of a unique 'sporting' hero, someone who was less a sportsperson in the conventional sense and much more of an entertainer: Dara Singh. Dara was the undisputed champion of professional wrestling and his bouts would often draw crowds in excess of 50,000.

The Seventies: Highs and lows

From the seventies, Indian performance in most sports, including hockey, plummeted. It was only in cricket, where India was also-rans earlier, that the country's performance brought some cheer. The year 1971 was a landmark year for Indian cricket when India defeated both the West Indies and England on overseas tours. When India began its tour of England in July, it had not won a single match out of the nineteen Tests that it had played earlier on English soil, beginning in 1932. Indeed, in its last two visits, the Indian team had been soundly beaten in all the eight Tests that were played. Compared to the West Indies, the English cricket side in 1971 could also lay claim to being the top team in the world. After the first two Tests had ended in rain-affected draws, the two teams headed to London's Oval ground for the final test. There were only 5000-odd Indian supporters in the ground to see the historic moment but they made the most of it. The London *Times* reported: 'The Indian supporters celebrated the winning boundary by Abid Ali by rushing from the terraces as the players made a dash for the pavilion.'[13] The iconic photograph of the joyous scene represented in equal measure the sheer thrill of beating the colonial masters at their own game and the liberation of Indian cricket from decades of mediocrity. The next day's *Times of India* confirmed the significance of the win on its front page: 'Indian cricket achieved its ultimate ambition here today—a victory over England in England.'[14] An editorial the next day said: 'Glorious to be living at this hour and to be an Indian! Days, months, years will pass, but our cricket team's magnificent triumph over England in England will remain unforgettable.'[15]

In hockey, India had slipped to the third place by the 1968 Olympics and in the 1972 Games could not better its bronze medal position. This was to be India's last Olympic medal against a full field if the gold medal in the boycott-hit 1980 Moscow Olympics—where most of the top hockey-playing countries did not participate—is not taken into account. There was a fleeting triumph in 1975 when India won its first and only hockey World Cup before a sell-out crowd of 50,000 at the Merdeka stadium in Kuala Lumpur. In Delhi, huge crowds of hockey fans were seen standing outside banks and government offices on the occasion, listening to the radio commentary. The celebrations following the victory were testimony to the popularity of hockey, especially in north India. The *Hindustan Times* reported: 'Delhi fans danced to the rhythm of drums and distributed sweets. In Connaught Circus, a huge clapping and dancing crowd followed two drummers and a group of *bhangra* dancers. A restaurant owner treated his customers for free when the news came out.'[16] On the return of the players, 10,000 people turned up at Delhi's Palam airport and there was a near-stampede. However, the 1975 victory proved to be a false dawn for Indian hockey. The very next year, India had its worst ever showing in the Olympics, finishing seventh in the Montreal Olympics.

The Eighties Onwards: The World Cup Victory and Its Impact

It was a coincidence that just as a national television audience was coming into being, spurred by the introduction of colour telecast during the 1982 Asian Games held in Delhi, India's greatest cricketing triumph, since the 1971 victory over England, occurred. On 25 June 1983 India caught everybody by surprise by winning the cricket World Cup. The win was completely unexpected since India had performed abysmally in the two earlier editions of the tournament and were considered novices in the limited-overs version of cricket. The image of India's young captain Kapil Dev holding aloft the cup at Lord's was seen by millions of viewers across the country. The viewership wasn't restricted only to households that owned TVs. Those without television sets watched the semi-final and the final— the only two matches shown live in India—in someone else's house or in common spaces.

If 1983 forged a fortuitous link between cricket and an expanding television audience, it ironically hastened the decline of football and hockey. Television coverage of international football opened the eyes of Indian sports fans to the vast difference in standard between Indian football and rest of the world. This was true even in Calcutta, which was the most football-obsessed city of India. The first international match to be shown live to the Indian audience was the final of the 1978 World Cup; by the next World Cup in 1982, the entire tournament was telecast live. This had the effect of impressing on football fans the 'gap between their own local heroes and the great international stars'.[17] In the case of hockey, the introduction of television coincided with a particularly heavy defeat and that too at the hands of Pakistan in the 1982 Asian Games final. The Indian goalkeeper, Mir Ranjan Negi, was vilified[18] (his reputation was partially redeemed after the success of the Bollywood film, *Chak de India*, based on his time as the coach of the Indian women's hockey team) and many Indians switched off from hockey forever. Success in international hockey has dried up since, with India winning Asiad golds in 1998 and 2014, but having no success in either the Olympics or the World Cup. Thus, an editor of a national daily lamented, 'One of the greatest tragedies of our hockey is that its most glorious phase preceded the era of live television in India.'[19]

It was from the eighties onwards that the popularity of cricket reached an all-time high in India. This was made possible by and intrinsically linked to the phenomenal growth of television during this period. The marriage between cricket and television was cemented from the early nineties when the Indian economy was unshackled from decades of state control. Private satellite and cable broadcasters were allowed to enter the Indian market for the first time, breaking Doordarshan's monopoly over cricket telecasts. The BCCI, which had a paltry Rs 200,000 in its coffers during the 1983 World Cup[20] and did not even have the money to reward the members of the Indian team, was quick to spot the immense opportunities presented by the happy convergence of an ever-widening television audience and an upswing in the fortunes of Indian cricket. It even dared to bring the World Cup, which had been held in England since its inception in 1975, to the Indian subcontinent in 1987.

It was not only the cricket board that made money. The players, who had got a pittance till the eighties, were now much sought after. The real game-changer, however, was the deal that Mark Mascarenhas struck with India's biggest sports star and one of the finest batsmen in the world, Sachin Tendulkar, in 1996, guaranteeing him USD 7.5 million over five years. Thanks to the Twenty20 revolution, which was aided by India winning the T20 World Cup in 2007, and the Indian Premier League, first played in 2008, Indian cricketers are now raking in big money without even playing for the national side. The IPL model, where city-based franchisees compete against each other, has been applied, with varying degrees of success, to other sports, including kabaddi.

A Vibrant Present

The dominance of cricket in India from the eighties, despite the occasional individual brilliance of a Prakash Padukone or Pullela Gopichand in badminton, Vijay Amritraj in tennis and P.T. Usha in athletics, has often mistakenly been touted as the reason for the decline of other sports. Happily, the last decade or so have been one of the best periods for Indian sport outside the cricket field. Since Usha narrowly missed a medal in the 1984 Olympics, India has won individual medals in several disciplines beginning with Leander Paes' bronze medal in tennis in 1996. This was astonishingly India's first individual medal in the Olympics in over forty years after Jadhav's bronze in wrestling in 1952. Following Paes, Karnam Malleswari won a bronze in women's weightlifting (2000) and army man (and now Union minister) Rajyavardhan Rathore a silver in shooting (2004), before shooter Abhinav Bindra in 2008 became the first Indian ever to win an individual Olympic gold medal. In the 2008 Beijing Games, Vijender Singh and Sushil Kumar won a bronze each in boxing and wrestling respectively, before India won its largest ever-tally of six medals—two silvers and four bronze—in the 2012 London Games. The sports where India tasted Olympic success in London were wrestling, shooting, boxing and badminton. Though India could not match its performance of London in the 2016 Rio Games, for the first time an Indian woman, badminton player P.V. Sindhu, won a silver medal.

India's performance in the last two Olympics, looked at in terms of population, number of competitors sent and the high expectations, was ordinary. But placed in the context of India's overall Olympic record, it was very good. There are three things to note of this sporting resurgence: first, women sportspersons, such as Saina Nehwal, Mary Kom, P.V. Sindhu, Sakshi Malik and Sania Mirza, have been at its forefront; second, there has been a decentring of sport with the smaller cities and hinterland contributing more than the metros; and finally, it is spread across several sports. India will not be a sporting superpower in the near future.

However, if this trend continues, it might at least find itself on the medal sheet of international competitions with more regularity.

XVII

Civil Service Reforms in India

S. Narayan

The existing structure of the civil services in India owes much to the pattern of administration that the colonial rulers introduced into this country. The process of securing control over the entire geography of India, which included the areas now in Pakistan and Bangladesh, took over a hundred years. There were also subsequent annexations of Sri Lanka and Burma (now Myanmar) and even Malaysia into this empire, though the administration in those areas was managed somewhat differently.

Pre-Independence

In the Indian Subcontinent, the concern of the colonial administration was the extraction of revenue. Since the structure of the economy was substantially agrarian, it meant getting it from revenues on land. In the presidency areas of Madras, Bombay and Bengal, the introduction of permanent settlement[1] ensured the settlement of land to the owners, rates of levy on the land as well as introduction of a machinery to collect revenues. The colonial rulers drew substantially on the experiences of the Mughals and the Muslim rulers who had come before them. Hence, rates of land revenue were fixed on criteria that had been adopted for hundreds of years. At the same time, the administration recognized the existence of large landholders and zamindars, as well as minor and major princely states that had their own systems of revenue collection. In areas not settled by the ryotwari[2] system, the collection of revenues was a tax on the landowner, and the zamindar or the prince was expected to hand over a portion of the revenues to the rulers.

The administrative and civil services structure grew out of these considerations of governance. In areas where the government was administering the ryotwari system, it was necessary to have an elaborate set of records for landholdings, land transfers and ownerships, birth and death data as well as an annual record of crops cultivated, conditions of the crops and yield, revenues due and collectible, and accounts for collection. This ensured the development of a hierarchy of officialdom that started at the village level with the village accountant and headman, through supervising hierarchies at different levels, to the administrative unit of a district, which was headed by a district collector, really the kingpin of the administration at that time. He was not only responsible for the collection of revenues, but also for the settlement of disputes, and as a magistrate, for awarding punishments. The responsibility of maintaining law and order lay with him, and in all respects, he was the eyes and ears of the colonial rulers.

In the zamindari areas and in the administered princely states, the role of the colonial administration was reduced to the extent that the revenue amounts, predetermined, were the responsibility of the owner. Hence, at the detailed village level the account-keeping machinery was not required to the extent it was required in ryotwari areas. Law and order, and settlement of disputes lay with the prince, who had his own administrative hierarchy.

The colonial system envisaged an overarching secretariat in Delhi (after it moved there from Calcutta), at the peak of which was the Viceroy, assisted by members in council. Most importantly, the administration in the presidency areas was through a governor, who had all the executive powers, until the Montague–Chelmsford reforms ushered in a period of provincially elected legislatures answerable to the governor.

After 1947

After Independence in 1947, the system of administration remained very similar to that before, with the addition that a similar pattern was introduced in all the states. The introduction of the Indian Civil Service personnel through a series of competitive examinations (in the Gladstone era) introduced a hierarchy of English-educated, committed set of civil servants into the administration who rose through ranks in the districts as sub-divisional officers, to district collectors, and eventually to positions of policymaking in the provincial and the Central government. After Independence, the civil service became the administrative service, and was supported by the police service, recruited through similar competitive examinations. The rights and privileges of the persons admitted to these services were included in articles 309 to 311 of the Constitution, and even the removal of these persons was protected by due process in the Constitution.

These new entrants occupy the highest levels of the civil services, manning almost all departments in the secretariats at the state as well as the Central government.

Broadly, the structure of the administration of civil services has remained the same for the last seventy years, though some regional variations have been introduced over the last seven decades. The problems that have arisen have primarily been due to the fact that much in India has changed.

First, and most importantly, the introduction of democratically elected legislators at the state and Central level resulted in direct accountability of these legislators to the voters and public at large. At a fundamental level, there was the district administration, primarily responsible for maintaining law and order, and administering according to set processes and regulations. And then there was the aspirant legislator, keen on providing development and amenities for this electorate. The morphing of the colonial district collector into a development administrator has had mixed success, as the political hierarchy increasingly felt emboldened to step into the realm of administration through requests, demands, and sometimes pressure. There was, and is, nothing in the system to prescribe coping mechanisms, and even today, the conflict between the politician and the administrator, especially at regional levels, is the subject of regular news.

Second, the role of the Central government and also the state governments changed substantially. No longer were the final arbiters in faraway London; and important fiscal, monetary, foreign policy, security and development decisions had to be taken at the government level, either by the Centre or in the states. There was also the cabinet of ministers and sectoral hierarchies of departments and their staffing as well as parliamentary accountability and requirements of legislative oversight. Suddenly, the remit of responsibilities of the civil services expanded. At the same time, the processes of decision-making remained mired in the 1900s. Files would originate at the lower levels of the bureaucracy and would meander upwards for decision.

Lord Curzon, Viceroy, in a note in August 1899 gives an example:

I will give, before passing on, an illustration of the prolixity of the existing system. A Despatch from Secretary of State arrived in one of the Departments of the Government of India in my predecessor's time. It covered three and a half pages of print. After being somewhat gingerly touched by a few clerks, it was taken in hand by an Under Secretary who paraphrased it in one and a half pages of print and then added a Note recording his own opinion in four and a half additional pages of print. This brave example was eagerly followed by his colleagues in an ascending scale; and by the time the Viceroy and Members of Council had noted on it, the recorded Notes amounted to 28 pages of small print, as compared with the three and a half pages of large print from the Secretary of State that had provoked this lamentable effusion. I need hardly add that no final decision was arrived at, and the case was left over to me for settlement.[3]

Such processes exist even today, holding up the decision-making process. Prime Minister Narendra Modi has expressed his unhappiness publicly on several occasions over the slow process of decision-making as well as the process rather than the output-oriented culture of administration.

Third, there has arisen considerable difference in the way that administrative processes in the states operate. This has led to the erosion of the processes. In the structure that has been followed since colonial times, decision-making has been based on documented reasoning, which originate in departments, then referred to others for comments, and finally decisions arrived at after a detailed examination of the issues involved. In several states, the regional parties in power have dispensed with systems, and decision-making is often top-down, ad-hoc and sometimes without examining the issues in detail. Such processes lead to later complaints as well as attempts at corrections. The ascendancy of regional parties, as well as the constant change between parties of differing ideologies in certain states, have resulted in the administration turning cautious in taking sensitive decisions, for fear of being found fault with by a succeeding administration.

Reforms

It is evident that the processes and procedures as well as the structure of the administration and the personnel who are manning it require a change of approach and mindset. It is interesting that civil service reforms have been attempted continuously by governments in India, and there have been close to fifty committees that have looked at administrative reforms and given their recommendations, starting in 1952. There have been recommendations that have focused on approaches to recruitment, measuring performance, accountability and ethics. There have also been recommendations that have highlighted the needs to build capacity, enhance accountability, competence, performance, and to recognize and reward leadership and performance. The first Administrative Reforms Commission, appointed in 1966, focused on dealing with public grievances, planning, personnel, Centre-state relations and the machinery of the Government of India and other procedures. The second Administrative Reforms Commission, appointed in 2005, gave its report in 2009 and included chapters on ethics, local governments, handling terrorism, right to information, e-governance and the organizational structure of the government. Suggestions include changes in the personnel procedures, in policy implementation and performance-based assessment.

The NITI Aayog has been quite vocal in demanding changes. 'It is not feasible for India to progress through the twenty-first century with nineteenth century administrative systems.'[4] The NITI Aayog has strongly recommended lateral induction into civil services at higher levels, of persons who are professionally qualified and bring a larger world experience to the government. There have been recent placements, even at higher levels of the bureaucracy, in pursuit of these policies.

The core question in the issue of civil service reforms appears to be whether the civil services as they are constituted, and indeed the systems and procedures within which they work, are suited to current-day expectations and needs. There are several aspects to be considered here.

To start with, there is now a clear difference between the levels of services expected at the state level and the Central level. There is a distinct difference between the two. At the state level, the civil services are substantially engaged in providing services, including health, public distribution of foodgrains, and education. The state government is also responsible for infrastructure, including roads, electricity and the provision of water supply, both for private use as well as for industry. It is responsible for a large number of services in urban areas that include water supply, sewage treatment and waste removal, and the maintenance of roads and street lights. It is also responsible for law and order and security, as well as for the collection of state revenues, most importantly the GST.

After the liberalization of industrial licencing and the opening up of the economy, the role of the state governments in industrialization has now moved to providing an attractive location for investment through provision of facilities, infrastructure and fiscal concessions, and not with setting up industry or finance corporations or setting up public sector units. Overall, the state administration has matured into a service delivery unit, and it is evident from policy pronouncements from state governments at the time of budget making, that they are mostly incremental additions to existing programmes.

In this scenario, the civil services should be focusing on efficiency and effectiveness of delivery and public satisfaction at all levels. The political hierarchy would also expect that the services expected by the public are being delivered regularly and efficiently. This requires an efficient, accountable and professional administration that is able to manage the departmental hierarchy in a manner that delivers these results. There are very few areas where innovative thinking or policymaking is required: perhaps in the area of infrastructure, transportation or energy policy. The structure of the civil service at the state level would, therefore, have to be different from that at the Central level. There is little need for brilliance or for tall trees. The services portfolio has matured and just needs to be delivered and improved upon, day after day.

The picture is somewhat different at the Central level. After the abolition of the Planning Commission, the closing of several centrally sponsored schemes and the enhancement in the devolution of share of total revenues to the states, the Central government has lesser responsibility for implementation than the states. Even the national programmes of Swachh Bharat, Smart Cities, food security, rojgar yojna are to be implemented at the state or sub-state levels.

The responsibility for the Central government lies in the conceptualization of these pan-India schemes, providing body and flesh to the programmes, and ensuring an enabling and facilitating environment for these programmes to work: in short, to conceptualize, detail and monitor national schemes. There are also departments of the Central government that are involved with areas beyond the remit of the state governments, most importantly defence, atomic energy and space, foreign policy, energy, including petroleum and coal, civil aviation, railways and shipping, finance and financial markets and exchanges as well as collection of direct and indirect taxes. It is clear from this list that each one requires domain knowledge for formulating and implementing policies and strategies, and that inadequate professional knowledge would be a dampener. Most importantly, it is evident that service in the state or in the district as a collector will in no way help the person concerned to acquire this expertise or experience.

If this argument is accepted, then there is a clear need to separate the higher administration of the civil services into two categories—those that are involved at the state level and those at the Central level. The Indian Administrative Service personnel, coming from public service delivery experience at the state level, should no longer be expected to perform the specific policy and strategic tasks at the Central level. This fact is already being recognized at the levels of state administration. State governments prefer to post local officers promoted to the IAS as district collectors and also in important development departments that interact with the public on services delivery. One chief minister remarked a few years ago that he could run the state without the IAS.[5]

At the same time, the talent pool of the IAS needs to be nurtured into specialization of specific sectoral expertise that include intimate professional knowledge of these areas. Coupled with continuous tenure of postings in a particular department, as is the practice in most developed countries like Japan, the UK and even the US, it is is bound to prove more impactful. It also follows that at the Central level, these ministries need to have domain knowledge experts at senior levels. There is no need, for example, for the defence secretary to be an IAS appointee.

The IAS, as presently structured into a career option, seems to have outlived its usefulness. Perhaps the time has come to rethink the IAS into a state cadre that would remain in the state, and Central cadre that would spend a few years in the state, and then move to the Centre. The specialization of the latter would be decided at the time of recruitment so that the candidate knows where he/she would be spending the rest of his/her career.

All this does not take care of the Curzon issue, of the process of decision-making and filing. This is a structural issue and Curzon notes:

> In Great Britain the offices of the Government are manned from top to bottom by clerks or Secretaries, all of whom have passed a severe and often special competitive examination, whose life service will be devoted to the department, and who acquire early and carry with them through their careers the traditions and a great deal of the unwritten knowledge of the office. Here the case is widely different. The lower grades of the departments are filled with non-gazetted officers of a class and attainment not comparable with those of the corresponding ranks in the English offices.

The process of decision-making, therefore, passes through several layers of different understandings and capabilities, before arriving at the highest levels. One of the important suggestions made in several administrative reform recommendations is the need for a department to speak with one voice—there cannot be views that differ at each level. The proposal needs to be debated within the department and a single view arrived at conveyed. This would require two steps, one for making sure that the record of discussions within the department are kept accurately and faithfully, and two, for reducing the clerical and other categories in the secretariat. More explicitly, while it would make sense at the state level, where specific programmes are implemented, to have a significant implementing, monitoring and review machinery manned at different levels with different skills, it would hardly be appropriate to consider this mechanism as relevant for deciding whether to launch a manned mission to the moon.

The suggestion above requires a serious revision of the manual of secretariat procedures that has been in vogue at the Central secretariat level for over a hundred years, and to replace it with a more decision-oriented system, where, focus shifts to outcomes that can be reviewed and monitored, if necessary, even by the prime minister.

There is an opportunity to move forward from the current manual filing system through various clerical levels and to introduce a more technology-based e-filing system that would be much more officer- and decision-oriented. An attempt has been made in the new secretariat at Amravati in Andhra Pradesh and decisions are all recorded on e-files. Now that the GST is in place, it should be possible to integrate the entire revenue collection services at different levels into a single platform.

Increasing urbanization has led to a large pressure on public services delivered at the city administration level. This includes water, removal of waste and sewerage, as well as roads and electricity. Even after the Constitutional amendments empowering local bodies, systems are not in place in many states. The problem appears to be a lack of adequate professional capacity to deliver these services. Some of the cities are larger than Singapore or Dubai, and yet the technical staff is not of that quality. As the country urbanizes, skilling of technical personnel at the level of local bodies will emerge as a major challenge.

A final point is about the recruitment, training and evaluation of the civil services. There are many useful recommendations in the administrative reform committees' reports that speak about building capacity, enhancing accountability and of performance-oriented assessment. It is a pity that many of these recommendations, extremely sound in nature, have not been implemented. The current government at the Centre, concerned as it is with performance and delivery, is well placed to make these changes happen.

XVIII

Clean or Not-Clean: India's Energy Dilemma

Subhomoy Bhattacharjee

There is a forest of solar panels atop the Coal India Ltd (CIL) head office in Kolkata to generate 140 kilowatt (kW) peak power on sunny days, which are most days in the tropical city. The former chairman of CIL, Sutirtha Bhattacharya, claimed that those panels above his office, the world's largest coal company, demonstrate where the future of coal lies. The panels by themselves are a puny component of India's current generation of over fifty-seven gigawatts (GW) from renewables (as on 31 March 2017) but they are an evocative signature of the direction where India would wish to steer its energy matrix.

Despite those powerful optics, the role of coal in the Indian economy remains massive. After two centuries of powering India's energy needs, coal puff will take time to be smothered out. Both the International Energy Agency (IEA) and the Indian government's NITI Aayog calculate coal to power over 50 per cent of India's electricity generation till 2040. 'The share of coal in India's commercial primary energy supply was 55 per cent in 2015–16 and is expected to remain high at 48–54 per cent till 2040. If one adds to it the role of coal in producing steel, cement and paper besides other industries, that percentage will be higher still.'[1]

But the critical element yet to fall in place in the Indian energy matrix is whether it is the government or the private sector that will drive production and distribution of coal, oil and gas. It is a tricky question no Indian government has been able to solve in the seventy years since Independence. It is also the primary reason for India's underspending on the sector. To make the private sector interested in investing in energy, the Tenth Five Year Plan (2002–07) correctly diagnosed the need to do four things. These were restructuring and privatization of public sector undertakings, rationalization of tariffs in the power sector, phasing out energy subsidies, and finally moving those subsidies that cannot be eliminated explicitly to Central and state budgets.

It has taken time to make them happen. The work on the first has just begun; the second, the centre's Uday scheme (we shall discuss this later) is the third iteration of a solution to rationalize power tariffs in fifteen years. Linkage of Aadhaar with those of beneficiaries has only now begun to yield results and states still expect the Centre to carry the can for the money spent on energy subsidy.

While the NITI Aayog is clear that all investments in the energy sector must be led by the private sector from here, the hurdles are of political economy. About 24 per cent of the Indian population has no access to electricity. That itself covers huge interstate variations. The government's own electricity measurement dashboard shows densely populated states like Uttar Pradesh has 49 per cent of its rural households without electricity, and those with access to it get it for only some hours in a day.[2] Forty per cent of India's population still makes do without clean cooking fuel. The government would love to make these numbers history, but is leery that freeing of pricing of all energy fuel at India's current per capita income levels could make these targets stiff. Coal mining is still, therefore, linked to end-use commitments for anybody other than CIL, even though it raises the cost of each tonne of coal mined. In the oil economy, it is only since July 2017 that petrol and diesel prices now move daily in tandem with international prices. Kerosene and even LPG prices are set by the government. Yet without the attraction of free pricing, few companies would want to make the long-term big investments in the sector.

As a result India's per capita energy consumption even in 2016 is 670 kgoe (kilogram of oil equivalent—the normalized unit to measure energy usage) while that of electricity consumption is 1075 kilowatt-hour (kWh) per year.[3] Both are just a third of the world average.

Still the solar signature on the CIL tower and the coal (pun intended) calculations demonstrate a welcome but pragmatic move towards fulfilling the energy needs of the Indian economy. Post 1947, Indian policymakers rarely ventured into such forward-looking agenda for a long time. The agenda, when it was formulated, hugged ministries instead of looking at the broad picture, and so made sporadic progress. Since growth in energy consumption has an almost one-to-one connection with the growth rate of GDP, the piecemeal agenda stalled the growth of the economy. As the stakes rose, the economy instead got into more than one political crisis.[4] There were several of those arising from energy management policies. The first occurred in December 1954 when the government introduced the phrase 'socialistic pattern of society' in its Industrial Policy Resolution. Industry was stunned. Ministers led by finance minister C.D. Deshmukh used every possible pulpit to assuage their fears. Yet 'every established industry ran to extract a promise from the government that doomsday was not around the corner for them. The move to nationalize J.R.D. Tata's Telco was scrapped, and the banks led by A.D. Shroff, cement by the Kotharis and jute by the Birlas got a reprieve. Coal did not . . . India had committed a fatal mistake. The energy economy was left to wobble with no promise of adequate government investment and none from the private sector to make up the slack.'[5]

Energy by Pieces

It would seem surprising today but the omission to count energy as an element of national five year plans sat well with the circumstances in which India won her Independence. The first half of the twentieth century saw a massive struggle between the

European powers to wrest control over oil resources across the globe. Among the many reasons the Axis Powers lost the Second World War was the efficiency with which the Allied Powers cut off their access to oil, in Africa, with the Atlantic blockade and the relentless bombing of the refineries in Germany. Transport economics had moved clearly to a dependence on oil as the fuel of choice. Coal was relegated to light up the cities and villages but its role as a means of transport was over.

As Independence arrived in India, its political leaders studied these developments. They also noticed that in comparison with its needs, the country was energy starved. India accounts for 17 per cent of the world's population but has only 0.6 per cent, 0.4 per cent and 7 per cent of the world's oil, gas and coal reserves respectively.[6] This meant the country had to depend heavily on imports even when the level of energy consumption was low by global standards. But with the memory of the two world wars vivid in their minds, the policymakers were also clear that India would not begin a fresh rush to colonize offshore sources to secure a reliable source of energy. This was a huge affirmation of faith in the emerging geopolitical order. It disregarded history that showed that rights over fuel had rarely led to good feelings among nations. Post the spread of the Industrial Revolution, the demands for fuel security made nations that had ambitions to grow fast become eager hunters for sources of energy. India's first government under Prime Minister Jawaharlal Nehru, including the newly set up Planning Commission, instead banked more on faith than a thought-through strategy to mine its coal reserves more aggressively—but only by the state—and import oil from the Middle Eastern countries, demonstrating the use of peaceful coexistence.

Both these plans were put in a compromising situation by unanticipated developments, chiefly among them the rise in prices of imported crude oil and the repeated crises in the Middle East. The external markets for coal were meanwhile allowed to go dry without anyone taking a conscious decision to do so. The economy had a flourishing trade in coal before Independence, where plenty of British managing agencies, such as Andrew Yule, competed with Indian interests represented by Gujarati and even Parsi agents. Earlier in the nineteenth century, there were even Bengali companies of whom Dwarakanath Tagore with his Carr–Tagore company was the biggest.

All of them were snuffed out or put on notice once India decided that eventually all coal and oil business had to be nationalized. Investments from the private sector naturally began to dry up but the state had little fiscal space to replace them. So it never got clear how New Delhi would, if at all, steer a higher production of coal and oil. For instance, P.C. Mahalanobis, the Indian government's first statistical adviser and author of the Second Five Year Plan, argued that it made no sense to fill up the ballast of the railway engines with coal to then lug more coal by wagons across the country to fuel other industries.[7] Imported oil could do the work better. The man who could secure the oil security for India was Gamal Abdel Nasser, the president of Egypt from 1956 to 1970. Nasser and Nehru came famously close but only politically. Egypt had hardly any oil to sell and Nasser was not exactly popular with the oil sheikhs of Saudi Arabia, Oman or Kuwait, especially after he began nationalizing foreign oil companies. There was another little hitch. Egypt's staple export was cotton; India also produced cotton. Neither needed the other's products.

The emergence of Cold War in the Middle East left India with very few options to source crude oil at cheap prices. While the Suez Blockade and the Six Day War had a relatively minor impact, India was badly hurt by the sharp spike in prices from the successive oil shocks of the early seventies.[8]

The Middle Eastern nations made no allowance for India's needs and limited foreign exchange reserves to pay for the high prices. This was a let-down. Nehru had been sure that he would not only get oil, but he would get it at the same price that the UK got it for. After all, Mumbai and London were roughly the same distance from Abadan in Iran. When international oil companies, such as Burmah Oil, raised the price of Indian petrol by an anna[9] in 1957, Nehru described it as 'loot' and speeded up the construction of a state-run oil refinery at Barauni in Bihar. Before the revision, the price of a gallon of oil imported from the Middle East by India cost just six pence more than the cost in the UK. A couple of years later in May 1960, the prime minister ran to Ankleshwar in Gujarat when India struck its first oil well beyond Assam. As he stood beaming at the site, a gusher began spouting oil, spraying some on him too. Even as the engineers ran to switch it off, Nehru said: 'I shall address the Parliament in this sherwani. Let everybody know that we now have our own oil.' He named the well 'Vasundhara'.

These were naive expectations and, worse, piecemeal. Naturally, there were a series of hits and misses. By the early sixties, India had set up its state-owned exploration company, the Oil and Natural Gas Corporation Limited (ONGC). Its first chairman K.D. Malaviya, notched up a big success when Iran offered it four offshore exploration blocks. India formed a joint venture with ENI and Phillips Petroleum to explore them and found oil in two of them, 'Rostum' and 'Raksh'; the oil was imported to Cochin. But soon thereafter, India was forced to surrender those two blocks in 1979 when the Shah of Iran was deposed. A decade later, ONGC set up its subsidiary—ONGC Videsh Limited (OVL)—in 1989 to prospect for oil abroad. But, of course, it did not have the balance sheet to purchase anything worthwhile for a long time.

India's major success in prospecting for domestic oil was the discovery of an offshore oilfield near the coast of Mumbai that came into operation in 1974. The field was discovered by a joint Russian and Indian team.[10] Bombay High, the over-forty-year field, has been India's oil mainstay but production has clearly plateaued. In the last ten years till 2015–16, oil production from all domestic sources rose by only 15 per cent while consumption of petroleum products has increased by 62 per cent. It is rather curious that India bade goodbye to the US-dominated oil companies in the seventies, again through nationalization of their Indian assets, but ended up hugging oil oligarchs of Russia post-2000. The OVL's success has been patchy with Rosneft, or with Venezuela, managing to generate equity returns but no oil supply was secured for imports back home.

While oil prospecting rarely gave a cheer, India could have considered itself lucky that it had a considerable amount of coal as reserves. The Indian Coalfields Report of 1946 authored by K.C. Mahindra introduced seminal changes in the regulations for the coal sector. It formed the bedrock of the Industrial Policy Resolution of 1946 made by Shyama Prasad Mukherjee as the industry minister. Under the Policy, the government made it clear that coal mines would be nationalized eventually. Not only did coal miners stop fresh investments in the sector, the broader industrial lobby too was not happy. By the time the Industrial Policy Resolution of 1956 came around with the understanding that the mines would be nationalized soon, the price of coal had risen and that disturbed the earnings of the Indian Railways. This was a huge fiscal challenge for the government.

The coal industry and the railways played a tug-of-war game in the sixties that only made the coal prices rise. There was a downstream impact too. Coal had become the fuel of choice for urban Indian homes and its price rise hurt both domestic budgets and prospects for the re-election of candidates. The government had to move fast. It used the plea that the conditions of the coal workers were too dismal to nationalize the mines. Coal India Limited was formed in 1975. This galvanized mining as the CIL pushed additional investments to extract more coal. But as it had no control over the evacuation of coal to the power plants, due to the shortage of wagons and lines, the conditions did not really improve. Pricing reforms, being encouraged in several sectors in the eighties, were not considered for energy goods.[11] One of those reforms was to erase a policy of freight equalization that allowed a tonne of coal to be priced the same across the country, irrespective of transport costs. It was introduced in 1952, but hardly served to encourage dispersal of industry. Because of the shortage of railway wagons, it was a dead letter.

This impacted the post-nineties economy that showed spurts of growth. Those spurts were hemmed in by crippling power shortages due to the lack of coal. A way out was offered by the then West Bengal chief minister Jyoti Basu, who advised Prime Minister P.V. Narasimha Rao that some coal mines could be offered to companies bypassing CIL, provided they made the requisite investment in building power or steel plants. With the support of the politically powerful communist parties, the government pushed through amendments to the Coal Mines (Nationalization) Act. The response from the industry, initially a trickle, became a flood as China created a global revival for commodities post the Asian financial crisis of 1997. By 1999, there was a rush for mines where several dubious business groups jumped in. From there, it was a short walk to the biggest energy crisis—the coal scam—laid bare by the national auditor's report on the sector in 2012.

Clearly, the rules to keep the private sector out of mining had hurt both oil and gas, as well as coal. After Bombay High, exploration of new areas for oil lagged for decades till new companies were allowed to enter after liberalization in 1991. Even now of India's nearly 3.17 million square km of sedimentary area, only 19 per cent has been somewhat explored for oil and gas.[12] But the scale of disaster in coal was much larger. The state went back on its policy to keep mining entirely to government-run companies, CIL and SECL, without making the changes explicit.

The compromise meant trouble. Prime Minister Manmohan Singh was convinced that new mines should be auctioned, but was equally convinced that the Parliament would not endorse it. By 2012 the effect of this policy paralysis was clear. The auditor noted that the government had suffered a potential loss of Rs 28 billion (USD 0.44 million) in handing out those mines without inviting auctions.[13] The finding was instrumental, among other things, in forcing the Manmohan Singh-led UPA government out of office and has kept the next NDA government on tenterhooks about selling any natural resource without auctions. The collateral damage from this policy is that the mines bought in auctions are now economically unviable as coal prices have crashed globally. Since Indian coal is inferior, the incentive to import has risen.

Energy Enterprise

After those hits and misses, India has finally arrived at a plan for energy security that incorporates environmental challenges with the need to keep coal fires burning. It does not envisage a large-scale switchover to gas instead of coal, though the latter has far more carbon footprint, because it would mean a massive spike in imports. Till 2027, the Central Electricity Authority (CEA) has projected no addition to the existing gas grid 'in view of an acute natural gas shortage in the country'.[14]

The government also claims, and quite reasonably, that India is now making a transition from a power deficit to a power surplus scenario. It has begun to export power to neighbouring countries. Also, because of the size of its economy, Indian demand influences international price trends for coal, oil and gas, though 'macroeconomic development and policies in China shape coal demand and supply, with implications elsewhere'.[15] China accounts for almost 50 per cent of the global coal demand, 45 per cent of coal production and more than 10 per cent of seaborne trade. Therefore, economic or policy changes in China affect the coal market.

For India, energy pricing matters because first of all it needs to make its citizens consume more energy. Of the 304 million people who do not get electricity, it is essential they do so to ensure the state can reach them digitally to supply cash subsidy, education and healthcare. All government agencies have pencilled in a higher growth rate for energy consumption than the trend rate for the past decade. That can only happen if the prices stay flat. Happily, both oil and coal prices have begun to soften as IEA reports show. Though it creates risk that this will cut global oil discoveries that have fallen to a 'record low in 2016 as companies continued to cut spending and conventional oil projects sanctioned were at the lowest level in more than seventy years'.[16] India has begun to see the impact of this slowdown as no companies have bid in response to its open average policy for oil and gas.

The other two arms of India's energy matrix are sustainability and economic growth. These four do not move in tandem. Low fossil fuel prices make them an affordable option, even when imported, if renewable energy prices do not fall as much. In India, even a minor difference in prices could create a long tail risk. For instance, several states have opened bids for solar power projects where companies have aggressively lowered prices in each round. The cash-strapped state electricity distribution companies suddenly find that bids made in late 2016 are several notches higher than the latest bids made in June 2017 and have asked the earlier companies to renegotiate. Rewriting contractual obligations by the buyers is a risky option reminiscent of what happened in the coal sector in its heyday. India has committed to develop 175 GW of renewable power by 2022, which means there is no need to build additional coal-based power stations beyond what has already come on steam by 2015. Alarmingly, CEA projections show, despite the sufficiency, another 50,025 MW of coal-based power capacity is already under construction. These projects can be made use of only after 2022 and have already sunk over Rs 40 billion of bank loans.[17] They are the new stress points for the economy. As it is in the past decade, India has ramped up on about 80 GW of coal capacity just when the global appetite for renewables is rising fast.

Harnessing the potential of renewables also demands developing corresponding hydro- and gas-based power plants. Hydro power has just not taken off in India (8.16 per cent by 2022). Compared with the expected global average of 25 per cent share of gas in the energy mix (by 2035), India will only reach 9 per cent by 2040.[18] Without these balances, it is difficult to envisage how renewables will deliver in India. Globally in 2016, renewables supplied more than half the global electricity demand growth, with hydro accounting for half of that share.

Clearly the Indian energy story has suffered from insufficient attention paid in the past to develop robust institutions, optimal pricing and the enforcement of regulations. As the contours of the new policy focus more on correcting these issues, they face a world order impatient with tinkering around with the past errors. India has added more than 10 GW of renewable energy in just one year. The asking rate, however, has gotten stiffer, which the solar panels on the CIL tower cannot hope to cover only through optics.

XIX

Democracy's Angry Crowds: Civil Society and Legitimacy in India

Subrata K. Mitra

Though democratic states derive their legitimacy from popular support, the relationship of civil society and democracy is not as straightforward as it might appear at first sight. After all, most democratic states are run by elected representatives, and public institutions do not necessarily provide much scope for the populace to play a role in their functioning. The same applies to the formulation and implementation of public policy. This is the crux of the question that Larry Diamond asks in his seminal contribution to the relationship of civil society and democracy: 'Is it primarily the elite who make, shape and consolidate democracy? Or, does the public matter?'[1] Drawing on recent Indian examples, one can add a further twist to this general question. How about the 'wrong' kind of public—lynch mobs and fanatic mobs—asserting their collective might to confront public authority, trying to protect minority rights?[2]

The complex relationship of civil society and democracy has engaged generations of activists and students of social theory.[3] Indian research on these issues of civil society activism draw on the life and contributions of Gandhi calling for direct action by people for the protection of democratic rights. As a young barrister in South Africa, Gandhi had discovered the potential of civil society for the assertion of democratic rights and transformed this 'experiment', with his

189

unique political skill, into the concept of *satyagraha*. On his return to India, he supplemented this with two further concepts—*swadeshi* and *Swaraj*—which became the firm basis of an enduring link between India's civil society and the abstract goal of independence from the British colonial rule. The mobilization of peasants, workers, women and former untouchables gave the moribund Indian National Congress a social relevance. Following Independence, this heritage became an enduring basis of the dynamism and resilience of India's electoral democracy. However, if Gandhian direct action showed the magical power of civil society activism under colonial rule, the success in Champaran met with its nemesis in the violence unleashed by the enraged masses in Chauri Chaura.[4] This duality of civil society activism—its assertion of democratic rights on the one hand, and its potential for rejection of minority rights and violence to life and property on the other—leads to the core question: does civil society activism in India enhance democratic consolidation, or does it stymie institutions of accountability and policymaking, and subvert the course of electoral democracy?

Frenzied Crowds, Entrenched Insurgency, Resilient Democracy: An Indian Paradox?

Agitating crowds pushing at police barricades, contesting public policies they consider illegitimate, and toppling dictators, have been much in evidence in recent politics.[5] Spread across vast distances in time and space, the agitation of these foot soldiers suggests a cross-national relationship between the agency of civil society and transition to democracy. Closer home, the East Asian variant of popular mobilization, with authoritarian, repressive and corrupt rulers as the foci of popular anger, provides some comparative features. In Indonesia, the Philippines, South Korea and Thailand, popular anger catalysed democratic transition. In each of these cases, the crowds were pitted against an elite viewed as corrupt, oppressive or venal. India represents a different context. Where does India, whose route to democracy has been different from both that of the

European mainstream and East and Southeast Asia, fit in this broad pattern?

In the liberal democratic imagination, the sense of outrage that runs through the crowds of Tahrir Square of Cairo, Lal Chowk of Srinagar, and similar multitudes from Thailand, South Korea, Indonesia and the Philippines connects them to the *citoyens* and *citoyennes* of Paris streets in July 1789 and the French Revolution that paved the way for popular democracy. How might one read this Indian mosaic? Other images add to the confusing signals that India sends out. Entrenched insurgencies, election candidates in the campaign mode, and serpentine lines of men and women patiently waiting to exercise their franchise exist side by side, each of them pressing its claim in the name of their democratic rights. The paradoxical character of these routine images hardly attracts media or scholarly attention.

The Indian route to democracy has been different from the European prototype. India is a functional democracy, where change occurs through the normal political process. A plethora of political parties, elections, pressure groups, judicial interventions and public commissions, security forces, and civil services at federal, regional and local levels, jostle for space and influence in the public sphere, generate and implement public policies—without intervention of civil society. And yet, side by side, there is the spectre of crowds on Delhi streets agitating against corruption and more recently, crowds in Hyderabad and Osmania University campus agitating for the creation of a new state of Telangana; the telegenic folk of stone-throwing Kashmiris agitating for 'azadi' (freedom) and political parties protesting against demonetization. These phenomena raise several key questions for both students of Indian politics as well as those with an interest in the theory of the transition to, and consolidation of, democracy.

Unlike in East Asian cases, elections with limited franchise were introduced in India in the 1860s. Since Independence, regular general elections at the Central, regional and local levels are held regularly and important political change takes place at these levels on the basis of electoral outcomes. Regulatory agencies and institutions of accountability function effectively. The existence of multiple modes of interest articulation and aggregation, combining conventional methods of campaign participation, voting, lobbying and contacting leaders and administrators with indigenous forms of protest have become an effective basis for governance, transition to democracy and its consolidation in India. The legacy of Gandhian satyagraha, which had blended participation in elections with limited suffrage and rational protest in a seemingly seamless flow under colonial rule, has developed many variants in India after Independence. These have taken radically different forms in regions with well-settled administrative structures, such as Gujarat and Karnataka, where the response of the Indian state to civil society activism differs greatly from that in more troubled regions like Kashmir, the northeast, and the 'red corridor' of India, linking the hill districts of central and eastern India with pockets of Naxalite strength in the south.

Are these acts of strategic protest with the ever-present danger of mobs spinning out of the control of their stewards and spilling over into violence the soft underbelly of Indian democracy or a supplementary route to the same goal of democratic consolidation? This broad question requires the empirical specification of 'civil society' in the Indian context, its linkages with democratic consolidation and an explanation of conditions leading to such a consolidation as opposed to the dissipation of democratic capital in violent destruction.

Civil Society, Democratic Transition and Consolidation: A Complex Relationship

The ambiguity of the concept of civil society and its location within the social and political space contributes to the uncertainty that marks the interpretation of how civil society activism is linked to democratic transition and consolidation. Equally underspecified is the incentive that leads to the formation of the crowd and its mobilization for a political purpose. For clearer understanding, it is important to note the typology of civil society activism (Table 3) and analyse the evolution of the specific types and their implication for democratic consolidation.

Table 3: A Typology of 'Angry Crowds'

Core values of the groups

Level of location	Materialist/secular	Identity/religion
National	Type 2 Anna Hazare movement	Type 4 Hindu nationalists
Local/regional	Type 1 Farmers of Singur Naxalites of Andhra Pradesh	Type 3 Khalistan movement

Locating Civil Society and Incentivizing Civil Society Activism

Civil society defines the space between the private sphere and the institutions of the state. As Larry Diamond defines it, civil society is 'the realm of organized social life that is open, voluntary, bound by a legal order or set of shared rules'.[6] Civil society activism involves private citizens acting collectively to make demands on the state or to express in the public sphere their interests, preferences, and ideal or to check the authority of the state and make it accountable. In terms of these roles and functions, civil society encompasses several organizations concerned with public matters. They include civil, issue-oriented, religious and educational interest groups and associations. Some are known as non-governmental organizations, or NGOs; some are informal and loosely structured.[7] In the Indian context, if one considers private spheres of family, caste, kin, religious groups and corporations as the private sphere of society and civil service and other institutions of the state as the state sphere, then the space between the two is occupied by the elusive civil society. This is the political space where the agency of the private sphere meets that of the state to negotiate an agenda that neither the state nor the private sphere is able or willing to implement. The moment for this is generated by crowds—like those that came together to demand the creation of Telangana, or to protest against corruption as part of the Anna Hazare movement.

A Typology of Civil Society Activism

Not all instances of civil society activism are the same. Based on their spatial location (local/regional as against national) and political interests (such as material issues, or the protection and promotion of religious values and/or ethnic identity) that motivate the participants, one can visualize four types of civil society activism (Table 3).

The 'Responsive' State and the Process of Evolution of Civil Society Activism

How these different types evolve and their consequence for democratization depends on a number of factors. Most important of these are the salience that the core elements of the civil society activists attach to their shared goal, the number and territorial catchment of the imagined community they draw on, and the response of the state. Based on comparable cases,[8] one can trace the evolution of sub-national movements (figure 9), as an exemplar of the evolution of Type 1.

Figure 9: Sub-National Movements

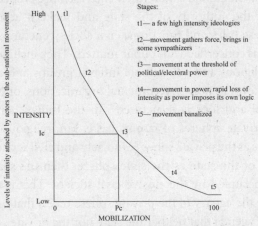

Levels of intensity attached by actors to the sub-national movement

INTENSITY

High — t1

Ic

Low

0   Pc   100

MOBILIZATION

Active nationalists as a percentage of the imagined community

Stages:

t1— a few high intensity ideologies

t2—movement gathers force, brings in some sympathizers

t3— movement at the threshold of political/electoral power

t4— movement in power, rapid loss of intensity as power imposes its own logic

t5— movement banalized

Ic—Critical threshold of intensity, beyond which nationalism becomes 'visible' over and above 'mundane' politics
Pc—Critical threshold of numbers beyond which those adhering to nationalism constitute a political force

Source: Adapted from Mitra and Lewis (eds.) (1996), p. 27.

As one can see from Figure 9, many demands for secession from the Indian state begin as very high-intensity movements led by a handful of activists. The Central government reacts with a double strategy of accommodation and repression, just as the secessionist movements promote their cause with a combination of protest and participation. Typically, such movements transform as they gain in strength. The average intensity of the movement comes down as numbers grow and the leadership seeks to exercise its authority over the followers. As the transformation of Assam into seven different states, or the creation of new entities such as Uttarakhand, Jharkhand, Chhattisgarh and Telangana shows, such movements eventually lead to the creation of new federal states with leaders of the separatist movement becoming new rulers. These post-Independence movements have a pre-Independence origin. The call for a federal division of powers advocated by the Indian National Congress in the twenties, when it organized its provincial committees on the basis of linguistically contiguous areas, originated from the need to safeguard regional and sectional identity. But economic policy, especially in a country with formidable problems of development, required central coordination. Out of these contradictory needs emerged 'cooperative' federalism—a form of power-sharing in which national, state and local governments interact cooperatively and collectively to solve common problems rather than acting in an adversarial mode.

With the second type of civil society activism, the state may concede the main elements of the agenda without much resistance if they are consistent with the goals of the ruling party or the coalition, though the negotiations might become stormy if the leaders of the civil society exceed their original mandate. This was the case with the Anna Hazare movement that became political when elements of Hindu nationalist groups began extending it their support. The 'navnirman' movement of 1974, which was keen on replacing the elected government of Gujarat, did not get much headway and came up against a roadblock to transform itself into a national movement, aimed at resisting the authoritarian rule of Indira Gandhi. The third type, promoting ethnic identity, has found accommodation within

India's flexible federalism but the state draws a clear line when such demands openly contradict the secular goals of the Constitution, as in the case of the Khalistan movement. The solutions offered by the state have sought to accommodate the economic and political grievances of Punjab while firmly rejecting the religious and territorial demands.

The fourth type, aimed at transforming the core values of the national state, as many suspect the Hindu nationalist groups aim at, has been thwarted by two different factors. The first is the growth of rival movements from within the same social groups and the second is competition between ideologues and office-seekers. The Patel agitation in Gujarat in 2015 led by the younger segment of the Patel community who felt they have been denied their just share of jobs and admissions to coveted educational institutes, illustrates the first of these deterrents. The Patels—entrepreneurial, self-reliant in the sense of not being dependent on state subsidies, and financially secure—represent an important social base of the BJP. The community has been among the most ardent supporters of Narendra Modi. The defection of a section of them under the leadership of Hardik Patel, the twenty-two-year-old leader of the agitation suggesting 'get rid of reservation or make everyone its slave',[9] was harking back to an emotive and violent phase of the anti-reservation movement in Gujarat in the eighties. India's complex quota system, which seeks to balance the principle of merit in recruitment to public services and highly-prized places in medical, engineering and other branches of education with a preferential treatment to designated communities belonging to Scheduled Castes and Scheduled Tribes, is the cornerstone of institutionalized distributive justice that underpins Indian democracy. The Patels, though normally content to pursue life within the broad framework of the law, have been ferocious agitators when the occasion demanded it.[10] The Bardoli Satyagraha of Sardar Patel, which had inspired Mahatma Gandhi, still remains a historical marker.

The second deterrent on the evolution of Hindu extremism into a national force and its 'ambivalent' moderation[11] calls for a detailed discussion.

The BJP is the most important voice of Hindu nationalism in India today. Literally, the Indian Peoples' Party, successor to the Bharatiya Jana Sangh (BJS) and set up on 21 October 1951, shortly after India's independence with the mission to promote an exclusive Hindu view of the nation, state and collective identity in India, the party today is the core of the national government. In its current form, the core ideology can be summed up under 'five principles', namely: nationalism and national integration; democracy; positive secularism; Gandhian socialism; and value-based politics. Right from the outset, the party became a dual presence, with a division of labour between the political wing espousing a hybrid liberal Hindu nationalism and the organizational wing, supported by the RSS which supplied the dedication, energy and staff to make the new party work. Its network of several thousand *pracharaks*—full-time, educated, unmarried, male staffers—was put at the service of the BJP, giving the party overnight an effective group of campaigners. The political strength of Hindu nationalism soon became clear once the Ram Janmabhoomi issue became a central argument that galvanized Hindu sentiments and eventually propelled the BJP to power in 1998.

The dilemma between the pursuits of office as opposed to the assertion of ideology persists. The Hindu nationalist movement is constantly caught in the dilemma between political mobilization versus electoral representation; integration versus accommodation; ideology versus populism; *shakha* (cadre) versus *janata* (mass, people).

How India Copes with Civil Society Activism?

Protest movements, including those with a certain degree of violence, are not uncommon in India. They emerge as an act of complaint against a specific grievance, gather momentum if they have a cause that is widely shared and an effective leadership with good communication abilities is available to mobilize these elements into a mass movement. Often, the violence that results when protesters disobey orders meant to prohibit their actions adds 'police outrage' as an additional support to their cause. The life cycle of the movement comes to an end when a settlement is made. As a matter of fact, as one has seen time and again, and most recently in the case of the Anna Hazare Movement against public corruption, protest movements become an additional entry point for new issues, leaders and political vocabulary in India's noisy but effective democracy. 'Rational' protest thus complements institutional participation, spreading the message of democracy, empowering those who have been outside the tent, and contributing to the resilience of democracy in a non-Western setting.

Has India found a unique, idiosyncratic route to democracy transition and consolidation, or is the Indian solution capable of being understood in general terms? The paths indicated in Figure 9 show the multiple routes that are available to civil society activists in India. Today, representatives of civil society can directly approach administrators and policymakers for implementation of state policies if they find them lacking, and call on regulatory agencies like the judiciary and the media to vent their grievances. The discussion of the four types of civil society activism (Table 3) has pointed to the political route where, turned into movements, such activists eventually enrich the social base of politics by contributing new leadership to supplement the existing group of elite.

Democracy transition occurs when the existing authoritarian rulers are thrown out. What follows might be chaotic, or even worse, and democracy transition might induct a new set of authoritarian rulers. Democracy consolidation happens when orderly, democratic rule takes place, possibly with the induction of new elite from below. This can be termed as 'rebels into stakeholders' as was seen in Telangana and the northeast.

India's hyperactive media, NGOs, proactive judiciary and national political parties articulate these regional and local phenomena. Thanks to the multiple modes of participation, state–society relations in India benefit from systematic intermediation of both modern and traditional institutions, creating an ethos of effective and continuous interaction that helps rebels become stakeholders. The combined effect of all these methods is to dull the sharp edges of class and ethnic conflict and to transform what could have become a state of polarized conflict into a series of protracted negotiations. As such, even while an effective electoral route to power exists, nevertheless the undemocratic route seems to have a parallel life of its own. This adds a touch of ambivalence to democratic consolidation in India.

Figure 10

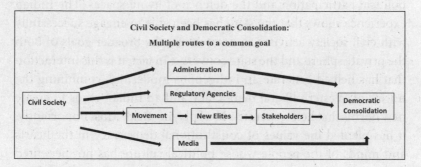

Conclusion

Thanks to the Gandhian legacy of the freedom movement, civil society activism, which gives citizens the room to manoeuvre between the state and society, continues to contribute to the deepening and broadening of Indian democracy. The Indian case reinforces the general lesson that while popular mobilization can bring down authoritarian rule, it is civil society activism that can check the growth of new autocracies and hone the newly gained rights into institutional norms of democratic consolidation.[12] The Indian experience bears out the range of functions that civil society fulfils with regard to the consolidation of democracy. Though India retains the draconian rules of colonial order (the Indian Penal Code and the Code of Criminal Procedure), in practice, the application of rules of order-keeping is moderated by the realization that civil society activists are also legitimate political actors. In reality, as one watches the negotiation of the state and society in India, one hears the magisterial voice of Charles Tilly who had castigated the reflex reaction of states criminalizing civil society activism as irrational.[13]

However, in order to be effective, civil society needs to be autonomous and resist manipulation by the state and business interests. In India, a strong and reliable civil society has been able to adapt structural change of the economy to the needs of the local people and at the same time served as a check on naked power. They have stimulated the political awareness of the masses, enhanced political participation and the defence of living spaces. The Indian experience shows that the state has been able to engage successfully with civil society activism in cases where the broader goals of both the private sphere and the state converge. In fact, it is this interaction that has helped generate an indigenous modernity, combining the norms of Western liberal democracy and an Indian ethos to create new norms that help generate a level playing field. Most importantly, it has planted the values of constitutional democracy in the hearts and minds of the people whose political culture has not benefited from the collective memory of the great battles for democratic rights as seen in eighteenth century Europe. The state has been able to extend the scope of Indian democracy through legislations like the Right to Information, which have helped civil society activism. On the other hand, the availability of this alternative route to the cherished political goals has cut the ground from under the feet of right-wing and left-wing radicalism.

XX

India As an Asian Power

Dhruva Jaishankar

Is India an Asian power? Obviously, it is a large country in Asia. But conceptually, the answer to that question has not always been so simple. For about half of its seventy-year independent history, India did not seek to project its influence meaningfully across Asia and in the Pacific. And only recently—over the last twenty-five years—has a significant role for India in Asia come to be recognized and desired by other relevant actors.

To understand how and why India has had to reengage with Asia over the past quarter-century, it is helpful to consider the emergence of modern Asia in three overlapping phases. The first was shaped by the process of decolonization between the end of the Second World War, in 1945, and the sixties. This era had its brief heyday between the Bandung Conference in 1955 and the Sino-Indian war of 1962, and was marked by Asian solidarity against colonialism and attempts to establish principles of non-alignment and peaceful coexistence. India played a remarkable leadership role during this period, not just as a normative power—a newly independent democracy that was actively shaping regional values—but in facilitating Asian engagement with the People's Republic of China, mediating during the Korean War, and facilitating Japan's re-entry into the international community.

The second phase saw pockets of rapid Asian economic growth and the celebration of 'Asian values'. The growth story was led by

Japan, followed by the tiger economies of South Korea, Hong Kong, Taiwan, and Singapore, and replicated to a certain degree by Malaysia, Thailand, Indonesia and the Philippines. These states benefited from political and security ties with the United States and the West, strong centralized governance and a focus on infrastructure, investment, manufacturing and exports. This period was also marked by the rise of a small-state-led institutionalism under the Association of Southeast Asian Nations (ASEAN), enabled by a relative vacuum of Great Power engagement. It lasted roughly from the Tokyo Olympics in 1964 to the end of the Cold War. For much of this period, India retreated. It became more preoccupied with its neighbourhood in South Asia and the Indian Ocean, and its position in international affairs was more heavily influenced by the dynamics of the Cold War. Moreover, with its economy remaining closed, India had only a marginal role to play in the Asian growth story of this era. Thus, for a time, Asia mattered less to India, and vice versa.

The third phase of Asia's emergence is ongoing. It began with the end of the Cold War in 1991, accelerated after 2001, and was felt in earnest after the global financial crisis of 2008. This period has been defined by the shift in economic and political power from the West to Asia, the rebalance of power within Asia in favour of China, and the reassertion of several other major powers on matters of Asian security and politics. This post-Cold War world has coincided with India's own economic liberalization. In the early nineties, India began to 'Look East', initially recognizing the economic importance and value of East and Southeast Asia. Gradually, China's growing assertiveness, ASEAN fragility, and uncertainty about US involvement in the region—as well as its own growing capabilities— compelled India to assume a bigger political and security role in the region. India, therefore, upgraded its 'Look East' policy to 'Act East' with the objective of ensuring a multipolar Asia.

Acting East necessitates further commercial integration with the region so as to provide another economic pole in the area. India will also have to become more active in deepening its diplomatic and security footprint not just in its immediate neighbourhood and the

Indian Ocean, but with partners such as the United States, Japan, Australia, and certain Southeast Asian states. Finally, India must remain active in Asian institutions so as to help preserve regional rules and norms, and help guide institutional evolution if necessary.

Asia 1.0: Colonization, Decolonization, and the Spirit of Bandung

It is impossible to appreciate India's engagement with Asia without understanding Asia's own evolution. The first phase of modern Asia's emergence—from roughly 1945 to the mid-sixties—was informed by the processes of colonization and decolonization, and resulted in most of today's states with their current geographical boundaries, their structures of governance, and their laws and languages.

The process of Asia's colonization by European powers, the United States and Japan was a traumatic one. It resulted in the brutal suppression of local populations, the destruction of traditional industries, and devastating warfare.[1] It also led to the exchange of populations, cultures and ideas across geographies, although often within a single colonial system. For example, an Indian diaspora, consisting of traders, labourers, and even professionals, developed in Burma (now Myanmar), Malaysia, Singapore, Hong Kong, and other British-controlled territories. It remains active and relevant to this day. The economic links were just as important, often replacing pre-colonial exchanges. There were also intra-Asian interactions in the military sphere, such as the use of Indian forces by the British in China during the Second Opium War and the Boxer Rebellion, and later against Japan during the Second World War.[2]

India played an important role in the process of Asian decolonization in the immediate post-War period. In March and April 1947, Jawaharlal Nehru—'by far the best-placed Asian leader to create and lead a broader Asian solidarity movement'[3]—hosted an Asian Relations Conference in Delhi. It was an idea that Nehru had discussed the previous year with Burmese leader Aung San, and considerable efforts were made to secure participation from the

likes of Vietnam and Indonesia. 'Asia is again finding itself,' Nehru
declared to the participants present from China, Korea, Turkey,
Iran, Afghanistan, Tibet, across Southeast Asia, and even Australia
and New Zealand.[4]

At the time, India's leadership in Asia was natural, and benefited
from the nature and timing of its independence movement. It was
a remarkable achievement, resulting in the single greatest act of
decolonization and democratization in history, and foreshadowed
similar movements in Southeast Asia. But it was not simply as a
normative leader that India engaged Asia. In the early years of the
post-War period, India served as a backchannel between the United
States and communist China, supported the repatriation of prisoners
of war during the Korean War in 1952, and facilitated Japan's re-entry
into the international community, as during Nehru's visit to Japan
in 1957.[5] At the Bandung Conference in Indonesia in 1955, India
along with a handful of other countries led newly independent Asian
and African countries to condemn colonialism, engage the People's
Republic of China, and establish principles of peaceful coexistence
that were to find continuing resonance over the years in Asia. As an
American newspaper noted at the time of the Bandung Conference:
'[A]t last the destiny of Asia is being determined in Asia, and not in
Geneva, or Paris, or London, and Washington. Colonialism is out
and hands off is the word. Asia is free. This is perhaps the historic
event of our century.'[6]

However, this optimism was short-lived. The 1962 India–China
border war buried the notion of India-led Asian solidarity. India's
frailties were exposed, the larger impulses of the Cold War began to
define the entire region, and the notion of peaceful coexistence in
Asia lay discredited.

Asia 2.0: Tiger Growth, Asian Values, and the ASEAN Way

By the early sixties, other developments were taking place that
presaged a second phase of modern Asia's evolution. Japan, which
had already industrialized following the Meiji Restoration in 1868,

recovered rapidly after the devastation of the Second World War. Benefiting economically from the Korean War and the United States' military presence, Japan had rebuilt itself sufficiently by 1964 to host the Olympics and launched its first high-speed railway. But it was not the only Asian economy to chart a path for growth on the security benefits of a US-led order, spending on infrastructure and public welfare, a focus on manufacturing, and access to Western markets for exports. A year later, in 1965, Singapore became independent, and initiated an ambitious national development agenda of its own under Lee Kuan Yew. South Korea, Taiwan and Hong Kong embarked on similar trajectories as Singapore, together becoming the 'Four Asian Tigers'.

This development also had consequences for governance. The notion of 'Asian values'—grounded in respect for authority, collective well-being, and social harmony—gained currency under Lee and Malaysia's Mahathir Mohammed, as an alternative to both Soviet-style socialism and Western liberalism. Other successful Asian economies of this period similarly saw value in strong centralized leadership, such as the Indonesia of Suharto and the Philippines under Ferdinand Marcos. As a consequence, the cultural dimension of the idea of Asia gained in salience. Asia's scope became more limited to regions that traditionally felt a Chinese cultural footprint, whether writing systems, religion, or other cultural attributes. 'Asian values' appeared to extend only to the region from Japan and Korea to Southeast Asia, and not westward to India and South Asia.[7]

The third feature of this new Asia was the advent of a regional institutional architecture defined by smaller states. In 1967, Singapore, Malaysia, Thailand, Indonesia and the Philippines formed ASEAN. The centrality of ASEAN—which eventually incorporated Vietnam, Laos, Cambodia, Brunei, and Myanmar—to regional trade agreements, summits, and security conversations in the region, arose out of a set of unusual circumstances. The United States' retreat from Vietnam in 1975; China's focus on its domestic growth under Deng Xiaoping; the Soviet Union's preoccupations with Afghanistan, Eastern Europe, and *glasnost*; Japan's continuing non-militarization; and Australia's remaining tensions with Indonesia, all contributed to a relative vacuum of major and middle powers exerting themselves in Southeast Asia.

In this period, India too was noticeable by its relative absence. The India–Pakistan wars of 1965 and 1971, and India's subsequent interventions during the eighties in Sri Lanka and elsewhere in the Indian Ocean, contributed to a focus on the immediate neighbourhood, at the expense of the broader Asian landscape. The Bangladesh and Afghanistan wars saw the dynamics of the Cold War creep closer to home. India also saw a deterioration of its domestic environment, including the rise of several insurgencies, such as the ones in Punjab and Jammu and Kashmir. The period of the Emergency in the seventies and political scandals in the eighties hobbled governance. But most importantly for Asia, India retreated from the economic dynamics that were starting to define the region. Trade in the seventies and the eighties was less than 15 per cent of India's gross domestic product, and overall growth rates were low, as the country continued to embrace autarkic economic principles.

The second phase of modern Asia—marked by 'tiger' growth, 'Asian values', and ASEAN centrality—really came into its own between 1980 and 1991. In the early eighties, mainland China began to acknowledge the need to replicate the growth models successfully pursued by Japan and the Asian Tigers and started to become integrated into the trade and supply chain networks of the Asia–Pacific. But by the nineties, doubts started creeping in about this model. In the early nineties, the Japanese economic bubble burst, and the Asian financial crisis of 1997 tainted the notion of Asian values.

Asia 3.0: China's Ascendance and the Asian Century

A third Asia has started to make itself apparent in the post-Cold War period. This period has seen the gradual economic integration of the region and more diversified economic growth. It is informed by the political circumstances of US primacy following the end of the

Cold War and the consequences of the rapid economic rise of China, especially following its entry into the World Trade Organization in 2001.

The global balance of economic power has shifted rapidly to Asia.[8] In 1992, the United States accounted for 32 per cent of the nominal GDP of what were later to become the G20 economies. The major Western European states (Germany, France, the UK, and Italy) enjoyed 29 per cent share and the six Asia–Pacific members (China, Japan, India, South Korea, Indonesia, and Australia) 27 per cent, of which Japan alone accounted for 19 per cent. By 2017, the balance looked quite different. The United States retained its 32 per cent share, but Europe's had shrunk to 18 per cent and Asia's had expanded to 37 per cent, of which China's was 20 per cent.[9]

This period has also been marked by the re-emergence of Great Power competition in the region. The primary competitive dynamic is between an ascendant United States and a rising China. The aftermath of the Tiananmen Square crackdowns of 1989, the 1995 Taiwan Straits Crisis, the 1999 bombing of the Chinese Embassy in Belgrade, and the 2001 Hainan Island incident were all eventually managed by Washington and Beijing, but hinted at a simmering adversarial relationship. After 2008, China's relations became overtly competitive not just with the United States, but also with Japan. In response, Japan under Shinzo Abe embarked upon transformative defence reforms to emerge as a more 'normal' military power. Following the ascension to power of Xi Jinping, the Southeast Asian disputants in the South China Sea, South Korea, and India began to bear the brunt of Chinese assertiveness. The deterioration of Sino-Indian relations after 2014, the South China Sea arbitration ruling of 2016, and China's response to North Korea's nuclearization proved to be important turning points. For India, China has presented a series of challenges, from regional security in South Asia and the Indian Ocean, to terrorism, the long-standing boundary dispute, imbalanced trade and India's position on global governance.

Thus, the third, and ongoing, era of modern Asia's ascendance has seen, paradoxically, growth and economic cooperation resulting in the greatest elimination of poverty in history and the accentuation of Great Power competition to Asia. While China's growth has created unprecedented opportunity, concerns about its opacity, unilateralism and mercantilism remain. Meanwhile, the reassertion of major and middle powers in the region—not just China, but also the United States, Japan, India and Australia—have raised questions about the viability of ASEAN centrality to Asia's institutional architecture.

Looking East, Acting East, Achieving Multipolarity

For India, the original impetus of its reengagement with Asia after the end of the Cold War was economic.[10] India's then prime minister, P.V. Narasimha Rao, embarked upon visits to China, South Korea, Thailand and Singapore, among other places. As Rao's biographer Vinay Sitapati notes: 'It was not just . . . capital that Rao found in East Asia; it was also an alternative economic model.'[11] Gradually, India's trade with Asian countries increased; private companies from Japan, South Korea, China, Thailand and Singapore entered the Indian market; and India reached trade and economic agreements with ASEAN, Japan and South Korea. ASEAN is now India's fourth largest trade partner; in terms of goods, China is first. Ongoing efforts by India to deepen economic integration with Asia include constructing the India–Myanmar–Thailand (IMT) trilateral highway, participating in Regional Comprehensive Economic Partnership (RCEP) talks, and negotiating an ASEAN–India Maritime Transport Cooperation Agreement.

Owing to India's growing economic promise—and with the efforts and encouragement of Asian leaders, such as, for example, Singapore's former prime minister Goh Chok Tong—it gradually became incorporated into the region's institutional architecture. It joined the ASEAN Regional Forum in 1996 and subsequently became a member of the East Asia Summit (EAS) and Asian Defence Ministers Meeting-Plus. At the same time, India integrated into new China-led institutions, such as BRICS, the Asian Infrastructure

Investment Bank and the Shanghai Cooperation Organization. At its own initiative, it has led a revival of the Bay of Bengal Initiative for Multi-Sectoral Technical and Economic Cooperation (BIMSTEC). Today, barring the Asia–Pacific Economic Cooperation (APEC) forum, India is well integrated into Asia's institutional architecture. APEC membership for India has been supported by several countries, including the United States, but has been complicated by India's approach to trade and questions about expanded membership for the institution. However, should existing institutions face further pressure or evolve, India is today far better situated to shape Asia-wide regional rules, laws, and norms.

India's entry into the security architecture of the region followed, but not without difficulties. The most important progress was made with the United States. Defence cooperation began to take off in the early 2000s, with the next steps in strategic partnership; the India–US civilian nuclear agreement; the acquisition by India of major US defence platforms such as the C-130J and C-17 transportation aircraft and P-8I maritime surveillance planes; and India being designated a major defence partner.

Starting in 2000, India also normalized relations with Japan, following sharp differences resulting from its 1998 nuclear tests. The growing convergence and cooperation resulted in quadrilateral (India–US–Japan–Australia) humanitarian operations after the 2004 Indian Ocean tsunami and maritime exercises in 2007. After China sent strong signals and changes in government took place in the four countries, progress slowed. Nonetheless, India now has frequent naval exercises with the United States (MALABAR), Japan (JIMEX) and Australia (AUSINDEX). Additionally, India has established regular high-level bilateral dialogues and trilateral India–US–Japan and India–Japan–Australia mechanisms. India has also initiated a different kind of security engagement with Southeast Asia. Among other initiatives, it has supported the Myanmar navy with technical assistance, provided facilities for Singapore to conduct artillery, mechanized force, and air exercises, coordinated maritime patrols with Indonesia and trained Vietnam's combat aircraft pilots.[12]

As a reflection of these institutional, economic and security changes, India's 'Look East' policy was upgraded to 'Act East'. This was meant to widen the scope to encompass the entire Asia–Pacific; shift the focus beyond economic considerations to political, security, and social ties; and attempt to make progress more action- and result-oriented. While institutional engagement and security partnerships are proceeding apace, India's commercial integration with Asia— and Southeast Asia in particular—has been underwhelming. Fast-tracking those efforts requires India to focus on developing northeast India and the Andaman and Nicobar Islands; improve air and land connectivity with Southeast Asia; reduce non-tariff barriers; leverage India's prowess in services, technology, and English language education; and liberalize visa regimes. Specific projects that are underway—completing the Kaladan Multi-Modal Project in Myanmar, extending and enhancing the IMT network, and connecting into Myanmar's Dawei deep-sea port project— would represent concrete efforts at improving India's connectivity with Southeast Asia.

India's role in Asia has undergone multiple changes as both India and Asia have evolved. Today, a more active Indian role in Asia is desired and sought after by many actors in Asia. With the imperative of creating a peaceful, interdependent, and multipolar Asia, India has little choice but to participate institutionally, integrate economically and become an active security provider across the region. Important strides have been made in these respects since the turn of the millennium, but an increased focus, particularly on the economic dimension, may yet be necessary if India is to achieve its objectives.

XXI

Indian Media at Seventy: Five Big Challenges

Nalin Mehta

Is there a connection between the long forgotten US battleship that blew up in the Havana Harbour in 1898 and the current state of the Indian media? You will be surprised!

When the *U.S.S. Maine* inexplicably blew up at the height of tensions between Washington and Spain, then masters of Cuba, the newly emerging American media barons, having just embarked on a contest for readership, saw a fantastic opportunity to capture paying readers by rallying them to the flag. The media in the US then was just as bloodthirsty as Indian TV networks are now. Enmeshed in a battle for supremacy with Joseph Pulitzer's *The World*, William Randolph Hearst's *New York Journal* immediately argued, without much proof, that a Spanish anti-ship mine had destroyed the *Maine* and its crew. Nothing quite matches a bout of self-righteous hysteria about the 'enemy' to draw in patriotic audiences. Hearst, who created America's largest newspaper chain, understood this better than most. He had dispatched reporters to Cuba to write on alleged Spanish atrocities. When his reporter cabled back: 'There is no war . . . request to be recalled,' Hearst famously replied: 'Please remain. You furnish the pictures, I'll furnish the war.'[1] Most historians agree the months of holier-than-thou press jingoism that followed forced the US–Spanish War engulfing the Philippines, Puerto Rico, the Caribbean, Guam and

Cuba. While the war ended Spanish colonialism, the American decision to start it was intrinsically rooted in the no-holds-barred journalism and battle for eyeballs that the newly minted media barons inaugurated.

Decades later, revisionist American naval historians concluded that the *U.S.S. Maine* probably sank from an internal explosion caused by the combustion of coal kept next to an ammunition magazine. Nonetheless, an aggressive media looking to capture readers with muscular nationalism combined with a suspicious explosion meant that such subtle explanations were easily ignored, with profound social, political and global consequences.

It is a story with useful pointers for those constantly puzzled about the bizarre loudness of much of India's media—especially the over-the-top breathlessness of TV news channels, and 'do aliens drink cow milk?' kind of exclusives. Were Hearst to visit an Indian TV news station today, he probably would not be surprised at all by the deliberate desperateness of permanent outrage spouted daily in the hope that somehow, anyhow, the viewer would stay on for just those few extra seconds. There are remarkable parallels between the shape of the Indian media in 2017 and the US media a hundred years ago: in numbers, penetration rates and competition.

The Indian media's current convulsions offer a paradox of Dickensian proportions:

> For the Indian media, it is unquestionably the best of times and it is also, unfortunately, the worst of times . . . We have never had such a wide audience or readership but our credibility has never been so tested. We have never seen such a flowering of TV channels and such a spreading footprint of newspaper titles, but the market is more consolidated than ever around the top few players. The quality of what we offer to our public has never been better but that same public can see that the ethical foundations of our actions have plumbed new depths. The impact of the media on India's public discourse has never been

so instant and its reach so pervasive, but many ask whether that impact is for good or ill.[2]

The state of the media is inextricably intertwined with the larger story of India and it is important to frame it by answering four key questions: what does the Indian media industry actually look like? How does its trajectory compare with that of media in other liberal democratic countries? Where is it going? And why should the media matter to every Indian? As the republic completes seventy years, these questions frame the five big challenges facing India's media industry:

World-famous, but Only in India

It is easy to get drunk with numbers about the Indian media industry. At a time when print newspaper circulations are rapidly shrinking in every major global media market, India, along with China, remains a global outlier for newspapers. It has the highest number of newspapers in circulation in the world;[3] produces the largest number of films each year; boasts of the second largest number of TV viewers at 780 million[4] and 476 million digital consumers. The numbers are not surprising, given our population.

However, it is striking that in global terms, India's media is not that big an industry. It was worth about USD 19.6 billion in 2016 with an annual growth of 9 per cent, which is barely a quarter of Google (USD 89.5 in revenues in 2016), a nineteen-year-old company, younger than most of India's TV channels.[5] As Star TV chairman and CEO, Uday Shankar, has pointed out: 'If the entire Indian media was a company, it would rank seventh or eighth in India. Media is a globally growing industry but our participation in that ecosystem is zero and India is hardly factored into the global thought process of technology or content.'[6] Indeed, Hollywood or the global TV market is not keen on developing India-specific products, which is not the case for China, or the United States. This is because, in global terms, India's media and the entertainment market are still not meaningful in monetary value. While this is slowly changing, India's media industry is world-famous, but only in the country.

Media Has Converged but Still Bound by Licence-Permit Raj Legacies

It is increasingly irrelevant to talk about print or television or digital or telecom companies as separate businesses in a world of digital convergence. Yet, regulatory constraints ensure the business models and politics of individual Indian media sub-sectors are still circumscribed by legacies of the licence-permit raj.

India remains the only major liberal democracy where private radio channels cannot broadcast their own news. The government of India, between October–December 2016, finished phase 3 of the auction for radio frequencies nationwide, where 266 frequencies were offered in ninety-two cities.[7] Yet, radio channels can only relay news that the All India Radio produces because of an old colonial straitjacket that saw radio news as being too volatile a medium to be allowed to go private.

In a country where retail prices of essential commodities are not controlled, and even diesel prices are being de-regulated, prices of TV channels (except HD channels) are regulated by the government. Until the eighties, the state didn't really invest in television, arguing that broadcasting was a luxury of the affluent that could wait till grandiose plans for economic progress bore fruit. The explosion of private broadcasting in the last twenty years transformed its status in governmental eyes from a bourgeois luxury into a *hoi polloi* essential, whose prices needed to be controlled.

In an effort to ensure that television prices didn't shoot through the roof, the Telecom Regulatory Authority of India (TRAI) ruled in 2006 that no individual pay channel could be priced at more than Rs 5.35 per month for consumers.[8] At first glance, this appears a sensible and consumer-friendly policy, but it is one which, in reality, has seriously distorted the economics of Indian television. This is because good content costs money. The price ceiling disincentivizes investments as channels know they can't recover costs from subscribers. Thus, channels only invest in programmes attracting advertising and remain hooked to the daily roulette of the ratings game with its vicious cycle of programming, appealing only to the lowest common denominator.

A network like HBO in the US is worth comparing. Emphasizing thoughtful, nuanced programming, HBO eschews advertising and is funded purely by the subscriptions of nearly 30 million customers. It has significantly fewer customers than its competitors, but due to secure and predictable income from the latter, it spends more on the quality of its programming. The first season of 'Games of Thrones' cost between USD 50–60 million to produce,[9] which is more than the entire annual programming budget of most major Indian networks.

If prices were decontrolled, would watching television be unaffordable for most Indians? Absolutely not. In a country with the world's largest terrestrial public broadcaster, this is a moot question. Doordarshan runs more than thirty free channels in two dozen different languages with a free DTH service. The state spends about Rs 3500 crores annually on public broadcasting services.[10] This is excluding channels run and financed separately by the Indian Parliament—Lok Sabha TV and Rajya Sabha TV. For high-cost programming like cricket, there is already a law in place to ensure that all private channels share their broadcasts free of cost with Doordarshan in the national interest.

The price cap actually distorts the market, artificially controlling ebbs and flows rather than protecting the viewer. It is a legacy of the fact that unlike print, which was already a vibrant industry in 1947, TV and radio were controlled by the state until the early nineties. TV came to India by accident in 1959, when the electronic giant Phillips left behind some television equipment as a gift after an exhibition in Delhi. India had only sixty-seven TV sets when Nehru died in 1964 and TV became a mass medium only in the eighties before the satellite boom of the nineties brought down the state monopoly on broadcasting.

Table 4: Estimated TV Sets in India: 1964–2016

Year	TV Sets in India
1964	67
1979	6,00,000
1982	20,00,000
1992	34,800,000
2000	84,000,000
2012	148,000,000
2016	183,000,000

Source: Nalin Mehta, *India on Television: How Satellite News Channels Changed the Way We Think and Act*. (New Delhi: HarperCollins, 2008), p. 43; Nalin Mehta, *Behind a Billion Screens: What Television Tells Us About Modern India* (New Delhi: HarperCollins, 2014), and BARC, 2017.

India today is the world's second largest TV market after China. While forces of globalization and liberalization since the 1991 economic reforms have changed the contours of the media industry, control mindset continues to bind the sector in subtle ways.

No Curbs on Political Ownership

India remains the only major liberal democracy where politicians and political parties can own traditional media platforms. For example, major investments in news television since the early-2000s have been from politicians, real estate, chit fund and money market companies and large corporations. This pervasive trend has led to these categories of owners having deep stakes in the majority of the news TV business in most Indian states. Such companies make up over 80 per cent of the news TV business in Andhra Pradesh, Karnataka and Odisha, between 60 and 70 per cent in Punjab, Maharashtra, West Bengal, Tamil Nadu and the northeast.[11] A decade ago, only a handful of states like Tamil Nadu had channels like Sun TV or Jaya TV, set up as propaganda arms of rival political parties. Now, this is the norm across India.

Politicians have as much of a right to free speech as everyone else and, in theory at least, each propaganda voice should cancel each other out. The trouble is twofold. First, it completely loads the democratic field in favour of political players with access to big under-the-table funding and crowds out less wealthy players. Second, the easy money that politicians bring into the game completely distorts the market, driving out all serious, neutral players.

One of the most under-analysed ways through which politicians control the news is by controlling cable operators. States like Chhattisgarh and Punjab have evolved their own models, where television is controlled by political parties through private TV networks, as well as cartelization of the cable industry. The practice of politicians buying into the TV business is a slippery slope. Several news channels have become conduits for black money and ill-gotten wealth. They also provide unfair advantage to their political owners and diminish the public space.

There are umpteen recommendations by the TRAI that warn against fixing the field in favour of politicians with the money to splurge; fair access in the political arena; unfair uses of state power and on grounds of equity—most recently in April 2014.[12] Several other countries already have such laws in place mandating strict limits against political ownership of commercial media outlets. India must follow suit.

Regulatory Twilight Zone

Information and Broadcasting ministers of recent years have suggested abolition of their ministry.[13] Notwithstanding political differences and ultimate intent, these comments by successive ministers point to the nature of the ongoing debate over the role of the state in sectors opened up after liberalization; the deep regulatory crisis affecting many of these; and the implications for governance.

In the early-nineties when first faced with the challenge of independent private television, the guardians of the state initially buried their heads in the sand, and then, in time-honoured fashion, blamed the proverbial foreign hand. The developments were described by an erstwhile I&B minister as 'diabolical invasion from the sky',[14] while another wondered 'Are we going to succumb as we did 250 years ago to gunpowder'.[15] Different arms of the government took different views—some for opening up, some against—and then, as with most things that politicians are unable to decide on in India, the Supreme Court came to the rescue, liberating airwaves from government control, giving legal sanctity to a private TV revolution and asking the Centre to create a new autonomous public authority to control and regulate the new reality. That was in 1995. Over two decades later, India is still waiting for such a law.

Members of Parliament did unite thrice—in 1995, 2002 and 2011—to pass or amend laws to govern specific aspects of the industry, on distribution and cable operators. They also united, expectedly, on a life-and-death matter: the right of the Indian people to watch cricket. A law was passed to ensure that Doordarshan could, in the 'national interest', telecast every international cricket game played in India without paying a single paisa for it. Yet, every attempt to create a new law encompassing the wider superstructure of the new reality of Indian television has failed (Table 5). Almost every I&B minister since 1995 has tried to put the genie of private TV back into the bottle. Every minister has stumbled.

Table 5: No Overarching Law—The Fate of Regulation

Sr. No.	Legislation/ Guideline	Problem/Status	Reason/Resolution
1	Cable Networks (Regulation) Act, 1995	Largely focused on distribution	Broadcasters based overseas and difficult to control
2	Broadcasting Bill, 1997	Introduced in Parliament but lapsed	Collapse of United Front government
3	Communications Convergence Bill, 2001	Lapsed	Collapse of thirteenth Lok Sabha

4	Cable Networks (Regulation) Amendment Act, 2003	Withdrawn in 2004, being introduced in three metros after court order	Political agitation by cable operators supported by the Delhi BJP
5	News Channel Uplinking Guidelines, 2004	Changed repeatedly	Pressure by TV networks
6	Broadcasting Services Regulation Bill, 2006	Draconian powers of news networks. Plans to introduce in Parliament for fresh consultation	Public and media outcry. Pressure by broadcasters
7	The Sports Broadcasting Signals (Mandatory Sharing with Prasar Bharti) Act, 2007	Legislated to ensure telecast of cricket matches on state network	Cricket nationalism
8	Cable Television Networks (Regulation) Second Amendment Bill, December 2011	Legislated to fast-track digitization	Supported by major industry players. Will increase subscription revenues

Source: Adapted from Nalin Mehta, *India on Television: How Satellite News Channels Changed the Ways We Think and Act.* New Delhi: HarperCollins, 2008, p. 120.

Each time a minister sought to bring in a big-picture law to regulate the new broadcasting realities in their entirety, their impulses were draconian, threatening to severely clip freedoms private networks had so assiduously carved for themselves. The last such draft of a law in 2007, for example, would have made it illegal for private channels to do live interviews with anyone in India without prior permission from a bureaucrat.

The incomplete transition of the controlling superstructure has translated into wide areas of legal uncertainty on broadcasting. It has meant severe infighting for control between overlapping arms of the state, resistance by new economic actors and the judiciary and the state governments taking on interventionist roles as arbiters in periodic crises over broadcasting. In practice, this has meant low predictability on the goalposts of the playing-field. It translated into governance by administrative notifications based on the whims and fancies of incumbent bureaucrats in control and an even larger role for the courts. Almost every order is legally disputed and quite often reversed or modified by the courts.

In all major liberal democracies, a single regulator runs all aspects of broadcasting. In India, the problem has been that even though TRAI was to create a level playing field for the new economy, the information and broadcasting ministry, which was the custodian of television in the days of socialist monopoly, never fully transferred its ownership. The old one remained with the new regulator, building tensions in the system and ensuring they remained in the fight for control. As a former TRAI chairman points out:

> The regulator there [in other countries] is in a way a single regulator . . . In India there have always been two regulators: one is the department and ministry and the other is TRAI because some functions are still with the Ministry of Information and Broadcasting and Department of Telecom. After all, DoT issues licences and manages spectrum, the Information and Broadcasting Ministry is responsible for the issue of licence of the DTH . . .
>
> We had a regulator earlier, which was regulating monopoly, then you got a new regulator to create a level playing field but the original regulator remained. So the ownership never got fully transferred. The endowment was not made, ownership was not transferred. So there is always a limited role for TRAI when compared to the FCC [in the USA] or [the UK's] OfCom.[16]

In the overlapping haze of regulation that is broadcasting, as many as ten different government institutions are legally empowered to issue directions on broadcasting: the I&B ministry as policymaker and final arbiter of content oversight, TRAI as a regulator of technical issues like carriage and pricing, the Telecom Disputes Settlement and Appellate Tribunal for appeals against decisions, the Ministry of Communications for licencing, transmission equipment, satellites, Internet protocol TV, and district-level committees that can monitor and censor 'certain programmes in the national interest'.[17]

Even the humble neighbourhood post office is involved in the regulations. All that is required to start a cable network is to fill a hundred-rupee form and register at a post office. There is no centralized system to track licenced cable operators and post offices are not even mandated to keep any record of renewals.

> How many got renewed, how many did not get renewed. No one knows. So you have a huge chunk of cable operators spread all over in the districts . . . also having a lot of political local interest for their business expansion. Most of them had some kind of an invisible hand who was taking care of all sorts of activities with muscle power.[18]

Digital Will Drive Media but Its Business Model Is Still Emerging

With the number of Internet-enabled mobile phones crossing 300 million in India, data costs spiralling downward after the entry of Reliance Jio, and the ubiquity of personal devices, everyone agrees that the future of the Indian media lies in the mobile and digital space.

The 2017 IPL auction for five-year broadcast and digital rights for 2018–22, which was won by Star India at a whopping Rs 16,347.5 crore (Rs 54 crore per match), illustrated how the media game is changing. 'For the first time in this country we are seeing a phenomenon where—for a media property—media, telecom and global technology and social media companies were bidding. A few other global e-commerce companies also examined it very closely. The competition was so diverse that it is anybody's guess at what prices these things will go.'

In 2014, Hotstar bought IPL digital rights for roughly Rs 300 crore. In 2017, for five-year digital rights, Facebook was willing to pay Rs 3,900 crore. 'Look at the multiples of growth. These companies have very different ways of looking at the commercial value of rights. It's a totally different mix now. The media is being buffeted by different forces.'[19]

While the future is mobile and bandwidth may be the new oil, the challenge is that viable business models are still emerging. Technology and social change has disrupted the old media. Yet, it is still an open question on how to make good money sustainably from the new media.

What companies from e-commerce to media are doing currently is to invest essentially for the long run, by throwing money to build audiences in the hope that one day these communities will be monetized. Even as the new media has created a personal revolution of sorts where everybody can now be a content creator, it has also created an uncertain landscape, where aggregators and platforms like Google and Facebook are positioned to have the bulk of revenues. Ultimately, profitability is crucial for making sustainable good content and as India's media companies change shape to digital-first models, the big question they all face is simple: how to make money from digital? How they answer it will reshape our information landscapes for the next decade.

XXII

New India Needs a New Model for Skill Development

Pawan Agarwal

India's large young population presents it a unique opportunity to become 'the human capital of the world'. The challenge, however, is to utilize the high proportion of young Indians, particularly the educated that are unemployed or underemployed. This is regardless of industry and businesses reportedly facing shortages of trained workers.

To address this paradox, the country's education and training system must develop and align with both domestic and overseas demand for qualified people. Vocational education and training (VET) and skill development (SD) should be central to India's development strategy. Developing a robust skill development ecosystem would better integrate education with the labour markets and act as an insurance against poverty.

This essay reviews the current scenario, making a case for a new approach and strategy to build a robust ecosystem for skill development for 'New India'. It then lays down the key elements of a new model and institutional arrangements required for skilling in India. It also takes a holistic view of the country's formal education and training system in order to build a synergy between the two.

Current Status

The formal VET system in India is small and underdeveloped. Merely 5.4 per cent of the country's existing workforce has formal vocational training compared to 68 per cent in the UK, 75 per cent in Germany, 80 per cent in Japan and 96 per cent in South Korea.[1] This does not include skill acquisition through informal channels, which is quite significant. In the formal sector, there is some vocational stream in schools, vocational training in Industrial Training Institutes (ITIs) for workmen, in polytechnics for skilling a supervisory workforce, and professional education as a part of the country's higher education system.

Skill Acquisition through Informal Channels

In India, skills are often 'inherited' and passed on from generation to generation, enabling individuals to carry on ancestral trade or occupations such as carpentry, plumbing, etc. Alternatively, some marketable expertise or skills are also acquired through apprenticeship to an ustad or skilled craftsman, enabling the individual to enter the large informal sector. Usually, skill acquisition takes place through informal channels with little or no emphasis on general or academic skills. Such people are mostly self-employed or are in low-paying jobs with little prospect of economic advancement. The formal sector, which is often better paying, requires skilled people with not only vocational but also at least basic academic skills.

VET at School Level

Vocational education at school level is small in India. There have been attempts to introduce the vocational stream over the past few decades, but these have failed to make much of an impact. Currently, only 6120 against 250,000 senior/senior secondary schools in the country offer vocational courses.[2] These together enrol less than 1 per cent of the students at the 10+2 level compared to over 50 per cent in

China and 55 per cent in Japan. In addition, about 13,350 ITIs offer vocational courses after Class X (a few courses are after Class VIII and Class XII) in various trades. Total intake in such courses is about 1.4 million, which is less than one-tenth of the students passing out of Class X.[3] Courses offered by the ITIs are not entirely aligned with the job opportunities available. A large majority of enrolment in ITIs is in the manufacturing trades that account for nearly two-thirds of all courses, while there are more job opportunities in the services sector. Further, the quality of vocational education and training provided both in the schools and ITIs is of poor quality, which is a major issue.

Vocational/Professional Education in Higher Education

After Class XII, students join universities and colleges for bachelors' degrees. There are 800 universities and 39,000 colleges enrolling about 34.6 million students in the country. Two-thirds of these students pursue general or academic education. The remaining ones are professional courses, largely confined to engineering and education. In addition, about 12,000 stand-alone institutions outside the university system offer two-year diploma courses.[4] These include polytechnics for engineering, nursing institutes and institutes for teacher education. Overall, higher education is skewed in favour of general or academic courses and vocational/professional studies are confined to some fields, such as engineering, IT and medical education, with fewer options in other fields. The quality of professional courses and mobility between degree and diploma courses are concerns. Certificate and diploma courses in polytechnics are often dead-end courses with no scope for further upward mobility and hence these are considered inferior qualifications.

Other Modes of Vocational Education and Skill Development

Apprenticeship training and short-term skilling are other major modes of vocational training and skill development in India.

Apprenticeship, the preferred VET model globally, is grossly underdeveloped. Currently there are just about 300,000 apprentices in the country[5] compared with more than 20 million in China. Recent reforms that provide for increased flexibility, enhanced compliance and higher stipends for apprentices are likely to increase the numbers. But far more coordinated efforts are needed to scale up apprenticeship significantly.

Recognizing the growing importance of skill development, Central and state governments have begun a plethora of skill development initiatives. Skilling courses range from a few weeks to a few months across many trades. The entire funding for such skilling comes from the government. Many private companies have emerged to deliver these training courses.

With a view to boost private initiatives in the training sector, the National Skill Development Corporation (NSDC) was set up in 2009. NSDC provides soft loans (and in some cases grants) for the purpose. It has also incubated setting up of industry-led Sector Skill Councils (SSCs) for creating national occupational standards (NOSs) and qualifications by job roles in various sectors. So far, forty SSCs have been established. A National Skill Qualification Framework (NSQF) to facilitate mobility across skill levels is also in place.[6] There have been efforts to consolidate the highly fragmented short-skilling space after the formation of a separate Ministry of Skill Development and Entrepreneurship in 2014.

Recent developments address some of the institutional issues but are mainly confined to short-term skilling. These have not had much impact on either the legacy VET system or on the formal education and training. VET reforms require a comprehensive approach and strategy that view it in conjunction with the formal education sector.

New Approach and Strategy

VET in the country is highly fragmented and underdeveloped and faces multiple challenges. In India, less than 10 per cent in the higher secondary classes (fifteen–sixteen years' age group) pursue vocational education. At the undergraduate level in higher education, about 30 per cent of students pursue a vocational/professional stream. The remaining students pursue academic education. This is very low compared with advanced and industrialized countries, where often three-fourths of all young people pursue vocational/professional or skill-oriented education and training in all age groups. Apart from the size of the VET sector, multiplicity in names of institutions is confusing and distorts public choice. There is also a mindset issue where VET is taken as an 'inferior' qualification. Thus, this sector requires a new strategy and approach. Five areas (summarized below) require attention:

1) **Capacity and public spending**—Consistent with India's demographic, economic profile and high growth performance, the VET sector has to grow rapidly. While the private sector dynamism could be leveraged, much of the investment must come from the government as VET often caters to the poorest and the most disadvantaged people. India spends less than one-tenth of its overall education spending on VET. But in many countries VET takes the lion's share, often exceeding 60 per cent of the overall public spending. There is also the opportunity to use idle capacity or overcapacity of the formal sector, for instance, engineering colleges for VET courses.

2) **Curricula, pedagogy, assessment and certification**—For the VET sector, curricula, pedagogy and assessment require an approach different from the academic stream. It is more practice-oriented and aligned with job roles, making a strong industry-connect a 'must' for this sector. The teaching-learning methodology should involve less lecturing, note-taking, and more hands-on activities to allow for experiential and interactive learning. Industry-led SSCs that provide the basic building block for curricula, pedagogy and assessment now address this issue to some extent, but more and better alignment is needed, particularly in the context of the old legacy system and formal education.

Apprenticeship fosters practical intelligence and enables better orientation for employability, compared to a single-track education system that leads to more youth dropping off the mainstream. Assessment and certification should not only establish equivalence between general and vocational education, but also provide for recognition of prior learning (RPL). This is particularly important for India since many people acquire skills informally. Finally, a unified qualification and credit framework is required to establish seamless link, between the VET sector and general education.

3) **Professional development and cadre of VET teachers—** There is a large gap in the demand and supply of trained vocational teachers. Currently, there is limited capacity for their training and professional development. In the absence of a separate cadre and limited career progression, the VET sector has failed to attract talented faculty. Systems and practices of hiring experienced practitioners and industry professionals should be streamlined in this respect and require a huge effort.

4) **Institutional framework—**Various types of VET institutions have little coordination among themselves. These have developed independent of each other. For instance, general education in schools and vocational training in ITIs are separated. So are vocational/professional training in polytechnics and stand-alone institutions vis-a-vis professional/technical education in universities and colleges. These are organized in silos with each having their own institutional arrangements for setting curricula, assessment and examination, teacher education, funding, regulation and governance. Thus, the institutional arrangements need to be rapidly overhauled.[7]

5) **Demand and cultural shift—**There is a preference and attraction for white-collar jobs and an aversion to working with one's in India. Thus, not surprisingly, general or academic education is preferred over the vocational option, resulting in lack of demand for VET education. Issues of societal perception

and attitudinal bias are complex and do not have easy solutions. However, the fact that VET graduates find jobs or become self-employed more easily as compared with others is changing public attitudes towards this sector and contributing towards its credibility. Further demand for professional/skill certification can be generated by making provision for the same in the recruitment rules for public sector employment and conditions of contract for public works. Regulatory bodies can also make skill training and certification mandatory to not only create demand for qualified people but also to raise productivity and economic performance. The private sector can play a supporting role in this regard.

A New Model

The desired model framework for skill development through vocational education should provide opportunities for truly academically minded students to pursue education in mainstream academics while allowing others to be educated in applied streams, vocational and professional areas as per their choice. VET should be fully integrated with education at all four levels, cover apprenticeship and continuing education and training (CET) through short-term skilling courses. The larger move should be towards a unified National Qualification and Credit Framework (NQCF) to cover both general and vocational/professional education.

Level One—Integration in Primary School

The importance of working with one's hands and the dignity of labour and manual work should be emphasized from Class VII onwards. This, following Mahatma Gandhi, is morally, educationally and socially appropriate. Such an emphasis will reduce the traditional Indian middle-class aversion to manual work and blue-collar employment. Soft skills and hands-on training should be part of the curricula for all elementary classes.

Level Two—Academic and Applied Streams in Secondary School

A scientifically designed aptitude test should measure cognitive skills for entry to Class IX and students could be split into academic and applied streams. Those with higher analytical abilities and capacity to think in abstract terms could go for the academic stream, while others should be admitted to the applied stream.

In classes IX and X, all subjects as per current practice should be taught but with different levels of sophistication. For instance, instruction in mathematics could be more abstract in academic stream, while in the applied stream, students can be exposed to illustrations of mathematical principles and the subject could be directly related to the use of mathematics in day-to-day life. There should be easy mobility from the applied to the academic stream. This would remove the stigma usually attached to the applied stream. There could be three categories of schools for classes IX and X: schools offering only the academic stream, those offering only the applied stream and hybrid schools offering both. Over time, enrolments in the applied stream should be at least half of overall enrolments.

Level Three—Professional Higher Secondary Schools

Another aptitude test after Class X should select students on their abilities beyond specific subjects or even linguistic and logical mathematical skills that standard IQ tests entail. These abilities should include musical intelligence, spatial intelligence, bodily kinaesthetic intelligence, interpersonal intelligence, intrapersonal intelligence and natural intelligence as key expressions of human ability that are relevant in a wide variety of professions. This test could be open to students from both academic and applied streams.

Most of the professional schools would be the normal schools of today. With some incremental investment, they can become professional schools. Such schools should provide students with skill sets for jobs or self-employment instead of an aimless pursuit of academic education. Professional schools could offer courses in agriculture and allied sector manufacturing and construction sectors and a wide variety of service-sector jobs.

ITIs could be re-branded as professional schools. As professional schools, ITI-curricula would include vocational skills as well as elements of general education, particularly languages, applied mathematics and soft skills. Some courses offered after classes VIII and XII should be discontinued so that entry to ITIs is uniform after Class X with a two-year duration of the course.

Level Four—Higher Professional Education

After higher secondary, students would transfer to two-year associate degree or three- or four-year bachelors' degree programmes, offered in professional colleges or general colleges. The duration of these programmes may vary by profession and job roles and entry could be based on national level college-entry tests. Two-year associate degree programmes could be offered in the 12,000 existing stand-alone institutions. Further, about 19,000 to 20,000 colleges (half of the total 39,000 degree colleges) offer three- or four-year programmes in various professional areas and 400 (half of the total 800 universities) offer exclusively professional programmes. All these professional universities are similar to the universities of applied sciences in other countries and higher professional education could come under their purview.

Professional universities or skill universities could be at the apex of professional education offering masters and doctorate programmes in various disciplines. Likewise, general universities that are either unitary or multi-disciplinary could be at the apex of general higher education.

Apprenticeship

Apprenticeship should be tightly integrated with professional education at level three and four. There could be two possible variants of this. In the first variant, students would work for four days in a week, followed by an academic course for one day, while in the other, students could study full-time for a year and a half and then follow up with six months of apprenticeship in a company/organization in a related field. The German model of dual education adopts the first variant and is the preferred model and should be encouraged. Larger focus on practice-oriented education, followed by a brief academic curriculum in short cycles has been found to support skills formation better.

Short-Term Skill Training

Short-term skilling courses would continue to be relevant and important. Such courses would be required for the young people dropping out of schools or leaving the system without any specific skillsets, and for Continuing Education and Training (CET) of those already in the workforce.

It would be preferable to study in small interrelated modules so that there is modular and credit accumulation that provides pathways into formal education and training systems. Short-term skilling opportunities should be locally available. Initiatives need to be taken so that skilling centres of good quality are available in all towns with a population of 10,000 or more throughout the country. Such courses should be fully or substantially funded by the government since they target the most disadvantaged sections of society.

National Qualification and Credit Framework (NQCF)

Finally, for easy mobility across the academic and applied (or vocational/professional) streams, there should be a National Qualification and Credit Framework (NQCF). It should cover both streams and ensure pathways either directly or with bridge courses for students throughout their educational career. Such a framework would provide guidelines for learning outcomes, pathways, assessment and accreditation of qualifications, allowing students to move easily between levels of study and institutions, receiving full credit for previous study. Both streams should be self-sufficient but mutually diaphanous and acknowledged as 'equivalent however different'.

Communication skills, grooming and personality development should be a necessary part of all education, right from primary to higher professional education. Entrepreneurship education and training should be expanded through schools, colleges and training institutions and in industry clusters to foster job creation.

New Institutional Arrangements

With major changes in the nature of work and rapid technological advances, boundaries between vocational and general education, professional and higher education, conventional and distance or online education have blurred. A new VET model and institutional arrangements should reflect this reality. A large number of bodies, often with overlapping mandates, have emerged both at the national and state levels. There is a need to merge several of them and redefine the mandates of others to achieve effective functional convergence of efforts and have an integrated approach to education and training in the country. New and legacy structures have to be integrated to achieve coherence and effectiveness.

In the VET sector, industry-driven SSCs could play a pivotal role. These should be strengthened to provide inputs on available jobs in each sector. SSCs could develop broad curriculum frameworks and assessment protocols for various job roles. Short-term skilling and professional education in schools and colleges should follow these guidelines and protocols. SSCs could play key roles in mentorship for entrepreneurship.

While a single school up to Class X for both academic and applied streams can continue, for higher secondary, there could be either a single school board with two separate wings or two separate boards for professional and general education. Once ITIs are reclassified as professional schools, state councils for vocational training would not be needed. These could be responsible for short-term skilling courses and renamed as state boards for skill development. A relook at the structure and functions of the National Skill Development Agency (NSDA), the National Council for Vocational Training (NCVT) and the National Skill Development Corporation (NSDC) is required. Further, both formal education and VET should be brought under a single ministry.

Higher professional education in colleges could be regulated by professional universities, which could continue to be under the oversight of a national regulator. The mandate of 'All India Council of Technical Education' (AICTE) that covers engineering education, management education, hotel management, pharmacy, architecture and applied arts can be broadened to include all professional education areas after Class XII. AICTE can be renamed 'All India Council for Professional Education' (AICPE) and the body can provide national protocols and standards for coordination across professional universities and colleges. AICPE should work closely with the SSCs.

Regional Directorates of Apprenticeship Training (RDATs) that handle trade apprentices and Boards of Apprenticeship Training (BOATs) responsible for graduate, technician and technician (vocational) apprentices could be merged to achieve better outreach and outcomes and a seamless interface with industry. SSCs could also be involved to increase the outreach.

Summary and Conclusions

A new India requires a new model for skill development with a holistic view of formal education and the VET sector. The latter in India is highly fragmented and underdeveloped. It faces multiple challenges and requires a new strategy and approach. The sector itself has to be scaled rapidly, for which much larger public funding is needed. Improved and fit-for-purpose curricula, better pedagogy and appropriate assessment methods along with robust industry-interface are essential. A large pool of high-quality VET teachers and instructors and ability to attract talent for the same is necessary.

XXIII

Corporate Governance in India: A Giant Leap in the Last Five Years

U.K. Sinha

Globally, the formulation of corporate governance norms and principles, their codification and strict enforcement under laws administered by the governments or regulators, does not have a long history. Developments like active lead by institutional investors, proxy firms or whistleblowers evolved even later. The realization of the importance of corporate governance came about as the role of corporations in the day-to-day life of large sections of population grew—either by their size and the impact they had on the larger economy, or by the way savings of households invested directly or indirectly in these corporations, or how millions of workers are engaged there. Corporate governance as a means to ensure business integrity and to create market confidence became more and more important since the mid-nineties—when global instances of fraud, malfeasance and lack of risk control became increasingly harmful. The Organization for Economic Co-operation and Development (OECD) came out with its first set of corporate governance principles in 1999; these were subsequently revised in 2004 and 2015. In 2002, the US enacted the Sarbanes-Oxley Act.[1]

The Case at Home

In Asia, in general, and in India in particular, the situation was also compounded by the fact that compared to the rest of the world, the holding of the dominant shareholder has been historically very high. In India, ten years ago the promoter shareholding was close to 60 per cent, which has come down to 50 per cent only recently. The temptation to treat the listed company as an extension of their family business so far as transparency or accountability is concerned was very strong.

Another factor in India, which gave the business promoters and the managements appointed by them high operational freedom was the fact that the political leadership of the newly independent country wanted rapid industrialization. In their anxiety to facilitate economic growth, they did not want to encourage monopolies or consolidation. The government felt it a duty to support the existing management lest the companies were destabilized or acquired by foreigners. For instance, institutional investors like the Life Insurance Corporation of India, the General Insurance Corporation of India or the Unit Trust of India were all government-owned or controlled and the underlying philosophy was not to question or destabilize them as long as the dividends and economic benefits accruing from these corporations were according to government expectations.

Besides, the Companies Act of 1956 regulated the affairs of Indian corporations, which concerned itself more with the procedures of running a corporation, issue of shares, dividends and schemes of arrangements. In the jurisprudence of the fifties, specific focus on corporate governance had little space. Post 1991, the financial sector reforms in India concentrated first on modernizing the trading system, developing world-class exchanges and settlement systems. Reforms in the primary market leading to disclosure-based free pricing, opening up the market for foreign portfolio investors and measures to usher in a competitive domestic funds industry followed.

By early 2000, the realization came that focus on internal governance of corporations, preventing abuse of dominance, public disclosures and dissemination of their affairs to the world at large in a transparent manner can be a very powerful tool to protect the interests of shareholders and help in generating trust in the market and its superintendence. A committee under the chairmanship of industrialist Kumar Mangalam Birla recommended important improvements, which were incorporated by the Securities and Exchange Board of India (SEBI) in 2000 through the mechanism of new provisions in the listing agreement between the stock exchanges and the listed companies. This effort was strengthened by taking a close look at the existing regulatory environment and the emerging challenges and revising the listing agreement based on the recommendations of the committee of N.R. Narayana Murthy—former chairman of the IT company Infosys.[2]

Efforts Since 2012

Minimum Public Holding, i.e. protection of small shareholders by preventing manipulation and fraudulent practices, requires that the shares under the free float, the proportion of stocks being traded in the market, for buying and selling, are large in number. Indian companies have comparatively large holdings by dominant shareholders. There were examples where the free float was even less than 10 per cent. One of the early measures taken was to change this situation. In 2012, SEBI insisted that all listed companies must reach the goal of Minimum Public Shareholding of 25 per cent within a year. The scheme was seriously monitored and implemented. Even state-owned enterprises were not spared, although they were given a longer compliance time period. Companies that failed to meet the deadline were promptly penalized giving a clear signal to the outside world about minority protection. Earlier, SEBI came out with a revised takeover code. One of the important provisions was to discontinue the earlier practice of paying a non-compete fee[3] to the selling shareholder. This ensured that the minority shareholder got the best price and there was no discrimination in favour of the selling shareholder.

SEBI came out with a consultation paper in 2013—Consultation Paper on Corporate Governance—that proposed the strengthening of the governance framework.[4] The proposals recommended an expansion in the role of the audit committee, a compulsory whistle-blower mechanism, prohibition of stock options to independent directors, performance evaluation of all directors and at least one woman director on the board of the company.

The Companies Act of 1956 was replaced by the Companies Act of 2013, which had for the first time specific provisions on corporate governance. The legislation drew heavily from the Consultation Paper of SEBI, mandating many of the provisions even for companies that are not listed on the stock exchanges. Specific provisions were made regarding the eligibility, role and functions of independent directors, specific procedures for dealing with related party transactions and providing a 'say' to minority shareholders, mandatory constitution of committees and other provisions for transparency and accountability, including a provision for performance evaluation of independent directors. Provisions for e-voting for shareholders' meeting have since been made mandatory.

SEBI's New Corporate Governance Norms

Laws in India mandate that while the criteria provided in the Companies Act are applicable to all, SEBI is free to treat these as minimum applicable provisions and can impose additional conditions for listed companies. From October 2014, SEBI introduced a number of additional requirements for listed companies.

Some of these criteria are:

Independent directors

- An independent director who has already served for a period of five years or more shall be eligible for reappointment for one more term only.

- The maximum number of companies in which a person can serve as an independent director has been restricted to seven (instead of ten as per the Companies Act).

Related Party Transactions (RPTs)

- A wider and more comprehensive definition with elements of Companies Act, 2013 and (Ind AS) 24.
- All RPTs shall require prior approval of the audit committee.
- Specific criterion provided for recognition of material RPTs:

    o 20 per cent of net worth.
    o 5 per cent of annual turnover.

- The companies shall prepare and disclose RPT policy in the annual report.

Others

- The principles of corporate governance have been laid down in the listing agreement, broadly based on OCED principles of corporate governance.
- Companies have been mandated to provide suitable training to independent directors and the details of such training imparted shall be disclosed in the annual report.
- Internal auditor to report to audit committee as a non-mandatory good governance practice.
- The board has to satisfy itself about the existence of a succession plan.
- The evaluation criteria of independent directors shall be laid down and disclosed in the annual report.

Finally, in order to strengthen enforceability of these provisions SEBI moved the corporate governance norms from the listing agreement to a new regulation—the Listing Obligations and Disclosure Requirements Regulation, 2015. Besides, stock exchanges have been empowered to regularly review and analyse the mandatory and time-bound disclosure by companies and take penal action. Delegating powers to exchanges to monitor corporate governance compliance and to penalize the corporations have been extremely successful.

Global Developments and Demand Side Interventions

In social and political life across the world, perceptible movements towards challenging authority, asserting individuals' rights, mass action, spontaneous reactions and wider protests are being noticed over the last decade. Regimes are being challenged, continuous and comprehensive evaluations are being demanded, authorities are being recalled before time, and the concept of fixity of tenure in institutional positions is being challenged successfully. From Turkey to Cairo, from Mexico to Brazil, small incidents, such as construction in a park or a rise in bus fare, is able to mobilize hundreds of thousands of people on the streets. It is also true that many in the crowd are not unemployed youth but decently employed/self-employed, well-educated persons who are indignant at their voices not being heard. Technology, of course, is helping generate a stronger momentum.

It stands to reason that if such sentiments are increasingly being demonstrated in political and social life then the same would also drive behaviour in dealing with authorities in charge of running corporations—where these 'ordinary' people have placed their hard-earned money. Therefore, it is hardly surprising that small stakeholders are challenging decisions by corporate boards. Even a hint of suspicion of conflict of interest or wrongdoing on the part of the companies is able to evoke strong reactions from shareholders. Shareholder activism is on the rise. Between 2014 and 2015 almost one-fourth of CEOs of Fortune 500 companies who were removed pre-maturely were due to shareholders' demand. Compensation and bonuses to CEOs are increasingly being questioned and in many cases, even national political leaderships have awakened to this disquiet amongst the shareholders. This is reflected in the British Prime Minister Theresa May's disapproval of the widening gap in the pay ratios of top executives and those of younger employees. Lack of gender diversity is another area attracting serious scrutiny.

Sensing these developments across the world, SEBI came out with a policy asking institutional investors to have voting policies, publish the policies on their websites and publicly disseminate their voting histories. The requirements began with mutual funds; pension funds and insurance companies followed suit. It is noticeable that even schemes of arrangements are being questioned by the institutional investors, who are often coming together before voting in order to take common stands that might reflect their disgruntlement. These demand side interventions have not only forced rethinking among corporate boards and managements, but have also generated a wider public debate.

Proxy Advisory Firms

Proxy advisers provide advice and analysis to institutional investors and other clients on the shareholder proposals brought to vote at Annual General Meetings (AGMs). They also execute votes in accordance with the instructions of their clients and engage in record keeping, and enabling a platform for voting. In addition, they provide recommendations on public offers. Further, proxy advisers provide consulting services to corporate clients on issues related to corporate governance, conduct corporate governance research and develop scores on corporate governance. Over the last five years, these firms have gained momentum and multiplied in numbers. SEBI regulations seek to provide that such analytical services and recommendations/advices are unbiased, independent, objective, and there is no conflict with other activities. Proxy advisers are to be registered and regulated under SEBI (Research analyst) Regulations, 2014. All the provisions of SEBI (Research analyst) Regulations, 2014, such as qualification and certification, capital adequacy, management of conflicts of interest and disclosure requirements, maintenance of records, code of conduct etc., also apply to the proxy advisers. SEBI has also placed certain restrictions on the conduct of experts who express their opinion in the media. The idea is to ensure disclosure and to avoid conflict of interest.

It is not surprising that the efforts taken by India have received universal recognition. The World Bank Report on ease of doing business has a component on minority investors' protection, where India's ranking jumped up from forty-nine in 2012 to thirty-four in 2013 and seven in 2014. In the latest report of the World Bank released in October 2017, India's ranking has further gone up to four.[5] This particular criterion in the World Bank ranking includes extent of shareholder governance and transparency, extent of director liability, extent of shareholder rights and extent of disclosure.

Emerging Trends and New Challenges

With governments increasingly withdrawing from commercial activities and even corporatizing traditional services like road, rail, water supply and sewage, the impact of private firms and corporations on society and environment is getting more and more substantial. Major multinational corporations have grown large, to the extent of exerting substantial influence over commercial and economic prospects all over the world. The risks arising from such influence were demonstrated by the global financial crisis that brought to light how the lack of good corporate governance and risk mitigation by companies can affect the lives of ordinary citizens across the world.

The emerging emphasis is now on risk mitigation, impact on environment and on the social fabric of society, and how sustainable the business model is. The fact that large institutional investors like pension funds or sovereign funds have significant holdings in the corporations they invest in has given further momentum to the demand on corporations to assess and report on parameters other than solely financial ones. The Oil Fund of Norway, which is close of USD 900 million in size and is equivalent to 1.3 per cent of all listed companies, has been forceful in its demand for close scrutiny of CEOs. It has, during the last two–three years, been successful in rejecting pay rises to many CEOs and demanded stricter accountability on performance.

The demand is also for disclosures keeping in mind not only the interests of shareholders, but all the stakeholders; workers, customers and society. Integrated reporting has now become a movement that has gained worldwide acceptance. SEBI first mandated a business responsibility report for the top 100 companies in 2012 and extended it to the top 500 companies. Finally, in early 2017, it has mandated integrated reporting. Some Indian companies have already started IR on a voluntary basis.

In mid-2017, SEBI recently proposed further strengthening of the corporate governance framework, for which a committee was set up. The committee has submitted its report recently where the focus is on ensuring further independence of independent directors and strengthening transparency, disclosures, board evaluation and improving safeguards against related party transactions. The effort to continuously strengthen governance and accountability is on.

XXIV

Tax Policy Design and Development: The Indian Story

Pinaki Chakraborty

Tax structure and the levels of taxation differ across countries based on their economic systems, public service delivery needs and the capacity to administer taxes. The primary objectives of a tax policy are to increase revenues irrespective of the forms of government, raise revenues equitably and fairly, minimize cost of raising taxes, encourage (or discourage) a particular economic activity, group and region.[1] Calibrating tax policy in a complex federal system like India has its own challenges. This essay discusses critical dimensions of India's tax policy reforms since Independence and evaluates its progress.

Levels and Structure of Taxes in India

A long-run trend in tax to GDP ratio is presented in Figure 11. India's tax to GDP ratio is often criticized as being low. There is no denying of the fact that further increase in tax to GDP ratio is possible and is the most desirable public finance option for an emerging market economy like India. However, if we take a long-run view, India's tax to GDP ratio (taking Centre and states together) was around 6 per cent of GDP in 1950–51. As per the 2015–16 budget estimates (or BE), it is now around 17.14 per cent of GDP. As evident, the relative importance of direct taxes has increased in recent years. This is attributed to major reforms in taxation post 1991. As evident from Figure 12, the share of direct tax was as low as 16 per cent of the total tax collections in 1991. This has increased to 34 per cent in 2015–16 (BE) (Figure 12). Since almost the entire direct collection is at the Union level, the share of direct taxes in total collection of the Union taxes will be even higher. As estimated for the year 2015–16, the share of direct tax collection in total tax collection was 50.14 per cent. This progressive change in tax structure away from direct to indirect taxes were due to the reduction and rationalization of direct tax rates, simplification of the tax structure and the introduction of technology in tax administration.

Figure 11: Tax to GDP Ratio: 1951-52 to 2015–16

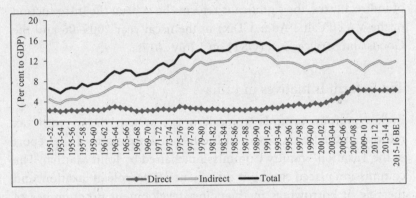

Source: Indian Public Finance Statistics, 2015–16.

Figure 12: Share of Taxes in Total Taxes: 1951–52 to 2015–16

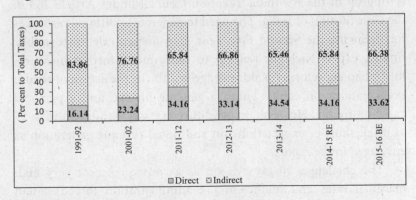

Source: Indian Public Finance Statistics, 2015–16.

Although combined tax-revenue as a percentage of GDP showed more or less an increasing trend till the last half of the eighties, it had started declining thereafter (more on this in the next section). The decline in tax to GDP ratio during the nineties was due to the drop in both customs duty and Union excise duty as a percentage of GDP. However, during the nineties, the direct tax effort increased sharply. It should be noted that as the Indian tax structure is heavily dependent on indirect taxes, the increase in the direct tax revenue effort could not compensate for the resultant revenue loss arising out of the decline in the tax effort of the indirect taxes. The peak rate of income and corporation tax also has declined sharply. In case of indirect taxes, the significant reforms have been the introduction of the VAT (Value Added Tax) in the fiscal year 2005–06 and the Goods and Services Tax (GST) on 1 July 2017.

Tax Reform Initiatives in India

India's journey towards a modern tax system began with tax reforms in the fifties, based on the recommendations of the report of the Taxation Enquiry Commission chaired by John Matthai. The commission placed emphasis on enhancing the role of taxation, and the role of borrowings in financing development programmes of the public sector. It also recommended progressive direct taxation with effective tax enforcement. The commission recommended the setting up of the All India Taxation Council under Article 263 of the Constitution of India. The need to generate additional resources for financing the Second Five Year Plan invited celebrated public finance expert Nicholas Kaldor[2] to recommend further measures for Indian tax reforms. Kaldor suggested the introduction of wealth tax, taxations on capital gains, a general gift tax, and a personal expenditure tax. However, expenditure tax was withdrawn in 1957 as it fell short of expectations on additional revenue generation as envisaged in the report.

The challenges of tax evasion as a consequence of very high marginal rates and inefficient tax administration forced Indian policymakers to attempt a series of reforms through the establishment of the Direct Taxes Enquiry Committee (DTEC)[3] headed by K.N. Wanchoo, and subsequently, the Indirect Taxes Enquiry Committee (ITEC)[4] headed by L.K. Jha. The major recommendations of the DTEC included measures to curb black money and tax evasion, reconstitution of the Central Board of Direct Taxes (CBDT) and introduction of a system of Permanent Account Numbers (PAN) for taxpayers. The most important recommendation of the ITEC was to introduce VAT in the country. The ITEC, however, took note of the limitations of the then prevailing tax administration structure and recommended a VAT system at the manufacturing level.

A comprehensive reform of the Indian tax system was first observed in mid-eighties in the Long Term Fiscal Policy (LTFP) statement of 1985. The LTFP recommended the introduction of VAT in line with the recommendation of the L.K. Jha committee. Though a modified VAT was tried at the manufacturing level, fundamental reform in the tax system in India was initiated in the early nineties based on the recommendations of the Tax Reforms Committee headed by Raja J. Chelliah. The Chelliah Committee focused on reforming both direct and indirect taxes as well the reforms in the tax administration and implementation of a modern tax system. With regard to the direct taxes, the committee recommended widening of tax bases and the moderation of the rates of direct taxes. For indirect taxes, the committee recommended introduction of VAT in place of central excise, and for customs duty, major recommendations were reduction in import tariff, reduction in the spread of rates, a simplified tax structure and abolition of many concessions and exemptions. It is noteworthy that the VAT was a consistent recommendation of various expert committees as an efficient restructuring of the indirect tax system in the country.

VAT—The First Step towards Rationalization

Post the Chelliah Committee recommendations, the rates of both direct and indirect taxes were reduced, processes simplified, and attempts were made to orient tax administration to a modern system. Though these reforms were particularly concentrated at the Union level, the domestic trade tax system remained complex and archaic. The transition to VAT from the pre-existing sales tax regime was a major reform in indirect tax as well as in the overall tax administration in India. The government decided in the year 1995 to introduce VAT to abolish multiple points of taxation and for rationalizing the overall tax burden. After protracted deliberation for almost ten years, most of the states replaced the age-old sales tax system with a VAT in 2005. Initially, a few states were reluctant to join the VAT system. By 2007, all the states were part of it. States' concern in moving to a VAT system was particularly driven by uncertainties with regard to the revenue outcome of VAT. The Union government had to assure the states about compensation of revenue in case of any losses. Also some states had particular concerns about the revenue neutrality of VAT as the tax structure differed across states. Producing states were concerned about phased reduction of the rate of interstate sales tax/central sales tax (CST) with the introduction of a destination-based VAT. However, post VAT, revenue growth of states was significant and the Union government did not have to make huge compensation to states.

Institutionally, VAT was one of the best examples of cooperation among Indian states in coordinating a consumption tax regime through the empowered committee of state finance ministers—a body which emerged not through enactment of law but as a necessity for coordination and implementation of a harmonized VAT system across states.

The VAT system had two major limitations. (i) It was applied only on goods and not on services; and (ii) it was levied only on intra-state trade with the provision for input tax credit (ITC). In other words, a comprehensive consumption tax reform was still not complete. Since CST continued in a VAT regime, there was a peculiar combination of intra-state VAT (i.e. VAT levied on the movement of goods within the state) based on the destination principle of taxation and an interstate sales tax or CST based on the origin principle of taxation.[5] This resulted in continuation of cascading of taxes and fragmented taxation of goods and services and significant tax on exportation from richer producing states to poorer consuming states.

While the VAT negotiations among the states were in place, in 2001, an expert group on taxation of services was set up. Separate task forces on direct and indirect taxes were set up by the Government of India in 2002. Under the prevailing service tax net, the expert group on taxation of services made specific recommendations to cover the sector. Among others, it suggested (i) integration of tax on services to a comprehensive central VAT on goods and services; (ii) sharing of powers to tax services with states; and (iii) incorporating a well-defined negative list of services relating to public utilities, health and education services, etc. The report of the advisory group on tax policy and tax administration for the Tenth Five Year Plan also provided a detailed roadmap for reforms in tax administration for direct taxes, customs duties, Union excises and more importantly for introducing VAT. The report of the task force on introducing the fiscal responsibility and budget management (FRBM) Act of 2003 made a significant recommendation of introducing an all-India goods and services tax (GST), with concurrent powers to tax services by the states. India has finally introduced the Goods and Services Tax (GST) on 1 July 2017. GST is considered as a landmark reform aimed at the unification of Indian markets. This reform is also cited as the best example of cooperation between the Union and the states in a federal setup.

GST in a Complex Federal System

While the original plan was to introduce the GST from 1 April 2010, the process got delayed by more than seven years. This delay is a reflection of the fact that political economy of tax reform is not an easy job in a complex federation like India. Indeed, the negotiations on VAT also had gone on for several years before it was finally implemented by states. Similarly, the GST was finally introduced after protracted negotiations between the Union government, twenty-nine state governments and seven centrally administered Union

Territories and to an extent with other stakeholders. The 122nd Constitution amendment paved the way for the implementation of GST. GST is expected to subsume major indirect taxes to provide a simple tax regime to develop a common market for India. The ultimate benefit of GST, however, would depend on the design of the tax, which is dependent on various provisions of the GST Bill and functioning of the GST council.

The significance of the GST as a landmark tax reform is evident from the fact that it required a Constitutional amendment to enable the Union government to tax consumption of goods and allow states to tax consumption of services. Following the amendment, both the Central and the state tax bases have merged, and both the Centre and state governments will collect taxes from this common base. The Constitutional amendment also enabled the creation of the GST council. The council's chairperson is the Union finance minister and all states have their ministerial nominees as members of the council. Since the creation of the council in November 2016, it has met on several occasions. On average, it has been meeting on a fortnightly basis for bringing clarity to the design, rate structure and mechanisms for compensation under GST. This is a commendable achievement. This also shows that the Indian federal system has begun to transform itself as a federation where both the Centre and states have learnt to trust each other, to the extent of giving up their exclusive taxation rights with respect to a particular tax base for a better system. This common tax base creation should result in an abolition of the fragmented tax regime, development of a common market, elimination of cascading of taxes and should help increase the growth of GDP by promoting trade, business and investment.

Taxes under GST

In line with the simple composite indirect tax system that exists in several other countries, the GST has subsumed a variety of existing Central and state taxes.

a) The Central taxes absorbed by the GST include central excise duties, additional duties of excise, additional duties of customs, special additional duties of customs, service tax and central cess and surcharges so far as they relate to the supply of goods and services.

b) Similarly, state taxes subsumed by GST are state VAT, central sales tax, luxury tax, entry tax, entertainment tax, taxes on advertisement, purchase tax, taxes on lotteries, betting and gambling and state surcharges and cess so far as they relate to supply of goods and services.

As of now, petroleum products, alcohol for human consumption, the real estate sector and electricity are kept out of the purview of GST. In other words, though most indirect taxes have come under GST, a large part of the economy in terms of sectors fetching significant revenues also remain outside its purview. Incomplete coverage of goods and services is an issue that the country needs to resolve as India moves further on the path of reforming indirect taxes for obtaining the full benefit of GST with a comprehensive coverage. There is little doubt though that the currently agreed structure is a vast improvement from the present design.

Introduction of the GST resulted in the abolition of age-old regressive central sales tax (CST). CST was a regressive tax levied at the point of production. The practice had resulted in a significant tax 'exportation'—i.e. change in share of taxes paid—from richer producing states to poorer consuming states contributing to fiscal inequality in the country. This precisely is the reason why some of the relatively richer producing states are not happy with the abolition of CST and were initially opposed to the idea of GST. It is expected that revenue gain due to expansion of base as a result of the destination principle of taxation and additional taxation of services should result in significant revenue gain to states after the input tax credit adjustment and loss of CST revenue.

Transitional Issues in GST

The government has declared that the remaining period of the financial year 2017–18 after the implementation of GST on 1 July would be treated as a period of transition. This implies that the government would be prepared to make calibrated changes as the situation unfolds, without a rigid view. But despite the fact that the GST council has been trying hard to be as clear as possible in drafting rules and conveying them to all the stakeholders for the successful implementation of the regime, several transition issues need to be addressed.

Amongst the several issues and implementation challenges being faced by the entire country, the key problem is of ensuring the dissemination of symmetric and timely information to all stakeholders. Given the completely new tax regime the country has now adopted, despite several guidelines/circulars/announcements, lack of clarity on multiple issues faced by very diverse industries/ sectors remains a concern.

Another challenge in the transition phase will be the modification of IT systems to make them GST-compliant. The multiplicity of rates, decentralized registration, generation of item-wise invoices with multiple copies, calculation of item-wise GST for multiple slab rates, and printing of such invoices containing numerous details, have increased the challenge. The experience of a few months after GST shows that such a mammoth technical upgradation of record-keeping and maintaining exercise seem to have created hardship for the traders, especially small businesses. The GST council is trying to address these issues. It has reduced the frequency of filing of tax returns now from monthly to quarterly basis. The council also has slashed rates on more than 175 items, reducing taxes on these from the existing 28 per cent in one of the biggest tax reductions since the new system kicked in.

A related transition issue is adherence to the anti-profiteering provisions. The anti-profiteering rules aim to ensure that the benefits of reduction in the rate of taxes on the supply of goods and services, or the benefit of input tax credit by way of reduction in prices, must be passed on to the buyers. This will definitely lead to some distortionary pricing in the interim period, the consequences of which can be manifold. But once the system stabilizes, competition and operation of market forces should result in automatic operation of the pass-through mechanism of input tax credit.

Has GST Compromised Federalism?

It is certainly true that the right to taxation is intimately linked with the right to decide on the rate of taxation. Post GST, individual state governments would not be able to decide on its rate structure in a particular state. That way, some might argue, for the sake of tax harmony, fiscal autonomy has been 'compromised'. This is true for the Central government as well. The Centre also cannot change the rates without the approval of the majority of the states in the GST council.

But if one examines the big picture, in a globalizing world, fiscal policy, especially tax policy, became ineffective a long time ago. To give an example: to attract global investment, India really cannot have a corporate income tax rate that is way above the rates in other emerging market economies trying to attract the same investments. The same is being reflected here, i.e. a process of harmonization of tax rates across the country through a process of negotiation in the GST council. In the former case, it is the market that forces a country to align rates to a particular reference; in the latter, it is happening through a process of negotiations. Even with fixed minimum rates, states would have ultimately converged to a particular reference rate. The larger question is whether rate harmonization alone is sufficient to attract trade and investment? Probably not. There must be harmonization of processes. If business and trade have to face different kinds of complexities in complying with tax laws in different states, rate harmonization would become ineffective.

Finally, post-GST fiscal architecture is an outcome of the Constitutional amendment. It is too late to reopen this issue.

Autonomy of all levels of governments, including that of the Union
government, has been tied to the GST council on matters of indirect
taxation. It is the responsibility of the council to work in a manner
that preserves and strengthens the fiscal autonomy of all the levels
of governments. The Centre, clearly, would have to take the lead in
this regard.

Appendix 1[*]

Sugarcane Characteristics across Major States

States	Region	Duration of Crop (months)	Irrigation Water Requirement in Lakh Litres/ha (equivalent no. of standard irrigations)[†]	Sugar Recovery Rate (per cent) TE (2014–15)
Uttar Pradesh	Sub-tropical regions	9.6	57.2 (7.6)	9.40
Bihar		12	37.5 (5)	9.03
Andhra Pradesh	Tropical regions	10.9	202.5 (27)	9.60
Maharashtra		13.5	196.1 (26.2)	11.30
Karnataka		13.1	256 (34.1)	10.73
Tamil Nadu		10.8	297 (39.6)	9.00

Source: (CACP, 2015–16).

† Note: Number of standard irrigation at 7.5 cm depth per hectare.

---

* Chapter VII: Towards Sustainable, Productive and Profitable Agriculture.

Appendix 2[*]

Change in Sectoral Shares in India (1970–2016)

Year	Services	Industry	Agriculture	Manufacturing
1970	37.6	20.5	42.0	13.7
1975	40.2	22.2	37.6	15.2
1980	40.3	24.3	35.4	16.2
1985	43.4	25.7	30.9	16.0
1990	44.5	26.5	29.0	16.2
1991	45.2	25.4	29.4	15.2
1992	45.5	25.8	28.7	15.4
1993	45.8	25.5	28.7	15.3
1994	45.3	26.4	28.3	16.2
1995	46.3	27.4	26.3	17.3
1996	46.3	26.6	27.1	16.9
1997	47.7	26.4	25.9	15.8
1998	48.5	25.7	25.8	15.0
1999	50.3	25.2	24.5	14.6
2000	51.0	26.0	23.0	15.3
2001	52.0	25.1	22.9	14.6
2002	53.1	26.2	20.7	14.9
2003	53.2	26.0	20.7	14.9
2004	53.0	27.9	19.0	15.3
2005	53.1	28.1	18.8	15.4

---

* Chapter XI: Indian Industry: Prospects and Challenges.

Year	Services	Industry	Agriculture	Manufacturing
2006	52.9	28.8	18.3	16.1
2007	46.4	34.7	18.9	18.9
2008	47.8	33.8	18.4	18.2
2009	48.5	33.1	18.4	17.8
2010	48.7	32.4	18.9	17.5
2011	49.0	32.5	18.5	17.4
2012	50.0	31.7	18.3	17.1
2013	50.6	30.8	18.6	16.5
2014	51.8	30.1	18.0	16.4
2015	53.0	29.6	17.5	16.6
2016	53.8	28.8	17.4	16.5

Source: Compiled by author from World Development Indicators Database, World Bank, available at http://databank.worldbank.org/data/reports. aspx?source=world-development-indicators; and Ministry of Statistics and Programme Implementation, Government of India, available at http://www. mospi.nic.in/data.

Appendix 3[*]

Change in Sectoral Shares in China (1970–2016)

Year	Services	Industry	Agriculture	Manufacturing
1970	24.9	40.3	34.8	33.3
1975	22.7	45.4	32.0	37.6
1980	22.3	48.1	29.6	39.9
1985	29.4	42.7	27.9	34.4
1990	32.4	41.0	26.6	32.3
1991	34.5	41.5	24.0	32.2
1992	35.6	43.1	21.3	32.4
1993	34.5	46.2	19.3	33.6
1994	34.4	46.2	19.5	33.3
1995	33.7	46.8	19.6	33.4
1996	33.6	47.1	19.3	33.2
1997	35.0	47.1	17.9	32.9
1998	37.0	45.8	17.2	31.5
1999	38.6	45.4	16.1	31.3
2000	39.8	45.5	14.7	31.8
2001	41.2	44.8	14.0	31.3
2002	42.2	44.5	13.3	31.1
2003	42.0	45.6	12.3	32.5
2004	41.2	45.9	12.9	32.0
2005	41.3	47.0	11.6	32.1

[*] Chapter XI: Indian Industry: Prospects and Challenges.

Year	Services	Industry	Agriculture	Manufacturing
2006	41.8	47.6	10.6	32.5
2007	42.9	46.9	10.3	32.4
2008	42.8	46.9	10.3	32.1
2009	44.3	45.9	9.8	31.5
2010	44.1	46.4	9.5	31.5
2011	44.2	46.4	9.4	31.3
2012	45.3	45.3	9.4	30.7
2013	46.7	44.0	9.3	29.7
2014	47.8	43.1	9.1	30.4
2015	50.2	40.9	8.8	30.0
2016	51.6	39.8	8.6	30.8

Source: Compiled by author from World Development Indicators Database, World Bank, available at *http://databank.worldbank.org/data/reports.aspx?source=world-development-indicators;* and National Bureau of Statistics of China, *http://www.stats.gov.cn/enGliSH/Statisticaldata/AnnualData/.*

Notes

Introduction

1. Vaishnav, Milan, and D.C. Danielle. 'A devil called policy paralysis', *India Today*, 18 May 2014. See http://indiatoday.intoday.in/story/policy-paralysis-upa-ii-corruption/1/362386.html.
2. Apart from the deceleration in GDP growth (5.7 per cent in Q1 of FY 18 as against 7.9 per cent in Q1 of FY 2017), the Centre for Monitoring of the Indian Economy (CMIE) estimated a loss of 1.5 million jobs during January to April in 2017.
3. India received wheat supplies under the US PL-480—a food aid programme of the United States administered in the sixties by president(s) John F. Kennedy and Lyndon B. Johnson. See https://history.state.gov/milestones/1961-1968/pl-480.
4. 'People practicing open defecation (percentage of population)', World Bank. See https://data.worldbank.org/indicator/SH.STA.ODFC.ZS.

Chapter I

1. Under that modus vivendi, India and China discussed their differences, like the boundary question, but did not allow the absence of a settlement to inhibit other cooperation such as trade, etc.
2. The proportion of merchandise trade in GDP has since dropped as world trade has shrunk.

Chapter II

1. A shorter and slightly abridged version of this essay was also submitted to the Lok Sabha Secretariat for their publication to commemorate seventy years of India's independence.

2. *Economic Reforms: Discussion Paper*. Ministry of Finance, Government of India, July 1993, p.1.

3. Mexico's sudden decision in 1994 to devalue the peso vis-a-vis the US dollar triggered abrupt capital flight and deep convulsions in the Mexican economy. The 'Tequila' effect is the informal moniker for the knock-on impact of the peso devaluation on other currencies of the region (Southern Cone and Brazil). The Tequila crisis was the first international crisis set off by capital volatility.

4. Reserve Bank of India, database on Indian economy. See https://dbie.rbi. org.in/DBIE/dbie.rbi?site=home.

5. All data in this paragraph estimated from: Reserve Bank of India, database on Indian economy. See https://dbie.rbi.org.in/DBIE/dbie.rbi?site=home.

6. All data in this paragraph estimated from: Reserve Bank of India, database on Indian economy. See https://dbie.rbi.org.in/DBIE/dbie. rbi?site=home.

7. Reserve Bank of India, database on Indian economy. See https://dbie.rbi. org.in/DBIE/dbie.rbi?site=home.

8. See: 'Competitive Monetary Easing—Is It Yesterday Once More?' Remarks by Raghuram Rajan, former governor of the Reserve Bank of India, at Brookings Institution, Washington, D.C., 10 April 2014. See http://www. bis.org/review/r140414b.htm.

9. External Sector is the portion of a country's economy that interacts with the economies of other countries. In the goods market, the external sector involves exports and imports. In the financial market it involves capital flows. Source: Wikipedia.

10. Monetary policy consists of the actions of a central bank, currency board or other regulatory committee that determine the size and rate of growth of the money supply, which in turn affects interest rates. Source: Investopedia.

Chapter III

1. Quraishi, S.Y. *An Undocumented Wonder: The Great Indian Election*. New Delhi: Rainlight, Rupa Publications, 2014.

2. Sen, A. 'Democracy as a Universal Value', *Journal Of Democracy*, *10*(3), 3–17. See http://dx.doi.org/10.1353/jod.1999.0055.

3. Quraishi, S.Y. *An Undocumented Wonder: The Great Indian Election*. New Delhi: Rainlight, Rupa Publications, 2014.

Chapter IV

1. Gopal, Sarvepalli. *Jawaharlal Nehru*. New Delhi: Oxford University Press, 1979, vol. 2, p. 162. *India: A Reference Annual, 1953*. New Delhi: Ministry of Information and Broadcasting, 1953, pp. 4, 315–16. Butler, David, and Ashok Lahiri and Prannoy Roy eds., *India Decides: Elections 1952–1989*. New Delhi: Living Media India, 1989, p. 56.
2. *Annual Reports 2014-15*. New Delhi: Telecom Regulatory Authority of India, 2015, p. 15.
3. 'Narendra Modi's Electoral Milestone: 437 rallies, 3 lakh km' *Times of India*, 30 April 2014. 'Fleet of 3 aircraft ensures Modi is home every night after day's campaigning', *Times of India*, 22 April 2014.
4. *India: A Reference Annual, 1953*. p. 317.
5. *Annual Report of the Registrar of Newspapers for India, 1958*. New Delhi: Ministry of Information and Broadcasting, 1959, p. 38.
6. Daily circulation figures are from the annual *Press in India*, published by the Registrar of Newspapers for India.
7. *India: A Reference Annual, 1953*. New Delhi: Ministry of Information and Broadcasting, 1953, p. 316.
8. *Mass Media in India, 1980–81*. New Delhi: Publications Division, 1982, p. 201.
9. *MMII, 1980–81*, p. 97.
10. *MMII, 1980–81*, p. 90. *India: A Reference Annual, 1964*. New Delhi: Publications Division, 1964, p. 125.
11. Jeffrey, Robin. 'The Mahatma Didn't Like the Movies and Why It Matters: Indian Broadcasting Policy, 1920–1990', *Global Media and Communication*. 2006, vol. 2, no. 2, pp. 207–27.
12. *Times of India Directory and Yearbook, 1979*. Mumbai: Times of India Press, 1979, p. 203. *India: A Reference Annual 1953*, pp. 330 and 204.
13. Jeffrey, Robin. *India's Newspaper Revolution*. New Delhi: Oxford University Press, 2010, third edition, p. 64.
14. Jeffrey. *India's Newspaper Revolution*. pp. 41–42.
15. *Statistical Outline of India, 1984*. Bombay: Tata Services Ltd, 1984, p. 94.
16. Mehta, Nalin. *India on Television*. New Delhi: HarperCollins, 2008, p. 42. *India 1990: A Reference Annual*. New Delhi: Publications Division, 1990, p. 279.
17. In 2015, India was estimated to have more than 60,000 cable providers. *TRAI Annual Report 2014–15*, p. 6.

18. Mehta. *India on Television*, for the contortions of governments confronted with irresistible pressures from impossible to control satellite-based TV.
19. *Press in India* for relevant years.
20. Kohli–Khandekar, Vanita. *The Indian Media Business*. New Delhi: SAGE Publications, 2013, fourth edition, p. 135.
21. Mehta, *India on Television*, p. 157.
22. Desai, Ashok V. *India's Telecommunications Industry*. New Delhi: SAGE Publications, 2006. It tells much of this story. See also: Jeffrey and Doron, *Great Indian Phone Book*, pp. 39–62.
23. *Annual Report, 2014–15*. New Delhi: Telecom Regulatory Authority of India, 2015, p. 4.
24. 'Indian Telecom Service Performance Indicator Report', press release no. 27/2017. 7 April 2017, p. 5.
25. Bamzai, Sandeep. 'A Network of Reliance', *India Today*, 14 January 2012.
26. See for example, the financial analysis of the Kolkata group—Ananda Bazar: 'ABP Group: a tale of contrasts', The Hoot, 10 April 2017.
27. Kohli–Khandekar, *Indian Media Business*, pp. 263–98.
28. Robin Jeffrey and Assa Doron. 'Mobile-izing: Democracy, Organization and India's First "Mass Mobile Phone" Elections', *Journal of Asian Studies*. February, 2012, vol. 71, no. 1 pp. 63–80.
29. Jeffrey, *India's Newspaper Revolution*, pp. 1–2.

Chapter V

1. 'India in an Asian Renaissance': speech by minister mentor Lee Kuan Yew at the thirty-seventh Jawaharlal Nehru Memorial Lecture, 21 November 2005.
2. Quoted in C.A. Bayly and T.N. Harper, *Forgotten Armies*. London, 2007, p. 324.
3. Ibid.
4. See Kripa Sridharan: 'India–ASEAN Relations: Evolution, Growth and Prospects' in Chandran Jeshurun (ed.), *China, India, Japan and the Security of Southeast Asia*. Singapore, Institute of Southeast Asian Studies, 1993, p. 118.
5. Sridharan, *The ASEAN Region in India's Foreign Policy*, p. 120
6. Ibid.
7. Kaul, M.M. 'ASEAN–India Relations during the Cold War', in Gordon and Henningham (eds.), *India Looks East: An Emerging Power and its Asia-Pacific Neighbours*, 2001, p. 54.

8. Southeast Asia underwent a period of 'Indianization', in which the nations of Southeast Asia were culturally suffused with Indian culture and civilization.

9. Sridharan, *The ASEAN Region in India's Foreign Policy*, p. 120

10. Satu P. Limaye, quoted in Michael Richardson, 'ASEAN Nations and India Warm Up', *International Herald Tribune*, 29–30 January 1994, as cited by Ishtiaq Hossain, 'Singapore–India Relations in the Post-Cold War Period', in M.C. Yong and Bhanoji Rao (eds.), *Singapore–India Relations: A Primer*. Singapore, 1995, p. 42.

11. See Sandy Gordon, 'India and Southeast Asia: A Renaissance in Relations?', in Sandy Gordon and Stephen Henningham (eds.), *India Looks East: An Emerging Power and its Asia-Pacific Neighbours*. Canberra, 1995, pp. 207–29.

12. India's re-engagement with Southeast Asia began in earnest in the 1990s after a lengthy period of 'benign neglect' during the Cold War. This strategic shift was first outlined as India's Look East policy by then Prime Minister Narasimha Rao in his Singapore lecture in 1994. Singapore remains a strong advocate of India's engagement and integration with ASEAN.

13. *India Today*, 15 January 1997.

14. Muni, S.D. 'India's Growing Identity with ASEAN'. Singapore: Institute of Southeast Asian Studies, trends, 31 August–1 September 1996, no. 72, p. 1.

15. Figures from Sridharan, *The ASEAN Region in India's Foreign Policy*, pp. 209–10.

16. Ibid., p. 207.

17. Nath, Ashok K. 'The Larger Emerging Economies of Asia – *Quo Vadis*', in Asia 21, Singapore, January 1997, p. 59.

18. *The Hindu*, 21 January 1997.

19. Cited in Prime Minister Manmohan Singh's speech at the fifth ASEAN–India Summit in Cebu, Philippines, 14 January 2007.

20. Rajiv Sikri, 'India's Foreign Policy Priorities in the Coming Decade', ISAS, NUS, Singapore.

21. 2015 statistics show that China's share of total ASEAN trade is 15.2 per cent while India's share is 2.6 per cent. See http://asean.org/storage/2016/06/table20_as-of-30-Aug-2016-2.pdf

22. Bhatia, Rajiv. 'India–ASEAN Relations: Progress and possibilities', *Institute of Peace and Conflict Studies*. Article no. 5296, 15 June 2017.

23. Sajjanhar, Ashok. 'Taking Stock of India's "Act East Policy"'. Observer Research Foundation, 2016. Web. 12 August. 2017. Issue brief no. 142, p. 2.

24. Bart Gaens and Olli Ruohomaki, 'India's "Look East"—"Act East" Policy: Hedging as a Foreign Policy Tool', *The Finnish Institute of International Affairs*, 2017. Web. 12 August. 2017. FIIA Briefing paper 222, p. 5.

25. New Delhi has recently proposed to further extend the Myanmar–Thailand link to Cambodia, Laos and Vietnam, and shorten travel from the Mekong river to India using water transport. This can be seen as an effort by India to further align itself with ASEAN and the Bay of Bengal Initiative for Multi-Sectoral Technical and Economic Cooperation (BIMSTEC). See 'India revives highway plan amid China's Belt and Road push', *The Straits Times*, 14 August 2017. See http://www.straitstimes.com/asia/south-asia/india-revives-highway-plan-amid-chinas-belt-and-road-push.

26. See Isabelle St. Mezard, *Eastward Bound. India's New Positioning in Asia.* Delhi, 2006.

Chapter VI

1. Dumont, Louis. *Homo Hierarchicus: The Caste System and Its Implications.* London: Weidenfeld and Nicolson.

2. It is believed by those who abide by the caste order that people are made up of different bodily substances. While these are intangible at the phenomenal level, they supposedly determine how pure a person is and where that person should be placed on the purity/ritual hierarchy. See McKim Marriot, 'Multiple References in Indian Caste System', in J. Silverberg, ed., *Social Mobility and the Caste System in India: An Interdisciplinary Symposium.* The Hague: Mouton, 1968.

3. Purusha Shukta is one of the hymns of the Rig Veda. It is thought that Purusha Shukta is interpolation into the Rig Veda, as it is different from other hymns.

4. Bougle, Celestin. *Essays on the Caste System.* Cambridge University Press, 1971. See also: 'The Essence and Reality of the Caste System', in *Contributions to India Sociology.* 1968, vol. 2, no. 1, pp. 7–30.

5. Ghurye, G. S. 'Features of the Caste System', in Dipankar Gupta, ed., *Social Stratification.* New Delhi, Oxford University Press, 1991, pp. 35–48.

6. This origin myth and the ones following it are from Dipankar Gupta, 'Continuous Hierarchies and Discrete Castes', in Dipankar Gupta, ed., *Social Stratification.* New Delhi: Oxford University Press, 1991.

7. The Balaji myth refers to the offsprings of the celestial coupling between Balaji or Srinivasa (another name for Vishnu in Andhra Pradesh) and Padmavati.

8. Jat numbers are from 1931 Census. Since then there has been no caste-specific census.

Chapter VII

1. https://www.un.org/development/desa/publications/world-population-prospects-the-2017-revision.html.

2. *Level and Pattern of Consumer Expenditure 2011–12.* Ministry of Statistics and Programme Implementation, National Sample Survey Office, Government of India, 2014.

3. The Falkenmark Water Stress Indicator marks a country water-stressed when annual per capita water availability is less than 1700 cubic metre and water scarce if it is less than 1000 cubic metre. See http://environ.chemeng.ntua.gr/WSM/Newsletters/Issue4/Indicators_Appendix.htm.

4. *Water and Related Statistics.* Water Resources Information System Directorate, Water Planning and Project Wing, Central Water Commission. Government of India, 2013, 2015.

5. *Guidelines for Improving Water Use Efficiency in Irrigation, Domestic and Industrial Sectors.* Ministry of Water Resources, Central Water Commission. Government of India, 2014.

6. http://eands.dacnet.nic.in/LUS_1999_2004.htm.

7. http://indiabudget.nic.in/ub2017-18/bh/bh1.pdf.

8. http://wrmin.nic.in/forms/list.aspx?lid=1279.

9. Gross Cropped Area (GCA) is the total area sown once and more than once in a particular year. When the crop is sown on a piece of land twice, the area is counted twice in GCA.

10. http://punenvis.nic.in/index2.aspx?slid=5814&sublinkid=995&langid=1&mid=1.

11. *Dynamic Ground Water Resources in India (As on 31st March 2011).* Ministry of Water Resources, River Development and Ganga Rejuvenation, Central Ground Water Board. Faridabad: Government of India, 2014.

12. *Agricultural Statistics at a Glance.* Ministry of Agriculture, Department of Agriculture and Cooperation, Government of India, 2014.

13. *Agricultural Statistics at a Glance.* Ministry of Agriculture, Department of Agriculture and Cooperation, Government of India, 2016.

14. One hectare is 10,000 square metres. It is a common unit of measurement in agricultural production.
15. *Price Policy for Kharif Crops.* Ministry of Agriculture and Farmers Welfare, Department of Agriculture Cooperation and Farmers Welfare, Commission for Agricultural Costs and Prices, Government of India, 2017–18.
16. NSSO. (2013–14). *Consolidated Results of Crop Estimation Survey on Principal Crops.* Ministry of Statistical and Programme Implementation, National Sample Survey Office, National Statistical Organisation. Government of India.
    CACP. (2013–14). *Price Policy for Kharif Crops.* Ministry of Agriculture and Farmers Welfare, Department of Agriculture, Cooperation and Farmers Welfare, Commission for Agricultural Costs and Prices. Government of India.
17. http://agripb.gov.in/abt_deptt/pdf/Pb%20preservation%20of%20Subsoil%20Act,2009.pdf.
18. http://k-learn.adb.org/system/files/materials/2012/04/201204-drip-irrigation-and-fertigation-technology-rice-cultivation.pdf.
19. Gulati, A., R. Roy, and S. Hussain. *Getting Punjab Agriculture Back on High Growth Path: Sources, Drivers and Policy Lessons.* New Delhi: Indian Council for Research on International Economic Relations (ICRIER), 2017.
20. Feed mill is any plant or factory that processes grains, vegetables or meat into animal feed.
21. Silage is fodder for cattle, sheep or other animals. A silage unit will be where it is prepared and stored. In starch factories, corn starch will be produced as part of the food processing industry.
22. http://eands.dacnet.nic.in/LUS_1999_2004.htm.
23. http://mahaagri.gov.in/level3detaildisp.aspx?id=6&subid=11&sub2id=1.
24. http://eands.dacnet.nic.in/APY_96_To_06.htm.
25. *Price Policy for Sugarcane.* Ministry of Agriculture, Department of Agriculture and Cooperation, Commission on Agricultural Costs and Prices. Government of India, 2015–16.
26. http://eands.dacnet.nic.in/APY_96_To_06.htm.
27. CACP, 2015–16.
28. http://eands.dacnet.nic.in/LUS_1999_2004.htm.
29. *Price Policy for Sugarcane.* Ministry of Agriculture, Department of Agriculture and Cooperation, Commision on Agricultural Costs and Prices. Government of India, 2016–17.

30. Based on data collected from micro-irrigation scheme implementation, department of agriculture, Pune. Government of Maharashtra (Note: data is from 1986 to March 2015).

31. https://www.maharashtra.gov.in/Site/upload/CabinetDecision/English/18-07-2017%20Cabinet%20Decision%20(Meeting%20No.138).pdf. Pp. 5–6. Marathi version: http://www.livemint.com/Politics/gLv0fWy012FI6Su0D5lQvJ/Maharashtra-makes-drip-irrigation-mandatory-for-sugar-cane-c.html.

32. http://pmksy.gov.in/microirrigation/Archive/MIAllocation201718.pdf.

Chapter VIII

1. Before this, national planning was confined mainly to the communist countries. Post the Second World War, the demands of reconstruction led many developed market economies to also adopt planning.

2. Although the model used for the Second Plan is now known as the Feldman–Mahalanobis Model, acknowledging its similarity to the model developed by G.A. Feldman in 1928, the two were developed independently. Nevertheless, while there are commonalities between the Soviet and the early Indian planning models, their modes of implementation were quite different.

3. The spectacular success stories of Taiwan and South Korea, which followed an overtly 'export-led' strategy began only about five years later.

4. The Third Plan saw the involvement of several eminent economists in developing and refining the original Mahalanobis model. The theoretical basis of this plan foreshadowed the 'two-gap' model of growth by Chenery and Strout developed in 1966.

5. There was a four-year 'Plan holiday' between the Third and Fourth Plans enabling recalibration of strategy. This was a political decision that planners had to incorporate into the plan model.

6. Roughly translated as: abolish poverty.

7. By the mid-seventies, savings rate in India had doubled compared with the early fifties and had surpassed that of the US.

8. In the Mahalanobis model, aggregate savings is related both to overall GDP and its sectoral composition. In the Harrod–Domar model it is related only to GDP. The Mahalanobis model could generate higher savings at lower GDP growth rates than the Harrod–Domar by manipulating sectoral composition.

9. Rajiv Gandhi is on public record as describing the then Planning Commission as 'a pack of jokers'.

10. The Eighth Plan, like the two previous plans, was 'realistic' with GDP growth target set at 5.5 per cent. The plan model remained the same as the two earlier plans, despite the change in the economic system.

11. In the earlier Plans, fiscal side was taken into account to the extent it affected availability of resources.

12. Planning Commission (2001), Approach Paper to the Tenth Five Year Plan, Government of India.

13. Three notable interventions of this plan were the National Highway Development Programme (NHDP), the Pradhan Mantri Gram Sadak Yojana (PMGSY), a rural roads programme, and the Sarva Shiksha Abhiyan (SSA), a universal primary education programme. The latter two interventions were again encroachments in the domain of states.

14. The Tenth Plan provided a consistent state-wise breakdown of the principal targets of the Plan in consultation with the state governments.

15. 'Inclusive growth' is first mentioned in the approach paper to the Eleventh Plan and has since become the dominant catchphrase in international development discourse.

16. The Eleventh Plan consolidated infrastructure initiatives of the Tenth under the rubric of 'Bharat Nirman'. Its other major innovation was the push to public–private partnerships (PPPs), particularly in power, roads and ports.

17. The Mahatma Gandhi National Rural Employment Guarantee Scheme (MGNREGS), the world's largest work-fare programme, was the principal intervention to address this issue.

18. A rough indication of this expansion is given by the fact that the Second Plan document was only 140 pages long whereas the Twelfth is nearly 1400.

19. Reacting to the charges of politicization of allocations during the Second and Third Plans, the Central government began allocating block grants on the basis of the Gadgil formula adopted by the NDC from the Fourth Plan onwards.

20. The states were to contribute a particular proportion of total funds in order to access the Centre's share.

21. NITI being the acronym for 'National Institution for Transforming India'.

22. Some form of a plan is necessary for accessing International Development Agency (IDA) funds that require a nationally owned Poverty Reduction

Strategy Paper (PRSP), which is nothing but a national plan under a different rubric.

23. The author's personal experience over the fifteen years he spent in the Planning Commission was that the most active users of the Plans were the private corporate sector, which saw the utility of a consistent economy-wide strategy for its own strategic planning.

Chapter IX

1. Nayar, Baldev Raj. *The Modernization Imperative and Indian Planning*. New Delhi: Vikas, 1972.

2. On the myriad challenges that she confronted on the domestic front, see Francine Frankel, *India's Political Economy: 1947–2004*. New Delhi: Oxford University Press, 2009.

3. The rationale for the Indian position is spelled out in K.B. Lall, 'India and the New International Economic Order', *International Studies*, 17, 3–4, 1978, pp. 435–61.

4. For a discussion of the factors that led to the Indian nuclear tests, see Sumit Ganguly, 'India's Pathway to Pokhran II: The Prospects and Sources of New Delhi's Nuclear Weapons Program', *International Security*, 23:4, Spring 1999, pp. 148–77.

5. Huntington, Samuel P. *Political Order in Changing Societies*. New Haven: Yale University Press, 1968.

6. Doshi, Vidhi. 'India's Long Wait for Justice: 27m Court Cases in Legal Logjam', *Guardian*, 5 May 2016.

7. Human Rights Watch, *Broken System: Dysfunction, Abuse, and Impunity in the Indian Police*. New York: Human Rights Watch, 2009.

8. '50 per cent of police posts vacant in UP; national average at 24 per cent', Press Trust of India, 2 April 2017.

9. Mohan, Vishwa. '3 cops to protect each VIP, just 1 policeman for 761 citizens', *Times of India*, 8 February 2013.

10. Chakravarti, Sudeep. *Red Sun: Travels in Naxalite Country*. New Delhi: Penguin Books, 2008.

11. Roy, Shubhajit. 'Why the Indian Foreign Service has a Quality and Quantity Dilemma', *Indian Express*, 4 August 2016.

12. Ramachandran, Sudha. 'The Indian Foreign Service: Worthy of an Emerging Power?' *Diplomat*, 12 July 2013. See http://thediplomat.com/2013/07/the-indian-foreign-service-worthy-of-an-emerging-power/.

13. Amarnath K. Menon and Gaurav C. Sawant. 'The Missile that Cannot Fire', *India Today*, 13 April 2012.

14. For a detailed discussion, see Sumit Ganguly and William R. Thompson, *Ascending India and Its State Capacity*. New Haven: Yale University Press, 2017.

Chapter X

1. Overview of Civil Society Organizations: India. Civil Society Briefs, Asian Development Bank, 2009.

2. In this paper, the terms non-governmental organizations and civil society organizations have been used interchangeably.

3. Edelman Trust Barometer: India, Edelman Trust Barometer Annual Global Study, 2017, vol. 1, no. 50.

4. See Rob Jenkins, 'NGOs and Indian Politics', in *The Oxford Companion to Indian Politics*, eds., Niraja Gopal Jayal and Pratap Bhanu Mehta. New Delhi: Oxford University Press, pp. 409–26. Tandon, Rajesh. 'The Hidden Universe of Non-profit Organisations in India', *Economic and Political Weekly*, 2017, vol. 52, no. 3, pp. 79–84.

5. Baviskar, B. S. 'NGOs and Civil Society in India', Sociological Bulletin, 2001, vol. 50, no. 1, pp. 3–15.

6. Sen, Siddhartha. 'Some Aspects of State-NGO Relationships in India in the Post-Independence Era', *Development and Change*. The Hague: International Institute of Social Studies, 1999, vol. 30, no. 2, pp. 327–55. See Rob Jenkins, 'NGOs and Indian Politics', in *The Oxford Companion to Indian Politics*, eds., Niraja Gopal Jayal and Pratap Bhanu Mehta. New Delhi: Oxford University Press, pp. 409–26.

7. Sampath, G. 'Time to Repeal the FCRA', *The Hindu*, 27 December 2016. http://www.thehindu.com/opinion/lead/Time-to-repeal-the-FCRA/article16946222.ece. Last accessed 4 July 2017. Balakrishnan, Ajit. 'Indian NGOs' Long March', *Business Standard*, 8 March 2012. See http://www.business-standard.com/article/opinion/ajit-balakrishnan-indian-ngos-long-march-112030800051_1.html Last accessed, 4 July 2017.

8. Chipko Movement is a non-violent forest conservation movement that was started in the seventies in the hilly regions of Kumaon and Garhwal to protest against tree felling. Under the leadership of Chandi Prasad Bhatt, a Gandhian social worker, Chipko, literally meaning embrace, was led by local villagers, particularly women, who would embrace trees to prevent

their felling. The activists outlined that rampant tree felling would lead to environmental degradation of the hills, increasing risks of landslides and flooding in the region.

9. Guha, Ramchandra. 'Environmentalist of the Poor', *Economic and Political Weekly*, 2002, vol. 37, no. 3, pp. 204–07.

10. The Jan Lokpal Bill, also referred to as the Citizen's Ombudsman Bill, is an anti-corruption bill drawn up by civil society activists in India seeking the appointment of a Jan Lokpal, an independent body to investigate corruption cases. See https://en.wikipedia.org/wiki/Jan_Lokpal_Bill.

11. See Rob Jenkins, 'NGOs and Indian Politics', in *The Oxford Companion to Indian Politics*, eds., Niraja Gopal Jayal and Pratap Bhanu Mehta. New Delhi: Oxford University Press, pp. 409–26.

12. Chandhoke, Neera. *The Conceits of Civil Society*. Oxford: Oxford University Press, 2003. See Rob Jenkins, 'NGOs and Indian Politics', in *The Oxford Companion to Indian Politics*, eds., Niraja Gopal Jayal and Pratap Bhanu Mehta. New Delhi: Oxford University Press, pp. 409–26.

13. Tandon, Rajesh. 'The Hidden Universe of Non-profit Organisations in India', *Economic and Political Weekly*, 2017, vol. 52, no. 3, pp. 79–84. Jalali, Rita. 'International Funding of NGOs in India: Bringing the State Back In', *Voluntas*, 2008, vol. 19, pp. 161–88.

14. 'Centre orders filing of cases against four NGOs', *The Hindu*, 28 February 2012. See http://www.thehindu.com/news/national/centre-orders-filing-of-cases-against-four-ngos/article2942708.ece. 'Kudankulam row: Cases against NGOs; German expelled', *Economic Times*, 29 February 2012. See https://economictimes.indiatimes.com/news/politics-and-nation/kudankulam-row-cases-against-ngos-german-expelled/articleshow/12077009.cms.

15. Haidar, Suhasini. 'US, Germany Slam India For New Funding Norms', *The Hindu*. 5 May 2017. See http://www.thehindu.com/news/national/us-germany-slam-india-for-new-funding-norms/article18385902.ece. Last accessed, 4 July 2017.

16. Baviskar, B.S. 'NGOs and Civil Society in India', *Sociological Bulletin*, 2001, vol. 50, no. 1, pp. 3–15.

17. PFI has also provided technical assistance for the roll out and implementation of the National Urban Health Mission (NUHM) across states and cities. Through its edutainment serial, 'Main Kuch Bhi Kar Sakti Hoon' (I, a Woman, Can Do Anything) that tackles social determinants of health and family planning, PFI provided a popular serial to Doordarshan,

the Government of India's television channel. To spread awareness on the Union government's national adolescent health programme, Rashtriya Kishor Swasthya Karyakram (RKSK), PFI contributed to developing behaviour change communication materials for peer educators in every village.

18. Naidu, M. Venkaiah. 'Seeking Synergy, Not Ideology: Government should Partner Civil Society, But the Latter's Advocacy should be Evidence-Based', *Times of India*, 1 June 2016. See http://blogs.timesofindia.indiatimes. com/toi-edit-page/seeking-synergy-not-ideology-government-should-partner-civil-society-but-the-latters-advocacy-should-be-evidence-based/. Last accessed, 4 July 2017.

Chapter XI

1. See D.R. Gadgil, *The Industrial Evolution of India in Recent Years*. Oxford University Press, 1938. Chatterjee, Basudev. *Trade, tariffs and empire: Lancashire and British policy in India 1919–1939*. Oxford University Press, 1992. Mukherjee, Aditya. 'Empire: How Colonial India Made Modern Britain', *Economic and Political Weekly*, vol. 45, no. 50, December 2010, pp.73–82.

2. Eckaus, Richard S. 'Planning in India', *National Economic Planning*, ed. Max F. Millikan. Cambridge: National Bureau of Economic Research, 1967. pp. 305–78.

3. Bhagwati, Jagdish N., and T.N. Srinivasan. *Foreign Trade Regimes and Economic Development—India*. Columbia University Press, 1975.

4. Wolf, Martin. 'Indian Exports', in 'Export Promotion Policies', World Bank staff working paper, no. 313. Washington, D.C.: World Bank, January 1979, pp. 68–70.

5. N. Swapna and N. Sujatha. 'Trends of IT Industry in Indian Economy— An Analysis', *Special Issue of International Journal of Computer Science & Informatics (IJCSI)*. 2012, vol. II, issue-1- 2, pp. 196-198. *Annual Report 2005–06* and *Annual Report 2015–16*. Ministry of Communications and IT, Government of India.

6. Rostow's economic model explains five stages of economic development. It moves from a traditional society to a transitional society, followed by take-off, drive to maturity and finally high mass consumption.

7. Amrit, Amirapu and Arvind Subramanian. 'Manufacturing or Services? An Indian Illustration of a Development Dilemma', working paper

no. 409. Washington, D.C.: Centre for Global Development, June 2015. Rodrik, Dani. 'Premature deindustrialization', working paper no. 20935. Cambridge: National Bureau of Economic Research (NBER), February 2015.

8. Kelkar, Vijay L., and Rajiv Kumar. 'Industrial Growth in the Eighties: Emerging Policy Issues', *Economic and Political Weekly*, vol. 25, no. 4, January 1990, pp. 209–22.

9. Author's computation from various government data sources and reports.

Chapter XII

1. The Maoist insurgency is a conflict between radical Leftists and the Indian state in parts of Adivasi-majority regions in Andhra Pradesh, Bihar, Chhattisgarh, Jharkhand, and Telangana that began around 2002. Its origins are traced to the older Naxalite movement of the sixties and the seventies.

2. The figures in this section are compiled from different sources for cultivation and ownership. They differ slightly because not all privately owned land is cultivated. The cultivation data are from 'Agricultural Statistics at a Glance, 2010'. See http://eands.dacnet.nic.in/. The data on operational holdings or ownership are from the 'Agricultural Census of 2010–11'. See http://agcensus.nic.in/document/agcensus2010/agcen2010rep.htm.

3. Irrigated or 'wet' land is roughly twice as productive as dry land in the same region.

4. This argument is made by many scholars, including Sukhamoy Chakravarty (*Development Planning: The Indian Experience*, New Delhi: Oxford University Press, 1987) and Sanjoy Chakravorty (*The Price of Land: Acquisition, Conflict, Consequence*, New Delhi: Oxford University Press, 2013).

5. Marginal farms are up to 1 hectare (2.5 acres) or less, whereas small farms are between 1 to 2 hectares.

6. Chakravorty, Sanjoy. *The Price of Land*. New Delhi: Oxford University Press, 2013, p. xxiii.

7. See Walter Fernandes, 'Sixty Years of Development-Induced Displacement in India: Scale, Impacts, and the Search for Alternatives', in *India Social Development Report 2008: Development and Displacement*, ed. H.M. Mathur. New Delhi: Oxford University Press, 2008, pp. 89–102.

8. Chakravorty, Sanjoy. *The Price of Land*, pp. xxiii–xxiv.
9. 'Rahul Gandhi kickstarts Congress's 2014 campaign in Uttar Pradesh', NDTV, 9 October 2013. See https://www.ndtv.com/india-news/rahul-gandhi-kickstarts-congresss-2014-campaign-in-uttar-pradesh-537167.

Chapter XIII

1. Economic Survey, 2015–16, economic division, Ministry of Finance, Government of India, 2016. Accessed at http://indiabudget.nic.in/budget2016-2017/survey.asp.
2. Economic Survey, 2016–17. Accessed at http://indiabudget.nic.in/es2016-17/echapter.pdf.
3. See, for instance, K. Srinath Reddy, Vikram Patel, Prabhat Jha, Vinod K. Paul, A.K. Shiva Kumar, Lalit Dandona: 'Towards achievement of universal health care in India by 2020: a call to action', *Lancet*, 26 February 2011, vol. 377, pp. 760–68.
4. 'State of the World's Children 2016'. accessed on 24 June at https://www.unicef.org/publications/files/UNICEF_SOWC_2016.pdf. Data on per capita incomes are from the World Bank accessed on 24 June 2017 at http://databank.worldbank.org/data/download/GNIPC.pdf.
5. 'Situation Analyses—Backdrop to the National Health Policy 2017'. New Delhi: Ministry of Health and Family Welfare, 2017.
6. Drèze, J., and A. K. Sen. *An Uncertain Glory: India and Its Contradictions*, Princeton: Princeton University Press, 2013.
7. Shiva Kumar, A.K., Lincoln C. Chen, Mita Choudhury, Shiban Ganju, Vijay Mahajan, Amarjeet Sinha and Abhijit Sen. 'Financing health care for all: challenges and opportunities', *Lancet*, 19 February 2011, vol. 377, no. 9766, pp. 668–79.
8. 'Situation Analyses—Backdrop to the National Health Policy 2017'. New Delhi: Ministry of Health and Family Welfare, 2017.
9. Patel, Vikram, Rachana Parikh, Sunil Nandraj, Priya Balasubramaniam, Kavita Narayan, Vinod K. Paul, A.K. Shiva Kumar, Mirai Chatterjee and K. Srinath Reddy. 'Assuring health coverage for all in India', *Lancet*, 12 December 2015, vol. 386, no. 10011, pp. 2422–35.
10. 'Assuring health coverage for all in India', *Lancet*, 12 December 2015, vol. 386, no. 10011, pp. 2422–35.
11. 'Financing health care for all: challenges and opportunities', *Lancet*, 19 February 2011, vol. 377, no. 9766, pp. 668–79.

12. The beneficiaries under RSBY are entitled to hospitalization coverage up to Rs 30,000 per annum on family floater basis, for most of the diseases that require hospitalization.

13. See http://www.cci.gov.in/sites/default/files/022014S.pdf.

14. http://timesofindia.indiatimes.com/city/patna/BHRC-directs-govt-to-pay-compensation-for-703-uterus-removals/articleshow/52095795.cms.

15. As in 13 earlier.

16. See presentation by vice-chairman, NITI Aayog: 'India 2031–32: Vision, Strategy and Action Agenda'. New Delhi, 21 April 2017.

17. Drèze, Jean and Amartya Sen. *An Uncertain Glory: India and its Contradictions*. New Delhi: Allen Lane, 2013.

18. http://economictimes.indiatimes.com/news/politics-and-nation/24-lakh-people-have-income-above-rs-10-lakh-but-25-lakh-cars-bought-every-year/articleshow/56201138.cms?utm_source=contentofinterest&utm_medium=text&utm_campaign=cppst.

19. http://indiabudget.nic.in/budget2016-2017/survey.asp.

20. http://indiabudget.nic.in/es2015-16/echapvol2-01.pdf.

Chapter XIV

1. World Population Prospects 2017, United Nations.

2. Speech by former president Pranab Mukherjee at the inaugural session of the visitor's conference 2016, 16 November 2016. See http://presidentofindia.nic.in/speeches-detail.htm?568.

3. 'India will become the world's most populous country by 2022, UN says', *Time*, 30 July 2015. See http://time.com/3978175/india-population-worlds-most-populous-country/.

4. CSO national account statistics.

5. India Labour Marker Update, ILO Country Office for India, July 2016; http://www.ilo.org/wcmsp5/groups/public/---asia/---ro-bangkok/---sro-new_delhi/documents/publication/wcms_496510.pdf.

6. Economic Survey, 2015–16, Ministry of Finance, Government of India. Chapter 7, vol. II, pp. 153–54. See http://indiabudget.nic.in/es2015-16/echapvol2-07.pdf.

7. Ibid.

8. LFPR is number of persons in the labour force per 1000 persons. Report on Employment-Unemployment Survey, Labour Bureau, India.

9. Ibid.

10. Report on Employment-Unemployment Survey, 2015–16, Government of India. Chandigarh: Ministry of Labour and Employment, Labour Bureau, vol. 1. See http://labourbureau.nic.in/EUS_5th_Vol_1.pdf

11. 'This is the most dangerous time for our planet', *Guardian*, 1 December 2016. See https://www.theguardian.com/commentisfree/2016/dec/01/stephen-hawking-dangerous-time-planet-inequality. Accessed on 15 February 2017.

12. 'Automation to replace lakhs of entry, mid-level IT execs: TV Mohandas Pai', *Economic Times*, 31 July 2016. See http://economictimes.indiatimes.com/tech/ites/automation-to-replace-lakhs-of-entry-mid-level-it-execs-tv-mohandas-pai/articleshow/53475940.cms

13. 'Which IT jobs will survive automation? Find out', *Economic Times*, 11 July 2016. See https://economictimes.indiatimes.com/wealth/earn/which-it-jobs-will-survive-automation-find-out/articleshow/53127553.cms

14. As in 24 above.

15. Quarterly Report on Changes in Employment in Selected Sectors (July 2015–September 2015); Government of India. Chandigarh: Ministry of Labour and Employment, Labour Bureau, March 2016.

16. World Bank, 2016, chapter 2, p. 126.

Chapter XV

1. All India Survey on Higher Education, 2015–16. MHRD, GoI.

2. Laha, Rozelle. 'IITs, IIMs think beyond govt funds and tuition fee', *Hindustan Times*. New Delhi, 13 May 2016. See http://www.hindustantimes.com/education/iits-iims-think-beyond-govt-funds-and-tuition-fee/story-0Xq5rfA7EWaJbyCXivxaWM.html.

3. Daniels, Ronald. 'Free the Public Universities', *The Chronicle is Higher Education*, 5 May 2016. See http://www.chronicle.com/article/Free-the-Public-Universities/236372.

4. https://www.timeshighereducation.com/world-university-rankings.

5. National Employability Survey Engineers, Aspiring Minds, 2016. See http://www.aspiringminds.com/sites/default/files/National%20Employability%20Report%20-%20Engineers%20Annual%20Report%202016.pdf.

6. '40 per cent shortage of faculty at IITs, central varsities: Prakash Javadekar', *Times of India*, 9 April 2017. See http://timesofindia.indiatimes.com/home/education/40-shortage-of-faculty-at-iits-central-varsities-prakash-javadekar/articleshow/58097774.cms.

7. 'Gujarat to get six new universities; Assembly clears bills', *Outlook*. Gandhinagar, 22 March 2017. See https://www.outlookindia.com/newsscroll/gujarat-to-get-six-new-universities-assembly-clears-bills/1012566.

8. 'Removing constraints in higher education: The argument that foreign investment benefits only a minority is flawed', *LiveMint*, 4 February 2016. See http://www.livemint.com/Opinion/i80yTtxj9xNIlhATWiIMIK/Removing-constraints-in-higher-education.html.

9. 'Higher Education in India: Twelfth Five Year Plan (2012–17) and beyond'. FICCI Higher Education Summit 2012. See https://learnos.files.wordpress.com/2012/11/ey-ficc_higher_education_report_nov12.pdf.

Chapter XVI

1. This paper is based on Ronojoy Sen's *Nation at Play: A History of Sport in India*. New York/New Delhi: Columbia University Press/Penguin, 2015.

2. Ashwini Kumar, quoted in Mihir Bose's *The Magic of Indian Cricket: Cricket and Society in India*. Abingdon: Routledge, 2006, p. 45.

3. *Times of India*, 13 August 1948.

4. Mellow, Melville de. *Reaching for Excellence: The glory and decay of sports in India*. New Delhi: Kalyani Publishers, 1979, pp. 48–49.

5. *The Economist*, 17 March 2012.

6. *Courier-Mail*, 13 November 1947.

7. *Courier-Mail*, 13 November 1947.

8. http://www.bharatiyahockey.org/granthalaya/hattrick/.

9. Kapadia, 'Rahim, Amal Dutta, P.K. and Nayeem: The Coaches Who Shaped Indian Football', *Football Studies*, October 2002, vol. 5, no. 2, p. 41.

10. Goswami, Chuni. *Khelte*. Calcutta: Ananda Publishers, 1982, p. 19.

11. Majumdar, Boria and Nalin Mehta. *Olympics: The India Story*. New Delhi: HarperCollins, 2008, p. 172.

12. Kapadia, p. 42.

13. *The Times*, 25 August 1971.

14. *Times of India*, 25 August 1971.

15. *Times of India*, 26 August 1971

16. *Hindustan Times*, 16 March 1975.

17. Guha, *India After Gandhi: The History of the World's Largest Democracy*. London: Picador, 2008, p. 736.

18. *Times of India*, 5 December 1982.

19. Gupta, Shekhar. 'Hockey just isn't cricket', *Indian Express*, 7 September 2002.

20. Haigh, Gideon. *Spheres of Influence: Writings on Cricket and Its Discontents*. London: Simon and Schuster, 2011, p. 4.

Chapter XVII

1. Lord Cornwallis, governor general of India, had all the lands surveyed and rental fixed according to soil and crop classifications and awarded titles to the owners for the land.

2. In the ryotwari system, the title holder was responsible for payment of annual revenues. In the zamindari areas, the zamindar or feudal owner was responsible for collection of revenues from all his farmers, and he had to pay a fixed rental to the crown. It led to considerable oppression of the small farmers by the zamindar, as the crown would not interfere, and would only insist on its share of revenues

3. Lord Curzon; Public A; August 1899, nos. 51–54, sourced from the National Archives.

4. Amitabh Kant, member secretary, NITI Aayog.

5. Mulayam Singh Yadav, former chief minister of UP, when the IAS in that state protested against the suspension of a young woman IAS officer.

Chapter XVIII

1. http://niti.gov.in/writereaddata/files/document_publication/NEP-ID_27.06.2017_0.pdf.

2. http://garv.gov.in/garv2/dashboard/garv.

3. Per capita energy or electricity consumption is the metric to monitor improvements in living standards, socioeconomic growth, etc. While it increased in transitioning economies such as India, it is still much less compared with high-income countries such as the US.

4. Bhattacharjee, Subhomoy. *India's Coal Story: From Damodar to Zambezi*. New Delhi: SAGE Publications, 2017.

5. Bhattacharjee, Subhomoy. *India's Coal Story*. New Delhi: SAGE Publications, 2017, chapter 2.

6. http://niti.gov.in/writereaddata/files/document_publication/NEP-ID_27.06.2017_0.pdf.

7. Chapter 18, para 15, Second Five Year Plan, Planning Commission. See http://planningcommission.nic.in/plans/planrel/fiveyr/welcome.html.

8. Right from the mid-fifties as the nations of the Middle East began to get independence, demands to nationalize their oil fields became strident. Egypt with hardly any reserves also made the additional demand to nationalize the largely French-run Universal Suez Canal Company, which it eventually did in July 1956. It led to a joint attack by Israel, British and French forces, which retook the Canal Zone. The stand-off brought Soviet Union to support the Arab nation and was finally resolved in a UN-led resolution the next year. The Six Day war of 1967 was a watershed moment in the Middle East, where the Israeli forces won decisively against the combined Arab forces of Egypt, Syria and Jordan. It has defined the politics, economics and life of the region like nothing else.

9. An anna was a currency unit used in India, equivalent to one-sixteenth Indian rupee.

10. http://www.cci.gov.in/sites/default/files/Indicus_20090420152009.pdf.

11. Trivedi, Prajapati. Administered Price Policy for Public Enterprises. See http://nacwc.nic.in/sites/writereaddata/cna/select-papers/1990-05-Administered_Price_Policy_for_Public_Enterprises.pdf.

12. Draft Energy Policy, NITI Aayog, Version June 2017.

13. Report No. 7 of 2012–13. Performance Audit of Allocation of Coal Blocks and Augmentation of Coal Production, Ministry of Coal. See http://www.cag.gov.in/content/report-no-7-2012-13-%E2%80%93-performance-audit-allocation-coal-blocks-and-augmentation-coal.

14. http://www.cea.nic.in/reports/committee/nep/nep_dec.pdf.

15. https://www.iea.org/Textbase/npsum/MTCMR2016SUM.pdf.

16. http://www.iea.org/newsroom/news/2016/november/world-energy-outlook-2016.html.

17. CRISIL Ratings Report. Top fifty stressed assets need haircut_19Jul2017.pdf.

18. Draft Energy Policy, NITI Aayog, Version June 2017.

Chapter XIX

1. Diamond, Larry. *Development Democracy: Towards Consolidation.* Baltimore: The Johns Hopkins Press, 1999, p. 218.

2. Ibid., p. 10.

3. Diamond's *Development Democracy: Towards Consolidation* is a seminal contribution that has generated a new branch of scholarship on the role of civil society in democracy transition and consolidation.

4. Champaran and Kheda Satyagraha (1917–18) are iconic examples of Gandhian civil society activism in action.

5. *The Economist*, 18 February 2017, p. 5.
6. Diamond. *Development Democracy: Towards Consolidation.* p. 221.
7. Ibid., p. 222.
8. 'The Rational Politics of Cultural Nationalism: Subnational Movements of South Asia in Comparative Perspective', *British Journal of Political Science.* 1995, vol. 25, pp. 57–78.
9. *The Hindu*, 28 August 2015.
10. Mitra. Subrata K. 'The Quota Movement in Gujarat: Implications for Modi and India's Democracy', ISAS Insights No. 289, 2 September, 2015 (ISAS, NUS), Singapore.
11. Subrata Mitra, *Studies in Indian Politics*, 2016, vol. 4, no. 1.
12. Diamond, 1999. Also see Sumit Ganguly and William Thompson, *Ascending India and its State Capacity: Extraction, Violence and Legitimacy.* New Haven: Yale University Press, 2017, p. 65.
13. Tilly, Charles. *The Formation of Nation-States in Western Europe.* Princeton: Princeton University Press,1975.

Chapter XX

1. See, for example, John Keay, *The Honourable Company: A History of the English East India Company*, London: HarperCollins, 1991; Nicola Cooper, *France in Indochina: Colonial Encounters*, New York: Bloomsbury, 2001; Catia Antunes and Jos Gommans, *Exploring the Dutch Empire: Agents, Networks and Institutions, 1600–2000*, New York: Bloomsbury, 2015; S.C.M. Paine, *The Japanese Empire: Grand Strategy from the Meiji Restoration to the Pacific War*, Cambridge: Cambridge University Press, 2017; Peter Hopkirk, *The Great Game: On Secret Service in High Asia*, London: Hachette, 1990; Stuart Creighton Miller, *Benevolent Assimilation: The American Conquest of the Philippines, 1899–1903*, New Haven: Yale University Press, 1982.
2. Silbey, David J. *The Boxer Rebellion and the Great Game in China: A History.* New York: Farrar, Straus and Giroux, 2012. Raghavan, Srinath. *India's War: The Making of Modern South Asia, 1939–1945.* New Delhi: Penguin Books, 2016.
3. Reid, Anthony. *A History of Southeast Asia: Critical Crossroads.* West Sussex: Wiley Blackwell, 2015, p. 415.
4. Ramachandra Guha, ed., *Makers of Modern India.* New Delhi: Viking, 2010, p. 341.

5. Dayal, Shiv. *India's Role in the Korean Question: A Study in the Settlement of International Disputes under the United Nations.* S. Chand, 1959. Halberstam, David. *The Coldest Winter: America and the Korean War.* London: Pan Macmillan, 2011. Hailey, Foster. 'Japan and India Drawing Closer', *New York Times*, 17 October, 1957.

6. Widyatmadja, Josef Purnama. 'The Spirit of Bandung', *Yale Global Online*, 6 April 2005.

7. Schell, Orville. 'Lee Kuan Yew, The Man Who Remade Asia', *Wall Street Journal*, 27 March 2015. Barr, Michael D. 'Lee Kuan Yew and the "Asian Values" Debate', *Asian Studies Review*, vol. 24, no. 3, September 2000, pp. 309–34.

8. Zakaria, Fareed. *The Post-American World.* New York: WW Norton, 2008.

9. World Economic Outlook Database, International Monetary Fund, April 2017.

10. Man Mohini Kaul, 'ASEAN-India Relations during the Cold War', in Frederic Grare and Amitabh Mattoo, eds., *India and ASEAN: The Politics of India's Look East Policy.* New Delhi: Manohar, 2001, p. 41.

11. Sitapati, Vinay. *Half-Lion: How P.V. Narasimha Rao Transformed India.* New Delhi: Penguin India, 2016, pp. 265–68.

12. Pandit, Rajat. 'India, Indonesia to host first air combat exercise with an eye on China', *Times of India*, 8 February 2017.

Chapter XXI

1. On 17 February 1898, Hearst's *New York Journal* carried the unequivocal banner headline, 'Destruction of the War Ship Maine was the Work of an Enemy'. *The World,* on the same day, carried the more cautious: 'Maine Explosion Caused by Bomb or Torpedo?' while *The San Fransisco Chronicle* went with the factual 'Battleship Maine Blown Up in the Harbor of Havana'. See James Creelman: *On the Great Highway: The Wanderings and Adventures of a Special Correspondent.* Boston: Lothrop, 1901, p. 178. Also see http://www.ucpress.edu/content/chapters/11067.ch01.pdf.

2. T.N. Ninan, chairman and chief editor, *Business Standard:* 'Indian Media's Dickensian Age', CASI Working Paper Series, nos. 11–03, December 2011. www.casi.sas.upenn.edu/khemka/ninan.

3. *Media for the Masses: The Promise Unfolds,* KPMG India-FICCI Media and Industry Report, March 2017, p. 95.

4. Laghate, Gaurav. 'TV Viewers in India More than All of Europe's', *Economic Times*, 3 May 2017. See http://economictimes.indiatimes.com/ industry/media/entertainment/media/tv-viewers-in-india-now-much-more-than-all-of-europes/articleshow/57438521.cms.

5. As in 4 earlier, p. 2. Numbers equalized from rupees to USD at September 2017 exchange rates.

6. Star TV CEO Uday Shankar in Nalin Mehta, *Behind a Billion Screens: What Television Tells Us About Modern India*. New Delhi: HarperCollins, 2017, p. xix.

7. In the second batch of this phase three auction, only sixty-six frequencies were sold. See http://www.livemint.com/Consumer/ GTMw2X88KGjxzMNM0dvKKL/FM-auctions-66-channels-fetch-Rs200-crore-200-remain-unsol.html.

8. *Telecom Regulatory Authority of India Consultation Paper on Issues Related to Tariff for Cable TV Services in CAS Notified Areas.* New Delhi, 22 April 2010.

9. http://www.forbes.com/sites/quora/2012/09/05/why-doesnt-hbo-allow-non-cable-subscribers-to-subscribe-to-hbo-go-a-la-hulu/http:// winteriscoming.net/2012/04/the-finances-of-game-of-thrones/.

10. Roughly about Rs 1500 crore on operating expenditure, Rs 1700 crore on salaries and Rs 300–400 crore on capital equipment. Figures from Jowhar Sircar, CEO, Prasar Bharti.

11. Computed by author on basis of Ministry of Information and Broadcasting records, publicly available information on listed TV companies, media reports and industry interviews in select states. The numbers are accurate as of January 2013.

12. TRAI first issued clear recommendations in this regard on 12 November 2008 and then on 28 December 2012. More followed on 12 August 2014.

13. 'Prakash Javadekar Wants to Abolish His Own Ministry', *Times of India*, 10 June 2014; http://timesofindia.indiatimes.com/india/Prakash-Javadekar-wants-to-abolish-his-own-ministry/articleshow/36316749.cms. 'Wisdom a Bit Too Late: I&B Minister Says Don't Need I&B', *Indian Express*, 14 May 2014. See http://m.indianexpress.com/article/india/india-others/ wisdom-a-bit-too-late-ib-minister-says-dont-need-ib/2060842/.

14. Bhatt, S.C. *Satellite Invasion of India.* New Delhi: Gyan Publishing, 1994, p. 86.

15. Swami, Praveen. 'Beating a Retreat: Why Doordarshan's New Channels Failed', *Frontline*, 14 January 1994.

16. Mehta, *India on Television*.
17. CII, *White Paper on Indian Broadcasting*, 2012, p. 5
18. Author's interview with Nripendra Misra, principal secretary to Prime Minister Narendra Modi and TRAI chairman 2006–09, and secretary, telecom 2004–05. Interview in New Delhi on 26 October 2012.
19. 'IPL bid aggressive but not outrageous', interview with Nalin Mehta, *Times of India*, 8 Sep 2017. See https://blogs.timesofindia.indiatimes.com/ academic-interest/ipl-bid-aggressive-but-not-outrageous-steep-inflation-in-tender-was-driven-hugely-by-digital-inflation/.

Chapter XXII

1. National Policy for Skill Development and Entrepreneurship 2015, Ministry of Skill Development and Entrepreneurship, Government of India.
2. Department of School Education and Literacy, Ministry of HRD, Government of India.
3. Ministry of Skill Development and Ministry of HRD.
4. All India Survey of Higher Education, 2015–16. Department of Higher Education, Ministry of HRD, Government of India.
5. Ministry of Skill Development and Entrepreneurship.
6. MSDE, 2015.
7. Agarwal, Pawan. *Indian Higher Education: Envisioning the Future*. New Delhi: SAGE Publications, 2009.

Chapter XXIII

1. The Sarbanes-Oxley Act of 2002 is an act passed by the US Congress in 2002 to protect investors from the possibility of fraudulent accounting by corporations. It was enacted in response to major public scandals such as Enron Corporation and WorldCom that shook investor confidence.
2. The committee laid down some recommendations to strengthen the corporate governance framework. Mandatory measures included audit committees, risk assessment and minimization procedures, code of conduct for all board members and senior management, and a whistle-blower policy for the company. Non-mandatory recommendations included instituting a system of training and evaluating the performance of board members.

3. Non-compete fee is paid to a selling shareholder, so that they do not re-enter the business and pose competition to the acquired company.
4. Consultative Paper on Review of Corporate Governance Norms in India. http://www.sebi.gov.in/sebi_data/attachdocs/1357290354602.pdf.
5. http://www.doingbusiness.org/data/exploretopics/protecting-minority-investors.

Chapter XXIV

1. Bird, Richard M. and Eric M. Zolt. 'Introduction to Tax Policy Design and Development', paper prepared for a course on practical issues in tax policy in developing countries, 28 April– 1 May 2003, World Bank.
2. Report of the Taxation Enquiry Commission, Ministry of Finance, Government of India. New Delhi, 1954.
3. Report of the Direct Taxes Enquiry Committee, Ministry of Finance, Government of India. New Delhi, 1971. See https://www.incometaxindia.gov.in/Pages/about-us/history-of-direct-taxation.aspx for a lucid history of direct taxation in India.
4. Report of the Indirect Taxation Enquiry Committee. Ministry of Finance, Government of India, New Delhi, 1978.
5. As per the origin-based principle, taxes are levied at the point of production while in case of the destination-based principle, taxes are levied at the point of consumption. Due to the origin-based CST, there was significant tax exportation from the richer producing states to poorer consuming states.

Contributors

SHIVSHANKAR MENON is currently a distinguished fellow of Brookings Institution, Washington, D.C.; chairman, advisory board, Institute of Chinese Studies, New Delhi; member, board of trustees, International Crisis Group; and a distinguished fellow of Asia Society Policy Institute, New York. He was previously the national security adviser to the prime minister of India (January 2010–May 2014) and foreign secretary of India (October 2006–July 2009). He has served as the Indian ambassador/high commissioner to China, Pakistan, Sri Lanka and Israel. In 2016 he published a book *Choices: Inside the Making of Indian Foreign Policy* (Brookings and Penguin Random House India, 2016). He has been a Fisher Family Fellow at the Kennedy School, Harvard University, 2015, and a Richard Wilhelm Fellow at Massachusetts Institute of Technology, 2015. He was chosen as one of the 'Top 100 Global Thinkers' by *Foreign Policy* magazine in 2010.

DUVVURI SUBBARAO was the governor of the Reserve Bank of India (2008–13). Prior to that, he was the finance secretary to the Government of India, 2007–08, and secretary to the Prime Minister's Economic Advisory Council, 2005–07. As a career civil servant for over thirty years, he has worked in various positions at the federal and state levels in India. On leave of absence from the civil service, he worked with the World Bank (1999–2004), where his job involved advising developing countries on macroeconomic management. Subbarao is currently a distinguished visiting fellow at National University of Singapore.

S.Y. QURAISHI, a civil servant, was the seventeenth chief election commissioner of India. He revolutionized voter participation in India. For this and other electoral reforms, he figured in 100 Most Powerful Indians of 2011 and 2012 by *Indian Express*. He has delivered lectures on democracy and elections worldwide. He is on the board of advisers of International IDEA (Institute of

Democracy and Electoral Assistance), Stockholm. He has been appointed the Global Ambassador of Democracy alongside eminent leaders like Kofi Annan. His book *An Undocumented Wonder: The Making of the Great Indian Election* has been a phenomenal success.

ROBIN JEFFREY is a visiting research professor at Institute of South Asian Studies, Singapore. His most recent book, written with Assa Doron, is *Waste of a Nation: Garbage and Growth in India* (Harvard University Press, 2018). He is the author, also with Assa Doron, of *Cell Phone Nation* (Hachette India, 2013). He published *India's Newspaper Revolution* in 2000, with two subsequent editions.

TAN TAI YONG, a historian, is the president of Yale-NUS College. He was the director of ISAS, National University of Singapore, from 2008 to 2015. He specializes in South and Southeast Asian History. He has published extensively on the Sikh diaspora, social and political history of colonial Punjab, decolonization and the partition of South Asia, and on Singapore's history. He has authored and co-authored several books, including *Singapore: A 700-Year History*, *Creating Greater Malaysia: Decolonization and the Politics of Merger*, *The Garrison State* and *The Aftermath of Partition in South Asia*.

DIPANKAR GUPTA is a sociologist and public intellectual. He was formerly a professor at the Centre for the Study of Social Systems, JNU, and was also associated with the Delhi School of Economics. His research interests include rural–urban transformation, labour laws in the informal sector, modernity, ethnicity, caste and stratification. He serves on the board of the RBI, National Bank for Agricultural and Rural Development (NABARD) and Max India. He has authored several books including *Justice before Reconciliation: Negotiating a 'New Normal' in Post-riot Mumbai and Ahmedabad*, *The Caged Phoenix: Can India fly?* and *Interrogating Caste: Understanding Hierarchy and Difference in Indian Society*. He is a regular columnist with *Times of India* and *The Hindu*.

ASHOK GULATI is currently the Infosys Chair Professor for Agriculture at ICRIER. Prior to this, he was chairman of the Commission for Agriculture Costs and Prices, Government of India; director at the International Food Policy Research Institute. He has written fourteen books and several research papers on Indian and Asian agriculture. He is a prolific writer in the media on agri-policies, and has been awarded the Padma Shri for his contribution to the field of agriculture policies in India.

GAYATHRI MOHAN is a consultant working on agriculture policy research at Indian Council for Research on International Economic Relations (ICRIER). During her tenure, she has conducted studies related to the agriculture-water nexus in India, in relation to rest of the world. She is an INSPIRE fellow, with a PhD in agricultural economics from University of Agricultural Sciences, Bangalore. Her areas of research interest include agricultural policies, development economics, natural resource economics and rural development.

PRONAB SEN is the country director for the International Growth Centre's India Central Programme. Earlier, he was the chairman of the National Statistical Commission; and principal economic adviser at the Government of India's Planning Commission. He was also the first chief statistician of India; and secretary, Ministry of Statistics and Programme Implementation, Government of India. A distinguished economist, he has taught at Johns Hopkins University and the Delhi School of Economics. As principal adviser, Perspective Planning Division of the Planning Commission, he was the author of the Approach Paper to four Five Year Plans and the principal author and coordinator of three Five Year Plans and Mid-term Appraisals.

SUMIT GANGULY holds the Rabindranath Tagore Chair in Indian Cultures and Civilizations and is a distinguished professor at the department of political science at Indiana University, Bloomington. He is authored, co-authored, edited and co-edited twenty-five books on contemporary South Asian politics. His most recent book, written with William R. Thompson, is *Ascending India and Its State Capacity* (Yale University Press, 2017).

POONAM MUTTREJA, executive director, Population Foundation of India (PFI), has over thirty-five years of experience in promoting women's rights, rural livelihoods, public advocacy, communications and behaviour change. She conceived and promoted the popular television serial 'Mai Kuch Bhi Kar Sakti Hoon' (I, a Woman, Can Do Anything). Before joining PFI, she served as the country director of McArthur Foundation in India. She serves on the board of several non-governmental organizations, and has co-founded SRUTI, Dastkar and the Ashoka Foundation. She is an alumnus of Delhi University and Harvard University's John F. Kennedy School of

Government. Poonam is a regular television and print commentator in India and internationally.

RAJIV KUMAR is the vice-chairman of NITI Aayog. He is also the founding director of Pahle India Foundation, New Delhi, and the chancellor of Gokhale Institute of Economics and Politics, Pune. He has served earlier as the secretary general, Federation of Indian Chambers of Commerce and Industry; director and chief executive of ICRIER; principal economist, Asian Development Bank, and economic adviser, Ministry of Finance, Government of India. His books include *Modi and His Challenges, Resurgent India: Ideas and Priorities* and *Exploding Aspirations: Unlocking India's Future.* A leading economist, he is a widely recognized economic columnist and a leading speaker on issues in Indian political economy.

SANJOY CHAKRAVORTY is professor of geography and urban studies at Temple University and a visiting fellow at the Center for the Advanced Study of India, University of Pennsylvania. His current research focuses on theoretical and empirical work on India, cities, inequality, and epistemology. He also writes fiction. His recent books include *The Other One Percent: Indians in America* (2016; a collaborative work on the Indian diaspora), *The Promoter* (2015; a novel), and *The Price of Land: Acquisition, Conflict, Consequence* (2013). His research has been supported by the National Science Foundation, the National Institute of Justice, the American Institute of Indian Studies, and the World Bank.

A.K. SHIVA KUMAR is a development economist and policy adviser who works on issues of human development, including poverty, health, nutrition, basic education and the rights of women and children. He is a board member of the Global Partnership to End Violence against Children; and is a senior policy adviser to UNICEF India. He also teaches economics and public policy at Ashoka University and Harvard's Kennedy School of Government. He is an alumnus of Bangalore University, the Indian Institute of Management, Ahmedabad, and Harvard University from where he did his master's in public administration and PhD in political economy and government.

AMITENDU PALIT is senior research fellow and research lead (trade and economic policy) at ISAS, National University of Singapore. Prior to joining academics, he worked for almost a decade in the Ministry of Finance in India and in various other ministries. An economist working on trade policies, regional developments, China–India relations and political economy, he is a columnist for *Financial Express* and a regular contributor to various global media. His books include *The Trans Pacific Partnership, China and India*, *China–India Economics* and *Special Economic Zones in India*. He appears as an expert on the BBC, Bloomberg, Channel News Asia, CNBC, Doordarshan (India) and All-India Radio.

SUMITA DAWRA is a member of the Indian Administrative Service (IAS), 1991 batch. She has a rich experience in public policy at various levels of governance in India, besides a good international exposure to public policy in China. Her experiences have helped her develop strong insights into using public policy as an effective tool for growth and development of countries. She has authored two books in public policy, namely—*China: Behind the Miracle* and *Poor but Spirited in Karimnagar: Field Notes of a Civil Servant*. Sumita is presently working as governance specialist with UNICEF India on a two-year deputation from service.

RONOJOY SEN is senior research fellow at ISAS and the South Asian Studies Programme, National University of Singapore. He has worked for over a decade with leading Indian newspapers, most recently as an editor for *Times of India*. His latest book is *Nation at Play: A History of Sport in India* (Columbia University Press/Penguin, 2015). He is also the author of *Articles of Faith: Religion, Secularism and the Indian Supreme Court* (Oxford University Press, 2010), and has edited several books. He has a PhD in political science from the University of Chicago and has read history at Presidency College, Kolkata.

S. NARAYAN (IAS, 1965 batch) with nearly four decades (1965–2004) in public service in the state and Central governments, in development administration, was the economic adviser to the prime minister during 2003–04. Prior to this assignment, he served the Government of India as the finance and economic affairs secretary, secretary in the Departments of Revenue, Petroleum, Coal and Industrial Development. In the Ministry of Finance, his responsibilities included formulation of macroeconomic policy for the government, tariff and taxation policies, as well as initiatives for modernizing the capital markets. His special interests include public finance, energy policy, governance issues and international trade. He has authored one book, edited two and written numerous policy papers, reports and book chapters. He also writes regularly in newspapers, both locally and internationally, on issues relating to public policy, governance, public finance, trade and energy. He has been a visiting senior research fellow at the Institute of South Asian Studies, National University of Singapore since 2005.

SUBHOMOY BHATTACHARJEE is a consulting editor at *Business Standard*. He writes on public policy—primarily finance and energy. His latest book *India's Coal Story: From Damodar to Zambezi* traces how India's coal reserves were at the centre of a major political scandal that nearly sent a prime minister to jail. It explores why since Independence, business and government in India could not settle the rights on energy security, creating the murky politics of coal and sketches the options for India's future energy security. He has read economics at the Delhi School of Economics, Delhi University. He has worked with the Government of India; with *Economic Times*, *Indian Express* and *Financial Express*; and is now a consultant with Research and Information System for Developing Countries, a New Delhi-based think tank. He is also a commentator of business news on various TV channels.

SUBRATA K. MITRA is the director, ISAS, and visiting research professor, NUS, and emeritus professor Heidelberg University, Germany. The dynamic interaction of culture and rationality has deeply influenced his research profile, which focuses on governance and administration, citizenship, hybridity and re-use, the evolution of the Indian state from classical to modern times, the transition to democracy and its consolidation, and security and foreign affairs of South Asia. His books *Culture and Rationality* (SAGE, 1999), *The Puzzle of India's Governance* (Routledge, 2005), *Re-use: The Art and Politics of Integration and Anxiety* (SAGE, 2008), *Politics in India* (Routledge, 2017), *Kautilya's Arthashastra: Classical Roots of Modern Politics in India* (jointly authored with Michael Liebig, NOMOS 2016, Rupa, 2017) represent different facets of his oeuvre.

DHRUVA JAISHANKAR is a fellow in foreign policy studies at Brookings India, New Delhi, and at Brookings Institution, Washington, D.C. He is also a regular contributor to Indian and international media. He was previously a transatlantic fellow and programme officer with the German Marshall Fund in Washington, D.C.; a research assistant at Brookings; and a reporter for CNN-IBN. He has been a visiting fellow with the Rajaratnam School of International

Studies; an IISS–SAIS Merrill Center Young Strategist; and a David Rockefeller fellow with the Trilateral Commission. He is an alumnus of Macalester College and Georgetown University.

NALIN MEHTA is a social scientist, journalist and author. He is a consulting editor with *Times of India* and the editor of the journal *South Asian History and Culture* (Routledge). He was previously the managing editor, Headlines Today; adjunct professor at IIM Bangalore; and has held senior positions with the Global Fund in Geneva, Switzerland, and UNAIDS. He also held fellowships at National University of Singapore, Australian National University, La Trobe University, and the International Olympics Museum. His books include *Behind a Billion Screens: What Television Tells Us About Modern India*, *India on Television: How Satellite Channels Have Changed the Way We Think and Act* and *Sellotape Legacy: Delhi and the Commonwealth Games*.

PAWAN AGARWAL is currently the CEO, Food Safety and Standards Authority of India in the Government of India. He is an IAS officer of 1985 of the West Bengal cadre. He has served in various capacities in the Central and state governments, such as the joint secretary, skill development, adviser, higher education, Planning Commission (now NITI Aayog) and in the HRD ministry and the University Grants Commission. He was the Fulbright New Century Scholar at Harvard University/Emory University; visiting scholar and fellow at ICRIER, New Delhi, and the Centre for the Study of Higher Education and the Australia India Institute at the University of Melbourne. He has authored *Indian Higher Education: Envisioning the Future* (SAGE, 2009).

U.K. SINHA served as the chairman of Securities and Exchange Board of India (SEBI) from February 2011 to 1 March 2017. Prior to this, he was the chairman and managing director at UTI Asset Management Company from 2005 until February 2011. Preceding this, he was the joint secretary in the Department of Economic Affairs at the Ministry of Finance and looked after capital markets, external commercial borrowings, pension reforms and foreign exchange management functions from June 2002 to October 2005. He has been conferred with many awards viz. CNBC-TV18 India Business Leader Awards (IBLA), 'Outstanding Contribution to Indian Business Award 2014', and *Economic Times*, 'Business Reformer of the Year Award 2014' to name a few. He was selected for the IAS in 1976. He holds MSc and LLB degrees.

PINAKI CHAKRABORTY is professor at the National Institute of Public Finance and Policy, India, and a research associate at Levy Economics Institute, New York. He is also the chairman of Kerala Public Expenditure Review Committee, appointed by the Kerala government. He was the economic adviser to the Fourteenth Finance Commission of India. He has held appointments as a visiting faculty at the University of Ottawa and the University of Carleton, Canada, Centre for Development Studies, JNU, and the Indira Gandhi Institute for Development Research, Mumbai. He has advised the governments of Nigeria, Kenya and some CIS countries in Central Asia. He holds a PhD in economics.